SHAKESPEARE:
THE ROMAN PLAYS

LONGMAN CRITICAL READERS

General Editor:

STAN SMITH, Professor of English, University of Dundee

Published titles:

K.M. NEWTON, *George Eliot*

MARY EAGLETON, *Feminist Literary Criticism*

GARY WALLER, *Shakespeare's Comedies*

JOHN DRAKAKIS, *Shakespearean Tragedy*

RICHARD WILSON AND RICHARD DUTTON, *New Historicism and Renaissance Drama*

PETER BROOKER, *Modernism/Postmodernism*

PETER WIDDOWSON, *D.H. Lawrence*

RACHEL BOWLBY, *Virginia Woolf*

FRANCIS MULHERN, *Contemporary Marxist Literary Criticism*

ANNABEL PATTERSON, *John Milton*

CYNTHIA CHASE, *Romanticism*

MICHAEL O'NEILL, *Shelley*

STEPHANIE TRIGG, *Medieval English Poetry*

ANTONY EASTHOPE, *Contemporary Film Theory*

TERRY EAGLETON, *Ideology*

MAUD ELLMANN, *Psychoanalytic Literary Criticism*

MARK CURRIE, *Metafiction*

ANDREW BENNETT, *Readers and Reading*

GRAHAM HOLDERNESS, BRYAN LOUGHREY AND ANDREW MURPHY, *Shakespeare: The Roman Plays*

BREAN HAMMOND, *Pope*

SHAKESPEARE: THE ROMAN PLAYS

Edited and Introduced by

GRAHAM HOLDERNESS, BRYAN LOUGHREY

AND

ANDREW MURPHY

LONGMAN
LONDON AND NEW YORK

Addison Wesley Longman Limited
Edinburgh Gate
Harlow, Essex CM20 2JE, England
and associated Companies throughout the world.

*Published in the United States of America
by Addison Wesley Longman Publishing, New York.*

© Addison Wesley Longman Limited 1996

First published 1996

ISBN 0 582 23770X CSD
ISBN 0 582 237696 PPR

British Library Cataloguing-in-Publication Data

A catalogue record of this book is
available from the British Library

Library of Congress Cataloging-in-Publication Data

Also Available

Set by 5K in 9/11½ pt Palatino
Produced by Longman Singapore Publishers (Pte) Ltd.
Printed in Singapore

Contents

General Editors' Preface

The outlines of contemporary critical theory are now often taught as a standard feature of a degree in literary studies. The development of particular theories has seen a thorough transformation of literary criticism. For example, Marxist and Foucauldian theories have revolutionised Shakespeare studies, and 'deconstruction' has led to a complete reassessment of Romantic poetry. Feminist criticism has left scarcely any period of literature unaffected by its searching critiques. Teachers of literary studies can no longer fall back on a standardised, received, methodology.

Lecturers and teachers are now urgently looking for guidance in a rapidly changing critical environment. They need help in understanding the latest revisions in literary theory, and especially in grasping the practical effects of the new theories in the form of theoretically sensitised new readings. A number of volumes in the series anthologise important essays on particular theories. However, in order to grasp the full implications and possible uses of particular theories it is essential to see them put to work. This series provides substantial volumes of new readings, presented in an accessible form and with a significant amount of editorial guidance.

Each volume includes a substantial introduction which explores the theoretical issues and conflicts embodied in the essays selected and locates areas of disagreement between positions. The pluralism of theories has to be put on the agenda of literary studies. We can no longer pretend that we all tacitly accept the same practices in literary studies. Neither is a *laissez-faire* attitude any longer tenable. Literature departments need to go beyond the mere toleration of theoretical differences: it is not enough merely to agree to differ; they need actually to 'stage' the differences openly. The volumes in this series all attempt to dramatise the differences, not necessarily with a view to resolving them but in order to foreground the choices presented by different theories or to argue for a particular route through the impasses the differences present.

The theory 'revolution' has had real effects. It has loosened the grip of traditional empiricist and romantic assumptions about language and literature. It is not always clear what is being proposed as the new agenda for literature studies, and indeed the very notion of 'literature' is questioned by the post-structuralist strain in theory. However, the uncertainties and obscurities of contemporary theories appear much less worrying when we see what the best critics have been able to do with them in practice. This series aims to disseminate the best of recent criticism and to show that it is possible to re-read the canonical texts of literature in new and challenging ways.

RAMAN SELDEN AND STAN SMITH

The Publishers and fellow Series Editor regret to record that Raman Selden died after a short illness in May 1991 at the age of fifty-three. Ray Selden was a fine scholar and a lovely man. All those he has worked with will remember him with much affection and respect.

Acknowledgements

We are grateful to the following for permission to reproduce copyright material:

Basil Blackwell Ltd for edited extracts from *Shakespeare and the Popular Voice* by Annabel Patterson (1989) pp 127–46; Cambridge University Press for the article 'Fashion it thus' by John Drakakis from *Shakespeare Survey* (ed.) Professor S. Wells, No. 44, pp 65–73; Cornell University Press for edited extracts from *Shakespeare's Rome: Republic and Empire* by Paul A. Cantor (1976) pp 206–35; Harvester Wheatsheaf for edited extracts from *Radical Tragedy: Religion, Ideology of Power in the Drama of Shakespeare and his Contemporaries* by Jonathan Dollimore (1984) pp 204–17; John Hopkins University Press and the author, Richard Wilson, for his article 'Is this a holiday?' from *ELH* vol. 54, No. 1, Spring 1987, pp 31–44; Oxford University Press and University of California Press for edited extracts from *Faultlines: Cultural Materialism and the Politics of Dissident Reading* by Alan Sinfield (1992) pp 1–28, copyright © 1992 The Regents of the University of California; Routledge and the authors for edited extracts from 'Lenten Butchery' by Michael D. Bristol from *Shakespeare Reproduced: The Text in History and Ideology* (ed.) Jean Howard and Marion O'Connor (Methuen, 1987) pp 207–24, and an extract from *Meaning By Shakespeare* by Terence Hawkes (Routledge, 1992) pp 42–60; Routledge for an extract from *Power on Display: The Politics of Shakespeare's Drama* by Leonard Tennenhouse (Methuen, 1986) pp 142–46; Routledge, New York and the author, Janet Adelman, for edited extracts from *Suffocating Mothers: Fantasies of Maternal Origin in Shakespeare's Plays* (1992) pp 176–92.

1 Introduction 'Shakespeare Dragged into Politics: Inner Story of Strange Conflict'

In the last decade or so, the fields of Renaissance studies in general, and Shakespeare studies in particular, have witnessed a major shift in emphasis and direction. This shift has come about in large measure because, in the early 1980s, a number of American and British scholars – largely in reaction against the poststructuralist modes of analysis then dominant – sought out a new direction for Renaissance studies. Poststructuralism had laid great emphasis on the ineluctable nature of language, and on its inability to sustain the distinctions through which it operates. For this reason, poststructuralist critics tended to focus their analysis intensely upon the text itself, paying relatively little attention to the context in which the text came to be written or to its immediate historical moment.[1] Two movements in the early 1980s sought to reverse this situation. In the US, the New Historicists revived an interest in the historical background to the text.[2] They endeavoured to avoid what they saw as the pitfalls of a traditional 'totalising' variety of historicism[3] by retaining some of poststructuralism's key insights and coupling them with a framework for viewing structures of power (largely derived from the work of Michel Foucault) which stressed the articulation of power with other practices and forms of writing and representation. The New Historicists attempted to place the text back into its context and to analyse the way in which the text could be brought to disclose the traces of the larger-scale political and social structural relations of its time.

In Britain, an equivalent reaction against certain forms of poststructuralism led to a similar renewed interest in history. The evolution in British critical thinking occurred against the background of the sharpening of the left–right divide within British politics and society, as the Conservative government, buoyed by a series of election victories, set about systematically reversing many of the institutional and social structures which had been put in place by post-war Labour governments. The new British historicism was, therefore, much more sharply politically inflected than its American counterpart. It represented in some measure a revival of a form of Marxist criticism, being heavily indebted, for example, to the classic Marxist-oriented work of Raymond Williams (especially his thinking on the nature of

1

ideology).[4] This political alignment is registered in the name which
Jonathan Dollimore and Alan Sinfield coined for the new movement
in Britain: 'Cultural Materialism'. 'Materialism', as Dollimore and
Sinfield note, 'is opposed to "idealism": it insists that culture does not
(cannot) transcend the material forces and relations of production.'[5]
Cultural Materialism is likewise distinguished from New Historicism
in the emphasis which it places on the continuity of connection
between the Renaissance text and the world of contemporary politics
and on the necessity of pledging a political commitment within that
contemporary world: '[Cultural Materialism] registers its commitment to
the transformation of a social order which exploits people on grounds
of race, gender and class.'[6]

  This shift in critical emphasis and analysis has been exceptionally
fruitful in the range of new scholarship to which it has given rise.
New-historicist criticism in the US has provided many interesting
studies of structures of social and political power and of what
Stephen Greenblatt has called 'the circulation of social energy'[7] in the
early modern period.[8] On the British side, in 1984, Jonathan Dollimore
provided a challenging reassessment of early modern drama in
his *Radical Tragedy*, arguing for a link between the drama and the
collapse of the institutions of State and Church (Crown, Court, central
administration, army, and episcopacy) at the onset of the English civil
war. 'If the causes of that collapse', Dollimore writes, 'can be discerned
in the previous decades then, at the very least, we might postulate a
connection in the early seventeenth century between the undermining
of these institutions and a theatre in which they and their ideological
legitimation were subjected to sceptical, interrogative and subversive
representations.'[9] In the following year, John Drakakis published, as
editor, a collection of essays under the title *Alternative Shakespeares*,
dedicated to seeking new (and more politically focused) avenues of
exploration of the texts of Shakespeare. In the same year, Dollimore
and Sinfield published another anthology of new Shakespeare criticism,
entitled *Political Shakespeare: New Essays in Cultural Materialism*, gathering
together essays on such subjects as the colonial context of *The Tempest*,
'the patriarchal bard', and the uses to which Shakespeare has been put
in education and in the media.

  This latter concern pointed toward a potential new field in
Shakespeare studies, namely the *uses* of Shakespeare: the way in
which Shakespeare has been constructed as a central cultural icon
and the manner in which his texts have been deployed for political
ends. 1988 saw the publication of a further collection of essays which
tackled this issue directly, uniting various strands of analysis under
the title *The Shakespeare Myth* and declaring that 'for every particular
present, Shakespeare is, here, now, always, what is currently being

made of him'.[10] The American scholar, Gary Taylor, also took up the issue of the cultural construction and reception of Shakespeare in the following year in his *Reinventing Shakespeare: A Cultural History from the Restoration to the Present*, and Michael Bristol provided an analysis of the appropriation and deployment of Shakespeare in the US in his 1990 book *Shakespeare's America, America's Shakespeare*.[11]

The effects of the past decade or so of radical new criticism have been registered by the conservative resistance which it has provoked within the academic world. In the US, the new scholarly disposition has come under attack from commentators such as Allan Bloom.[12] Likewise, traditionally minded Renaissance scholars such as R.A. Foakes and Brian Vickers have sought to mount something of a rearguard action, to defend Shakespeare from the criticisms and challenges of the radicals.[13] Such academic resistance is mirrored by a parallel debate within the greater cultural and political field. In August 1993, the British Sunday newspaper, the *Observer*, ran a lengthy feature article by Peter Watson in its Review section under the headline ' "Presume not that I am the thing I was" ' and subtitled 'The Battle of the Bard', charting the rise of New Historicism and Cultural Materialism and tracing the reactions provoked among conservative critics. 'The battle and the bitchiness are far from over', Watson writes, 'the Bard is still up for Grabs'.[14] Likewise, at the 1993 Conservative Party Conference in the UK, the British prime minister, in the midst of his keynote address to the party, took the time to launch a counter-attack against a group of some 500 academics who had published a letter in the British press condemning the government's policies on the study of literature in general and the study of Shakespeare in particular. Mr Major, waving a copy of the letter in the air, and pledging to speak to such academics in a language of which they themselves might approve, declared: 'Me and my party ain't going to take what them on the left says is OK. Right?'[15]

This present collection of recent work on Shakespeare's Roman plays has been assembled in the light of the developments and confrontations outlined here. Taking our cue from the general editors' goal for the series – that it 'aims to disseminate the best of recent criticism, and to show that it is possible to re-read the canonical texts of literature in new and challenging ways' – we have attempted to include in our collection what we consider to be some of the most interesting work on the Roman plays which has been produced by those critics who can be said, very broadly speaking, to fall within the New Historicist/Cultural Materialist critical spectrum.

To set the scene for our anthology, we would like to begin by considering a work which we have not included here: Derek Traversi's *Shakespeare: The Roman Plays*. Traversi's book was written in the early 1960s, before the advent of poststructuralism, at a time when the views of such critics as G. Wilson Knight (who celebrated the imperial dimension of Shakespeare's work) still held sway.[16] It bears many of the hallmarks of the New Critical approach to literature which had dominated literary criticism since the 1930s, in the wake of the influential work of F.R. and Q.D. Leavis, I.A. Richards, and the American expatriot T.S. Eliot in Britain, and John Crowe Ransom, Cleanth Brooks, and R.P. Blackmur in the US. Traversi's book usefully serves to provide an indication of the traditional critical practice against which many of the scholars included in this volume defined their own critical objectives.

In common with much of the criticism of the time, Traversi stresses the *personal* dimension of the plays, focusing intently on 'character'. Of Coriolanus, Traversi writes:

> We are required to share as spectators the difficult nature of his choices, to participate in the burden which his vocation imposes upon him. In the great tragedies this same sense of participation, of sharing in an action proceeding from the presence of a flaw in a single exalted nature, receives its highest expression, adding a new and universal dimension to individual perversity and its expiation through the ruin which it brings upon itself and in the Roman dramas this tragic content is finally allied to the more detached public vision of the earlier chronicles.[17]

Traversi harks back to the classicism of A.C. Bradley here in positing a 'tragic flaw' in the main character as the engine which drives Shakespeare's tragedies forward.[18] The hero of the play is seen less as being himself participant in a greater political, social, and ideological structure, than as a solitary individual, burdened by the weight of his particular 'vocation'. For Traversi, 'participation' indicates not the connectedness of the hero with the structures of which he is a part and which he himself manipulates, but, rather, the identification, on an individual basis, of the reader of the play with the play's central character.

Traversi posits a distinction between the Roman plays and the other tragedies, in that, in the Roman plays, the 'tragic content is finally allied to the more detached public vision of the earlier chronicles'. In this, he touches on one of the central themes of such criticism: the division of the world into discrete private and public realms, which may overlap to some limited extent (or, as here, be 'allied to' each other), but which are, finally, separate from each other. There is no sense in such analysis that, as more recent critics would suggest, the realms of the 'private' and the 'public' are *constructs* rather than essential, stable and unchanging actualities and that, in common with the 'public', the category of the 'private' is in certain crucial ways politically, as much as socially, constituted.

Just as the 'private' represents an immutable, essential category for Traversi, so too we find him positing a set of values, meanings, and ideals which transcend the purely local or historically particular. Thus he writes of the 'depth and universality of the dramatic conception' in the Roman plays and suggests that 'In the process of being removed from England to Rome the study of personal motivation in politics achieves a greater degree of impersonality and so, by the very nature of things, a wider human relevance, a greater universality (12). In viewing the plays in this way, Traversi is following a tradition which dates back to the seventeenth century and to Ben Jonson's assertion, some seven years after Shakespeare's death, that his fellow dramatist 'was not for an age, but for all time'. This view proposes that the work of Shakespeare is a repository of certain values and fundamental truths which are applicable transhistorically and transculturally. To take this view is, of course, to deny the historical and cultural context in which the works actually appeared: to close off any analysis of the *particularities* of the texts and their historical contingency. It also, of course, promotes the texts to the status of a kind of cultural 'standard'. If Shakespeare's plays embody transcultural values, then a people to whom the plays are in some way unintelligible must not be part of the community of civilised cultures. Appreciation of Shakespeare becomes a pre-requisite of qualifying for a global cultural 'passport'.

Traversi's tacit political programme becomes clearer when we register some of his comments on social and political structures. Shakespeare, he tells us, 'accepts the necessity of order in public affairs'(12) and Traversi sees the trajectory of the tragedies as tracing the results of 'misplaced attempts to follow the illusion of absolute autonomy at the expense of natural and freely accepted order'(17). The emphasis here on 'order', specifically on order as something like a bulwark against chaos and political crisis, is, again, typical of much of Renaissance scholarship of the time – deeply indebted, as it was, to Tillyard's *Elizabethan World Picture*. Tillyard posited an early modern mindset locked into a commitment to a worldview which united the entire cosmos, from macrocosm to microcosm, in a set of neat, orderly analogues (in brief, as divine:human, so king:subject, husband:wife, etc.). The problem, of course, is that the question of what *constitutes* order, and, moreover, of *who* constitutes order, goes unexamined here. Like Shakespeare's universal truths, order is taken to be 'not for an age, but for all time'; the idea of order is simply something which is 'natural and freely accepted'.

If we now turn to the opening selection of our anthology, Richard Wilson's ' "Is This a Holiday?": Shakespeare's Roman Carnival', the contrast is both the style and the thrust of the analysis should be clear. Where Traversi's texts appear virtually to be hermetically sealed, viewed by Traversi entirely within their own terms and held in splendid isolation from their historical context, Wilson strives throughout his essay to open up the text of *Julius Caesar* to its particular historical moment, in a variety of different ways. In a manner characteristic of much of New Historicist/Cultural Materialist writing, Wilson begins outside the text, with a document peripherally related to it: Thomas Platter's account of a visit to London, during which he witnessed a performance of *Julius Caesar*.[19] Wilson uses this short piece as an avenue into an exploration of the text itself and the particular context in which it was written and performed.

Wilson sees the text as being both a reflection of the political temper of the times and itself deeply implicated in that politics. Thus, for Wilson, the play is politically constituted, but, equally, the institution of drama itself serves political ends. In the first instance, Wilson traces, through the programme espoused by Brutus, the emergence of a new political doctrine characteristic of the modern state 'whereby subversion is produced in both consciousness and society to legitimize the order that subjects it'. At the same time, Wilson sees the theatre itself as participating in that process. For Wilson, the theatre serves to stage the emergent hegemonic doctrine, revealing its underpinning mechanisms. But this staging, occurring as it does in a carefully contrived and controlled environment, itself serves finally simply to reinforce those mechanisms. As Wilson writes: 'this early Globe play reflects candidly on the process whereby hegemony is obtained through the control of discourse, a process in which the inauguration of the playhouse was itself a major intervention.' Wilson contrasts the licensed and carefully policed arena of the theatre with the politically volatile and imperfectly controlled world of traditional carnival, which carries within it the potential for genuine political action. Thus, for Wilson, the world of the Globe becomes itself, like Caesar's 'Roman carnival' in *Julius Caesar*, 'a model of authoritarian populism, the true regimen of bread and circuses'.

Like Richard Wilson, John Drakakis also begins his essay on *Julius Caesar* with an anecdote peripheral to the text, this time taken from Thomas Heywood's *An Apology for Actors* (1612), in which Heywood rehearses an apocryphal anecdote about the historical Julius Caesar's supposed acting talents. Drakakis uses the story as a launching point for an investigation of the politics and practice of representation, proposing that '*Julius Caesar* is not so much a celebration of theatre as an unmasking of the politics of representation *per se'*. Drawing on the work of theorists such as Robert Weimann, Drakakis seeks to interrogate the relationship between representation and ideology. Like Wilson, he is not just concerned with the internal world of the text of the play, or with the relationship between the text and its immediate historical context, but also attends to the politics of the *institution* of theatre.

For Drakakis, representation emerges in *Julius Caesar* as an essential strategy of ideological formation. The effect of the play is to make this process manifest: 'Brutus, like Cassius before him, conjures . . . a representation of a Caesar that the play never allows us to observe as anything other than a wholly fabricated identity.' In this sense, the play serves to anatomise the mechanics of ideological construction. Drakakis sees the theatre less as a direct instrument of the state than as 'an unstable institution proceeding gingerly into a terrain fraught with considerable political danger'. Drakakis thus differs from Richard Wilson in his assessment of the political and ideological role of theatre, aligning himself much more closely with the position which Jonathan Dollimore adopts in *Radical Tragedy*. For Drakakis, the tendency of the theatre 'to produce *and* to interrogate ideologies', combines with other factors to render the institution profoundly – and fruitfully – ambiguous and liminal:

> when we consider the timing of performances, the constraints of official censorship, the social heterogeneity and consequent volatility of public theatre audiences, along with the desire for respectability amongst practitioners, and the attempts to secure influential patronage, it becomes clear that the liminal status of a theatre such as the Globe effectively guaranteed its relative 'openness' to the production of contradictory cultural meanings.

Thus, in contrast to Wilson, Drakakis sees the theatre as being in a relationship of continuity with the practice of carnival, rather than being a neutralising subversion of it. As he writes: 'the liminal position of the theatre, which it shared with other forms of festivity, far from simply ventriloquizing the discourses of political domination, engaged in forms of representation through which other, potentially subversive voices could be heard.'

If we turn to our final selection in the *Julius Caesar* section, Alan Sinfield's 'Theaters of War', we find a kindred form of analysis which, nevertheless, provides a rather different focus from that of Wilson and Drakakis. Where the latter deploy contemporary seventeenth-century texts as their point of entry to Shakespeare's play, Sinfield begins his essay firmly in the twentieth century, with an advert from the *Armed Forces Journal*. Noting that 'the conferral of cultural authority is a principal role of Shakespeare in our society', Sinfield investigates the manner in which Shakespeare and Shakespearean authority are appropriated by the military-industrial complex to lend cultural weight to the business of selling armaments. In a subtle reading of the advertisement's various codes (the text of the advert, the graphics, the nature of the images used, and even small details such as variations in spellings within the text – the Globe 'thea*tre*' vs the 'thea*ter* of military operations') Sinfield demonstrates the way in which Shakespeare is used to provide 'a legitimation of imperial enterprise'. Sinfield's piece is thus a graphic illustration of the Cultural Materialist commitment to our own political moment as well as to the original historical moment of the text itself.

From his analysis of the deployment of a general cultural token of 'Shakespeare' by Royal Ordnance, Sinfield goes on in the article to provide a short history of the deployment specifically of the text of *Julius Caesar*, noting the various ways in which the text has been adapted to different political ends and philosophies over the centuries (or excluded from the stage because it was not in keeping with the political temper of the times). He registers the fact that, while George Washington staged an amateur production of the play 'in the garret of his executive mansion in Philadelphia, with himself a Brutus', in Britain *Julius Caesar* 'was not performed at all from the time of the American Revolution, through the French Revolution, until well into the nineteenth century'. Sinfield continues his history of the deployment of the text up through the 1978 BBC/Time-Life video production of the play.

Sinfield ends his analysis with a proposal of his own for a theatrical interpretation of the text, promoting the plebeians and their tribunes to a central and crucial role, arguing that 'the tribunes' political program is vastly superior to that generated among the ruling elite, for instead of plotting to murder Caesar, they exhort the people to act openly, constitutionally, and collectively against the alterations to the constitution proposed by Caesar's party.' For Sinfield, the point of such a production would be 'to check the tendency of *Julius Caesar* to add Shakespearean authority to reactionary discourse' and, as such, his projected production of the play is very much in line with one of the aims which he sets out for Cultural Materialism in this article: this form of critical practice seeks, he writes, 'to discern the scope for dissident politics of class, race, gender, and sexual orientation, both within texts and in their roles in cultures'.

Our collection moves on from *Julius Caesar* to the second of the Roman plays, *Antony and Cleopatra*, and we begin with a short piece from Leonard Tennenhouse's *Power on Display: The Politics of Shakespeare's Drama*. *Antony and Cleopatra* is a very different play from *Julius Caesar*, with the central relationship between the titular characters tending to draw critics into feeling that, as Tennenhouse puts it, 'sexuality . . . appears to transcend politics in the play'. As Tennenhouse further notes, 'even the most dedicated historical critic feels hard pressed to maintain his or her concern for the vicissitudes of state power in this play'.

The interest of Tennenhouse's own discussion lies in the manner in which he contrives to combine an analysis of the play's engagement with the issue of sexuality with an analysis of the play's political thrust. Tennenhouse considers *Antony and Cleopatra* to be very much a post-Elizabethan play. He sees it as a text which is struggling to come to terms with the passing of an era in which the sexual and the political were deeply intertwined in the figure of Elizabeth.[20] In the Jacobean era, what Tennenhouse calls 'the iconic bond' between political and sexual desire is sundered and the image of the woman invested with political power shifts: 'no longer conceived as a legitimate means for access to membership in the corporate body, the aristocratic female has the potential to pollute.' Tennenhouse thus sees *Antony and Cleopatra* as 'Shakespeare's elegy for the signs and symbols which legitimized Elizabethan power. Of these, the single most important figure was that of the desiring and desired woman, her body valued for its ornamental surface, her feet deeply rooted in the ground.'

We follow the Tennenhouse extract with a piece from Janet Adelman. Though Adelman is really neither a historicist nor a Cultural Materialist, the piece complements Tennenhouse's analysis quite nicely, in that, where Tennenhouse concerns himself with the presentation of images of the female in *Antony and Cleopatra*, Adelman, in her essentially psychoanalytic reading of the text, takes up the issue of how 'maleness' is constructed in the play. Adelman's piece also provides an interesting contrast with Tennenhouse, in that, where he sees female identity as being negatively valenced in the text, Adelman sees it as representing, essentially, a positive force.

Adelman notes the way in which the text of *Antony and Cleopatra* is framed by two verbal pictures of Antony: Caesar's as I.iv.56–71 and Cleopatra's at V.ii.76–100,[21] arguing that 'Antony begins in Caesar's landscape of scarcity but then finds himself in Cleopatra's bounty'. For Adelman, 'what is at stake in this trajectory is the relocation and reconstruction of heroic masculinity'. Caesarian masculinity, Adelman suggests, 'is founded on differentiation from the female – and on the psychic scarcity that is the consequence of that differentiation'. By contrast, Antony's final fate in the play is to be figured as possessing a form of masculinity which is productively aligned with the female. Antony's masculinity

> is finally founded on incorporation of the female: in Cleopatra's vision of him, his bounty flows from him as though it were an attribute of his own body . . . In his capacity to give without being used up, he replicates the female economy of breast milk, self-renewing in its abundance; leaving behind Caesar's male economy of limited resources, he becomes like Cleopatra, feeding and renewing the appetite in an endless cycle of gratification and desire, making hungry where most he satisfies.

One of the refreshing aspects of Adelman's analysis is that it serves in a sense to recuperate the figure of Cleopatra – so often characterised in analyses of the text as an emasculating destroyer of Antony's manhood, rendering him, in the words of the play itself, 'a strumpet's fool' (I.i.13).[22] For Adelman, the attraction of the play is its evocation of an alternative kind of manhood. She is, however, alert to the fact that this evocation is severely constrained by the text – Cleopatra's 'imaginative act' of reconceiving Antony is, she notes, 'hedged around with conditions', being 'deeply retrospective, as much a lament for a dream that is irrevocably gone as a recreation of it in the present'.

We follow Adelman's piece with a short chapter from Jonathan Dollimore's *Radical Tragedy*. Dollimore, as might be expected, sees the narrative of *Antony and Cleopatra* in more fully political terms, arguing that the play is a particularly clear demonstration of the way in which ideology 'constitutes not only the authority of those in power but their very identity'. For Dollimore, the presentation of Antony in the play illustrates the struggle between dominant/residual ideological codes on the one hand and emergent codes on the other. Dollimore aligns Antony with an older conception of power, centred on notions of individual honour and *virtus*. Caesar, by contrast, is indicative of a new conception of power, which emerged in the early modern period, in which, as Dollimore notes (quoting Mervyn James), 'the monopoly both of honour and violence *by the state* was asserted' (our italics). For Dollimore, Antony becomes in the play the site of contention of these two modes of power, and the dissolution of the residual code to which Antony is faithful (and by which he is constituted) is necessarily accompanied by the sundering of Antony's very identity, evidenced, for instance, in such speeches of Antony's as

Sometime we see a cloud that's dragonish,
A vapour sometime, like a bear, or lion,
A tower'd citadel, a pendant rock,
A forked mountain, or blue promontory
With trees upon 't that nod unto the world,
And mock our eyes with air.

     . . .

That which is now a horse, even with a thought
The rack dislimns, and makes it indistinct
As water is in water.

     . . .

My good knave Eros, now thy captain is
Even such a body: here I am Antony,
Yet cannot hold this visible shape . . .

                                 (IV.xiv.2–14)

In presenting this analysis, Dollimore is greatly indebted to the concepts of ideology evolved by Raymond Williams's Marxist analysis of structures of power.[23] If we next turn to our first selection in the *Coriolanus* section of this anthology, we will find, in Annabel Patterson's chapter, a rather more traditional form of historicism. Patterson's piece is taken from her 1989 book *Shakespeare and the Popular Voice*. But even as she differs from Dollimore in terms of theoretical underpinnings of her work, Patterson nevertheless shares his desire to retrieve from within early modern dramatic literature (specifically, in Patterson's case, the work of Shakespeare) a sense of a radical critique at play. As Patterson writes in the introduction to her book, she 'take[s] the position that Shakespeare was one of our first cultural critics, in the sense of being capable of profound, structural analysis'. Patterson sees *Coriolanus* as representing Shakespeare's invitation to his audience

> to contemplate an alternative political system; and, more significantly still, to experience an entire dramatic action devoted to these questions: who shall speak for the commons; what power should the common people have in the system; to what extent is common power compatible with national safety?

Patterson reads the text directly against its immediate historical background, stressing the importance for the play of the Midlands Rising of 1607. As the rising grew in part out of concern over food shortages, before expanding to take in a greater programme of grievances and desire for reform, Patterson sees a strong link between this agrarian unrest within the early Jacobean state and the grievances of the plebeians and their struggles with the aristocracy in

Shakespeare's Rome. Patterson advances her analysis through a process of detailed, closely observed historical investigation, carefully sifting through royal proclamations, parliamentary records, and contemporary speeches and sermons to establish a body of evidence in support of her claims. She concludes that the fundamental concern of *Coriolanus* lies with conceptions of power, with Coriolanus embodying a militaristic code of power, while the text itself struggles to come to terms with constitutional issues, with 'how it is possible to define and limit such a previously unspeakable concept as *common* power' (our emphasis).

Michael Bristol's essay on *Coriolanus* presents a more traditional Marxist analysis. Bristol sees the play in terms of a conflict of class interests and, for him, the primary struggle within the text concerns the question of the legitimation of authority. In Bristol's analysis, Coriolanus appears as an anomalous figure who disrupts the normal pattern of authority formation within the world of the play, interrupting the expected dialectical rhythms of political engagement, which Bristol compares to the traditional struggle between the principles of Lent and of carnival (thus, for Bristol, 'carnival' has a rather different emphasis than it does for Richard Wilson and John Drakakis). Coriolanus, in Bristol's view, prompts a 'legitimation crisis', provoking a 'profound divergence over the question of the derivation of authority and the source of social initiative'. Bristol maintains that when the threat represented by Coriolanus is finally eliminated in the play, legitimation finally 'takes the form of a class compromise, in which the party in power is able to reestablish dominance over the popular element'. In the process, Bristol suggests, 'the threat of calamity provides the means for incorporating and channeling the energy of popular initiative'. But *Coriolanus* leaves us, Bristol maintains, with a set of profound questions regarding the way in which order is reconstructed at the end of the play:

> Is this an authentic and exemplary resolution of crisis? Is it a case of making the best of a bad situation? Or is it an instance of the thwarting of a genuine collective will by a dominant minority, using a general strategy of dramatized crisis, sacrifice, and the claims of a 'national emergency' to control and redirect the energy of a popular majority?

Our final selection on *Coriolanus* is taken from Terence Hawkes's *Meaning by Shakespeare*. Hawkes's piece is, in many ways, quite similar to Alan Sinfield's essay on *Julius Caesar*, in that it is firmly grounded in the twentieth century. Like Michael Bristol, Hawkes sees *Coriolanus* as being a play which is primarily concerned with the issue of class politics. Hawkes maps the play's own engagement with issues of class confrontation on to one of the major class conflicts of twentieth-century Britain: the General Strike of the mid-1920s. Like Sinfield, Hawkes provides a brief history of the political uses to which the play has been put over the years, noting, in particular, the attraction which the play has had for those who hold extreme right-wing political views. He then goes on to document a particular production of the play planned for Stratford-upon-Avon during the course of the General Strike. The production was to take place on 23 April 1926, as part of the Shakespeare birthday celebrations.

Where in her piece on *Coriolanus* Annabel Patterson meticulously sifts through contemporary seventeenth-century sources to build up a picture of the original immediate context of the play, Hawkes in his essay is equally meticulous in investigating the background of the 1926 performance of *Coriolanus*, sifting through a variety of materials to establish the significance and implications of the play for this particular twentieth-century moment of its history. Hawkes adeptly details the way in which the performance became a lens focusing the various political conflicts taking place in Britain at the time, noting, for example, the vigorous objections of the wife of the vicar of Stratford (who styled herself 'A Fascist and a Conservative') to the suggestion that, on the day of the birthday celebrations, the flag of the Soviet Union might be included alongside those of the many other nations which were flown in the centre of Stratford in honour of the playwright's birthday.

The headlines of the *Wolverhampton Express* in covering the 1926 birthday controversy are the lines which we have chosen as the opening title of our introduction: 'Shakespeare Dragged into Politics: Inner Story of Strange Conflict'. In fact, however, what we, and the critics whose work we have selected here, have been endeavouring to do is not so much to 'drag Shakespeare into politics' as to show how Shakespeare and Shakespeare criticism always have been deeply political, even if the politics have, in many ways (both consciously and unconsciously) been unarticulated or unacknowledged. The project of Cultural Materialism and (to a significantly lesser extent) New Historicism, is not (just) to initiate a politically inflected criticism, but to make explicit the politics inherent in *all* criticism and all forms of literary discourse.

It is for this reason that we end our selection not with Terry Hawkes's essay but with a chapter from Paul Cantor's book *Shakespeare's Rome: Republic and Empire*. In finishing here, we end, in a sense, where we began: with a very traditional piece of criticism which leaves unexamined its own political foundations and assumptions. Cantor's chapter is concerned with *Cymbeline*, a play which, while it has a Roman dimension, is not traditionally included under the rubric of 'The Roman Plays'. It is rather what might be called a 'Brittano-Roman' play.[24]

Most of the critics in this volume note the connection between Shakespeare's Rome and Shakespeare's England. *Cymbeline* makes that connection explicit and posits a historical continuity between Rome and England. Cantor notes the manner in which this continuity is established in the play, commenting on how *Cymbeline* 'dramatizes the liberation of Britain from Roman domination' and observing that:

> *Cymbeline* demonstrates that Britons can meet Romans on Roman terms – on the battlefield. The play acknowledges the grandeur that was Rome, but suggests that such grandeur is past, superseded by that of a young nation, awakening to its strength and potential.

And again:

> Clearly, Britain is proper heir to Roman civilization and values . . . And yet, it is equally clear, the time has come for Britain to declare its independence of Rome and Roman values. The play depicts Britain's struggle to come into its own as a strong but gentle nation, seasoned with courtesy, humanity, and a respect for the human heart.

Cantor appears here almost as a kind of naïve Christian, extolling the virtues of a set of New Testament values which are continuous with, but superior to, the talmudic tradition of the Old. In the process, he fails to attend to the *imperial* politics which provides the true link between Rome and Britain. This, after all, was the point of England's mythologising for itself a narrative of Roman origins, with roots in the various mediæval histories which provided an originary myth, presenting Britain as continuous with Rome and with Troy.

According to these accounts, Brutus, the great-grandson of Aeneas, survivor of the sacking of Troy and founder of Rome, ventures forth on an adventure-filled voyage, during the course of which, in Geoffrey of Monmouth's twelfth-century account, he has a dream in which he is told:

> beyond the setting of the sun, past the realms of Gaul, there lies an island in the sea, once occupied by giants. Now it is empty and ready for your folk. Down the years this will provide an abode suited to you and your people; and for your descendants it will be a second Troy. A race of kings will be born there from your stock and the round circle of the whole earth will be subject to them.[25]

In this myth, then, the centre of imperial power moves ever westward, from Troy, to Rome, to the British city of 'Troynovant' (London), taken (erroneously) to mean 'New Troy'. As Britomart discovers in Edmund Spenser's *Faerie Queene*: 'For noble *Britons* sprong from *Troians* bold, / And *Troynouant* was built of old *Troyes* ashes cold' (III.ix.38.8–9).[26] Cantor obliquely alludes to this trajectory in the concluding line of his piece when he proposes that 'in Shakespeare's Roman vision, the eagle flies westward and vanishes in British sunlight'. But no attempt is made to analyse or interrogate this imperial narrative. We are left, instead, with an image of the nascent imperial Britain as 'a strong but gentle nation, seasoned with courtesy, humanity, and a respect for the human heart'. In contrast with Cantor's humanistic assessment, one might note that the prophecy which Geoffrey has Brutus receive – that 'the round circle of the whole earth will be subject to' his descendants – proves to be remarkably prescient. As Edward Said has noted, by the beginning of World War I, Britain and the other western imperial powers 'held 85 percent of the earth's surface in some sort of colonial subjugation'.[27]

Disputes over the way we approach Shakespeare are not simply a matter of local scholarly disagreements, or of arcane academic infighting. Our orientation toward these texts and the interpretations we place upon them are, in fact (as John Major's conference speech demonstrates), of central importance. Analyses of Shakespeare and of the manner in which the playwright and his works are deployed effect deep intellectual, social and political resonances and reverberations within our culture. Alan Sinfield sums up these issues very succinctly when he writes in 'Theatres of War': 'What we make of Shakespeare is important politically because it affects what he makes of us.'

Notes and References

1. To suggest that poststructuralism blindly ignores history by focusing exclusively on textuality and language is an oversimplification. For a more complex sense of the relationship between poststructuralism and history, see Robert Young, *White Mythologies: Writing History and the West* (London: Routledge, 1990). For example of an exceptionally rich interplay of poststructuralism, history, feminism and politics, see the work of Gayatri Chakravorty Spivak.

2. For an extremely useful introduction to the theory of New Historicism and the various debates surrounding it, see H. Aram Veeser (ed.), *The New Historicism* (London: Routledge, 1989).

3. Most famously (or notoriously) exemplified in E.M.W. Tillyard's *Elizabethan World Picture* (London: Chatto & Windus, 1943).

4. See, for example, Williams's *Marxism and Literature* (Oxford: Oxford Univ. Press, 1977).

5. Jonathan Dollimore and Alan Sinfield, *Political Shakespeare: New Essays in Cultural Materialism* (Manchester: Manchester Univ. Press, 1985), p. viii.

6. Ibid.

7. See his *Shakespearean Negotiations* (Berkeley and Los Angeles: University of California Press, 1988), ch. 1.

8. For a very interesting collection of articles indicating the range and thrust of New Historicist practice, see Stephen Greenblatt (ed.), *Representing the English Renaissance* (Berkeley and Los Angeles: University of California Press, 1988) – this is an anthology of articles originally published in the New Historicist journal *Representations*.

9. Jonathan Dollimore, *Radical Tragedy: Religion, Ideology and Power in the Drama of Shakespeare and his Contemporaries* (Brighton: Harvester, 1984), p. 4.

10. Graham Holderness (ed.), *The Shakespeare Myth* (Manchester: Manchester Univ. Press, 1988), p. xvi.

11. Other books on the topic have followed. See, for example, Jean Marsden (ed.), *The Appropriation of Shakespeare: Post-Renaissance Reconstruction of the Works and the Myth* (Hemel Hempstead: Harvester Wheatsheaf, 1991) and Michael Dobson, *The Making of the National Poet: Shakespeare, Adaptation and Authorship, 1660–1769* (Oxford: Clarendon, 1992).

12. See Bloom's *The Closing of the American Mind* (New York: Simon & Schuster, 1987).

13. See Foakes, *Hamlet Versus Lear: Cultural Politics and Shakespeare's Art* (Cambridge: Cambridge Univ. Press, 1993) and Vickers, *Appropriating Shakespeare: Contemporary Critical Quarrels* (New Haven: Yale Univ. Press, 1993).

14. The *Observer*, 22 August 1993, pp. 37, 38. For a similar treatment of these issues, see 'Good, Bard or Indifferent' in the *Guardian*, 13 October 1994, pp. 2–4.

15. Patrick Wintour and Stephen Bates, 'Major Goes Back to the Old Values', the *Guardian* 9 October 1993, p. 6. The letter was originally drafted by a group of twenty-one Professors of English, whose number included Catherine Belsey, Jonathan Dollimore, Terence Hawkes, Graham Holderness, Lisa Jardine, and Alan Sinfield – all of whom are primarily associated with work in the field of Renaissance studies. The original letter, together with a list of the further signatories, was reprinted in the *THES*, 11 June 1993, p. 15.

16. See Knight's classic text *The Imperial Theme: Further Interpretations of Shakespeare's Tragedies, including the Roman Plays* (Oxford: Oxford Univ. Press, 1931; London: Methuen, 1951). As Alan Sinfield notes below, 'at the time of the Falklands/Malvinas expedition, [Knight] reiterated his belief in "the Shakespearean vision" of "the British Empire as a precursor, or prototype, of world-order" '. On Knight's colourful career, see (in passing) Richard Wilson, 'Shakespeare and the Economic Cycle' in *Critical Survey* 7:1 (January 1995).

17. Derek Traversi, *Shakespeare: The Roman Plays* (London: Hollis & Carter, 1963), p. 14. Subsequent references are included in the body of the text.

18. See A.C. Bradley, *Shakespearean Tragedy: Lectures on Hamlet, Othello, King Lear, Macbeth* (London: Macmillan, 1957).

19. New Historicist critics in particular have been much given to the deployment of an anecdote as an opening gambit in their critical analyses. On the significance and force of the anecdote, see Joel Fineman's 'The History of the Anecdote: Fiction and Fiction' in Veeser (ed.), *The New Historicism*. See also forthcoming work by Annabel Patterson on the anecdote and the writing of history in Holinshed's *Chronicles*.

20. For a good account of the iconography and political symbolism of the Elizabethan era, see Roy Strong, *The Cult of Elizabeth: Elizabethan Portraiture and Pageantry* (London: Thames & Hudson, 1977).

21. The references here are to the Arden edition of the play, edited by M.R. Ridley (London: Methuen, 1954). Students are also encouraged, however, to look at the text as it was originally published – see Charlton Hinman, *The First Folio of Shakespeare* (New York: Norton, 1968), or John Turner's edition in the Shakespearean Originals series (Hemel Hempstead: Harvester Wheatsheaf, 1995).

22. For a lively, if somewhat extravagant, calling to book of male critics of *Antony and Cleopatra*, see Linda T. Fitz, 'Egyptian Queens and Male Reviewers: Sexist Attitudes in *Antony and Cleopatra* Criticism', *Shakespeare Quarterly* 28 (1977), pp. 297–316.

23. See, in particular, ch. 8 of Williams, *Marxism and Literature*.

24. For an incisive historicist analysis of *Cymbeline*, see Leah Marcus, *Puzzling Shakespeare: Local Reading and its Discontents* (Berkeley and Los Angeles: University of California Press, 1988).

25. Geoffrey of Monmouth, *The History of the Kings of Britain* (London: Penguin, 1966), p. 65.

26. Edmund Spenser, *The Faerie Queene*, ed. Thomas P. Roche and C. Patrick O'Donnell (New Haven: Yale Univ. Press, 1981), p. 515.

27. Edward Said, 'Yeats and Decolonization' in *Nationalism, Colonialism, and Literature* (Minneapolis: University of Minnesota Press, 1990), p. 71.

2 'Is This a Holiday?': Shakespeare's Roman Carnival*

RICHARD WILSON

Richard Wilson's article on *Julius Caesar* examines the play from within the politically charged traditions of Carnival. Wilson makes use of the paradigms of Carnival evolved in the work of the Russian theorist Mikhail Bakhtin, while also drawing on the work of historians such as Natalie Zemon Davis and Christopher Hill concerning inversion and subversion within the early modern social and political world. Wilson's piece provides an interesting contrast with the essays which we have included from John Drakakis and Michael Bristol, which also take up the issue of carnival, but with different emphases.

Julius Caesar was the first Shakespearean play we know to have been acted at the Globe and was perhaps performed for the opening of the new Bankside playhouse in 1599. The Swiss tourist Thomas Platter saw it on September 21, and his impressions locate the work within the different practices that went to make the playhouse. To our minds, accustomed to a decorous image of both Shakespeare and ancient Rome, it is just the collision of codes and voices which makes the traveller's report seem so jarring and bizarre:

> After lunch, at about two o'clock, I and my party crossed the river, and there in the house with the thatched roof we saw an excellent performance of the tragedy of the first emperor, Julius Caesar, with about fifteen characters; and after the play, according to their custom, they did a most elegant and curious dance, two dressed in men's clothes and two in women's.[1]

Along with the chimney-pots, feather hats and chiming clocks in the play itself, we can absorb the shock of 'the house with the thatched roof,' but the elegant jig of Caesar and the boy dressed as Caesar's wife is too alienating a mixture for us of the 'merry and tragical.' Even the Swiss visitor thought it a curious local custom, and

*RICHARD WILSON, ' "Is This a Holiday?": Shakespeare's Roman Carnival', *English Literary History* 54:1 (Spring 1987), pp. 31–44.

he was lucky to see it, because by 1612 'all Jigs, Rhymes and Dances after Plays' had been 'utterly abolished' to prevent the 'tumults and outrages whereby His Majesty's peace is often broke,' alleged to be caused by the 'cut-purses and other lewd and ill-disposed persons' who were attracted by them into the auditorium in droves at the close of each performance.[2] Platter was an observer of a theatre already expelling gatecrashers and purging itself of the popular customs that had legitimized their unwelcome intrusion. He was witnessing what Francis Barker admits were 'the seeds of an incipient naturalism growing up' inside the Elizabethan theatre, and the inauguration of a new kind of drama in England, where clowns would learn to 'speak no more than is set down for them,' and laughter – as Hamlet prescribes – would be conditional on the 'necessary question of the play.' Authority in this theatre would come to be concentrated in 'the speech' written in what Hamlet proprietorially tells the players are 'my lines' (3.2.1–45), and the mastery of the author as producer would be founded on the suppression of just those practices which Platter thought so picturesque: the unwritten scenario of the mummers' dance, transvestite mockery, Dick Tarlton's 'villainous' comic improvisation, and the raucous collective gesture of disrespect for 'His Majesty's peace.' Elite and popular traditions coexist in embarrassed tension in Platter's travel diary, where the excellence of the classical tragedy consorts so oddly with the curiosity of the antic hay. The diarist did not realize, of course, that the sequence he recorded represented the scission between two cultures and for one of them the literal final fling, nor that 'the house with the thatched roof' was the scene, even as he applauded the performance of bitter social separation.[3]

The opening words of *Julius Caesar* seem to know themselves, nevertheless, as a declaration of company policy towards the theatre audience. They are addressed by the Roman Tribune Flavius to 'certain Commoners' who have entered 'over the stage,' and they are a rebuke to their temerity: 'Hence! home, you idle creatures, get you home / Is this a holiday?' Dressed in their festive 'best apparel,' these 'mechanical' men have mistaken the occasion for a 'holiday,' and to the rhetorical question 'Is this a holiday?' they are now given the firm answer that for them, at least, it is an ordinary 'labouring day' (1.1.1–60). This is an encounter, then, that situates what follows explicitly within the contemporary debate about the value or 'idleness' of popular culture, a debate in which, as Christopher Hill has written, 'two modes of life, with their different needs and standards, are in conflict as England moves out of the agricultural Middle Ages into the modern industrial world.'[4] And as Flavius and his colleague Marullus order the plebeians back to work, it is a confrontation that confirms Hill's thesis that the Puritan attack on popular festivity was a strategy to control the emerging manufacturing workforce. The Tribunes oppose 'holiday' because it blurs distinctions between the 'industrious' and the 'idle,' just as their counterparts the London Aldermen complained the theatres lured 'the prentices and servants of the City from their works.' In fact, the Tribunes' speeches echo *The Anatomy of Abuses* (1583) by the merchants' censor Philip Stubbes, and in so doing the actors of the Globe were disarming one of the most powerful, because pragmatic, objections to their trade. As Thomas Nashe protested when the first playhouse was opened on the South Bank in 1592, professional players were not to be confused with 'squirting bawdy comedians'; they were distinct from 'the pantaloon, whore and zany' of street theatre. Their patrons were 'Gentlemen of the Court, and the Inns of Court, and captains and soldiers' (a clientele corroborated by the 1602 police raid on the playhouses), and the citizens could rest assured that 'they heartily wish they might be troubled with none of their youth nor their prentices.' So theatre-owners such as Philip Henslowe were careful to obey the ban on 'interludes and plays on the Sabbath,' closing their doors on city workers (as James I complained) on the only afternoon when they were regularly free. If working men were present to hear the beginning of *Julius Caesar* and stayed despite it, the implication is clear that they had no business to be there. Theatre, we infer, is now itself a legitimate business with no room for the 'idle.'[5]

The first scene acted at the Globe can be interpreted, then, as a manoeuvre in the campaign to legitimize the Shakespearean stage and dissociate it from the subversiveness of artisanal culture. As historians such as Peter Burke have demonstrated, revelry and rebellion were entangled in Renaissance popular entertainments, and it was no coincidence that insurrections such as the Peasants' Revolts of 1381 and 1450, the Evil May Day riot of 1517, or Kett's Rebellion of 1549 should have been sparked off at seasonal plays or have had vivid carnivalesque features. The juridical function of folk drama had been to cement the ties and obligations of an agrarian community, and when these were threatened in the transition to capitalist social relations, it was through the 'rough music' of folk customs – mummings, wakes and charivaris – that the new masters were called to ritual account. The world of carnival, with its travesty and inversion, was a standing pretext for protest; but if, as happened increasingly in the early modern period, rulers chose to ignore the 'wild justice' of festivity, there could be what Burke calls 'a "switching" of codes, from the language of ritual to the language of rebellion,' when 'the wine barrel blew its top.'[6] This is what happened spectacularly in the bloody Carnival at Romans in 1580, and it was what happened less explosively in London during the crisis years of the 1590s, when hunger and unemployment drove 'disordered people of the common sort' (in the Aldermanic phrase) 'to assemble themselves and make matches for their lewd ungodly practices' at Shrovetide, May Day or Midsummer festivals when, like the workers in *Julius Caesar*, they could still 'cull out a holiday' from the industrial week. Associating all revels with rebellion, the authorities were instinctively sure that riotous 'apprentices and servants drew their infection' from the playhouses where people also caught the plague; but, as Nashe insisted, this analogy was a kind of category mistake, which miscalculated the new theatres' social role. If the playhouse was, as coroners reported, the site of 'frays and bloodshed,' it was as the target of violence, not the origin, as when apprentices rampaged traditionally on Shrove Tuesday to 'put play houses to the sack and bawdy houses to the spoil' (in 1617 wrecking the Cockpit Theatre with the loss of several lives). The rough music of charivari was hollered in anger from outside the playhouse walls.[7]

'The disorders of the 1590s were the most serious to menace the metropolis in the decades up to the Civil War,' writes the urban historian Peter Clark in a recent essay, and what concerns him is how this unprecedented metropolitan crisis was contained.[8] The answer must lie at least partly in the success with which the language of carnival as a discourse of legitimation was commandeered by the commercial players and then tamed. For as scenes like the opening of *Julius Caesar* remind us, and as history, in Foucault's words, 'constantly teaches us, discourse is not simply that which translates struggles or systems of domination, but is the thing for which struggle takes place.'[9] It was no mere evasion of authority, therefore, which led to the theatre being situated on the criminalized southern bank of The Thames, where Platter and his party rowed to unbrace and recreate themselves after lunch. In the complex zoning of the metropolis that dates precisely from this time, Southwark was to occupy the position of a policed and segregated annex to the business and residential districts on the river's northern side. Within its licensed liberties, the Bankside was to have the status of a permanent but strictly circumscribed carnival in the city's economy of repression and indulgence, a disposal-valve in its regulation of productivity and waste. Suspect and sinistral, until the final suppression of Hogarth's Southwark Fair in 1762, the South Bank was to function as the unconscious of the capital of trade. Nor, in this geography of desire, was it accidental that the Globe was built beside those very institutions that, in Foucault's analysis, shaped the discourses of modern subjectivity. Ringed by reconstructed prisons such as The Marshalsea and The Clink, and flanked by the newly refounded St. Thomas's Hospital, the playhouse meshed with a chain of buildings charged with those dividing practices whereby the productive subject was defined by isolation from its negative in the sick, the mad, the aged, the criminal, the bankrupt, and the unemployed: separated, as Flavius urges and the 1569 Charter of St. Thomas's decreed, from 'all Idle, Begging people.'[10] The wooden operating theatre of St. Thomas's survives as the celebrated arena where the body was cut into diseased and healthy parts. The 'Wooden O' of the Globe next door, which must have resembled it in design so much, operated in analogous ways on the body politic to divide and control the visceral language of carnival, separating out productive revelry (or art) from the idleness and infection of rebellion.

If Thomas Platter was a naive theatre critic, as a sociologist he was shrewder. 'England,' he observed, 'is the servants' prison, because their masters and mistresses are so severe.' The foreign visitor could see what has been confirmed in detail by Lee Beier in his study of masterless men and the vagrancy problem in Shakespearean England, that the public order system which Foucault dated from the founding of the Paris General Hospital in 1656 was already being established in London by 1599.[11] It was a system based, however, less on crude severity than on the strategy of self-regimentation and surveillance which Brutus proposes in *Julius Caesar* when he argues for a controlled and strictly rational rebellion:

> And let our hearts, as subtle masters do,
> Stir up their servants to an act of rage,
> And after seem to chide 'em. This shall make
> Our purpose necessary, and not envious.

> (2.1.175–8)

The Shakespearean text belongs to a historical moment when a revolutionary bourgeois politics has not naturalized its own productive processes, and Brutus's realpolitik is a complete statement of the technique of the modern state whereby subversion is produced in both consciousness and society to legitimize the order that subjects it. Unruly passions and apprentices are both checked in this regime, as Hal also demonstrates in his career as agent provocateur in Eastcheap, by being known and hated: incited to be rejected. This is a system of discipline whose subtlety, as Brutus recognizes, depends not on how it obstructs but on how it manipulates desire, so that sexuality, for example, will no longer be so much forbidden as the very ground through which power controls the community and the individual. And it is just this 'subtle, calculated technology of subjection,' as analyzed by Foucault, operating in the new factory, hospital or school of Elizabethan London, which surely explains why Bakhtin says so little in his work on the subversiveness of carnival about either Shakespeare or England. His ideas were recently applied to Elizabethan drama by Michael Bristol, who argues for what he terms the 'carnivalization' of

Shakespearean literature. The argument is not convincing because, as Umberto Eco has remarked, what Bakhtinians crucially forget in their idealization of carnival is precisely the revenge of Lent: that is to say, the confinement of desire within a dialectic of transgression and containment. If carnival were always so emancipatory, Eco adds, 'it would be impossible to explain why power uses circuses.'[12]

The conditions of modern subjectivity are inscribed within the Shakespearean text. Thus, when Portia tries to persuade her husband to share 'the secrets of [his] heart' by divulging the plot she calls the 'sick offence within your mind,' she challenges him: 'Dwell I but in the suburbs / Of your good pleasure? If it be no more, / Portia is Brutus' harlot' (2.1.268–306). Body, language and thought are all held in ideological subjection in the bourgeois order Brutus represents, but when he succumbs to Portia's emotional blackmail he destroys himself by failing to quarantine desire in the suburbs of his self, where it should have been confined like the brothels of the Bankside. In *Julius Caesar* carnival – the language of desire and the flesh – is a discourse that is always mastered by the dominant. Thus, the opening scenes take place on the Roman 'feast of Lupercal:' February 14, St. Valentine's Day and the approximate date of Mardi Gras. So Shakespeare's revelling artisans connect with those 'bands of prentices, 3,000 or 4,000 strong, who on Shrove Tuesday do outrages in all directions, especially in the suburbs,' in contemporary accounts, and whose Kingdoms and Abbeys of Misrule have been researched, in their European manifestations, by Natalie Zemon Davis.[13] In the play their carnival ceremonies have been appropriated by Caesar to legitimize his intended coronation. Antony therefore runs in the 'holy chase' to 'touch' Calphurnia for fertility (1.2.7–8), while Caesar himself performs in the Shroving game by pretending to give 'the rabblement' the freedom that they shout for. This would be the tactic of King James's *Book of Sports* (1618), of royalist propagandists such as Herrick, and ultimately of the Restoration, when (contrary to Bakhtin's thesis) the rituals "of May-poles, Hock-carts, Wassails, Wakes" could be harnessed to the legitimation of a program of social conservatism. It belongs to the world of what Hill calls "synthetic monarchy," of Elizabeth's Accession Day anniversary and the Stuart revival of "touching." And by this appropriation of the discourse of festival Caesar turns politics into theatre as 'the tag-rag people clap and hiss him, according as he pleas'd and displeas'd them, as they do the players' (1.2.255). He is the Carnival King, a Lord of Misrule who governs by exploiting his subjects' desires with his 'foolery' (1.2.232), manipulating 'fat, Sleek-headed men' (1.2.190), as he indulges Antony in plays and music when he 'revels long a'nights' (2.2.116). Provoking them 'to sports, to wildness, and much company' (2.1.189), Caesar is the master of revels who knows that 'danger' belongs to the 'lean and hungry' who can discipline the body to their purposes. So his Roman carnival becomes a model of authoritarian populism, the true regimen of bread and circuses.[14]

According to Anne Barton the theatre image in *Julius Caesar* is uniquely positive and 'the actors are no longer shadowy figures: they are the creators of history.'[15] This may be true, but it oversimplifies the process that the play rehearses whereby discourses, which are the means of struggle, are themselves shaped by that struggle as it unfolds. It unfolds in the Shakespearean text like carnival itself, as a masquerade in which successive ideologies which had seemed to be authoritative are 'discovered' and discarded as power is displaced. On Mardi Gras the aim is to see without being seen behind the carnival mask; and here the eye of power strips the mask of discourse from its antagonist, revealing – as Cassius demonstrates with his satirical broadsheets 'wherein Caesar's ambition shall be glanced at' – the naked drives discursive practices hide (1.2.315). Thus the plebeians who are masterless in their holiday guise are exposed by the Tribune's Puritan analysis of Caesar's 'idle creatures'; but Puritan discourse is itself 'put to silence' when it tries to 'pull the scarfs' from Caesar's images (1.2.282). That demystification belongs to the knives of the aristocratic fraction, whose mask of constitutionalism – with its common law reverence for ancient custom and contempt for the absolutist yoke – is worn 'like Roman actors do' (2.1.226), until Antony seizes the pulpit/stage in turn and reveals the carnivorous butchery their Lenten rhetoric conceals. This is the radical potentiality of Renaissance tragedy that Jonathan Dollimore and others would mobilize as a critical weapon: the revelry with which one discourse decodes the authority of another, as Antony deconstructs the discursivity of the 'honourable men' (3.2.120–230). With 'their hats pluck'd about their ears, / And half their faces buried in their cloaks' (2.1.73–4) or masked by handkerchiefs (2.1.315), the plotters who meet in Pompey's theatre assume the anonymity of carnival and arrogate its dispensation to kill a scapegoat in their coup against Caesar, just as the real rebels of the Dutch Revolt had started their uprising against the Spanish governor at Carnival in 1563 dressed in motley and jester's cap and bells. In the Renaissance, as Stephen Greenblatt contends, 'theatricality is one of power's essential modes'; so when their 'antic disposition' is ripped from these revellers, it is fittingly by the consummate theatricality and power of speech of a champion gamesman and seasoned masker. 'A masque is treason's licence' in Jacobean drama, but the incremental logic of this revelry will be to strip all power, including that of rebels, of its legitimacy, exposing the face of bare ambition beneath the 'veil'd look' (1.2.36) of rites and ceremonies (3.1.241).[16]

The Carnival at Romans in 1580 described by Emmanuel Le Roy
Ladurie provides a paradigm of Renaissance festival as a 'psychological
drama or ballet' whose players danced or acted out class struggle
through the 'symbolic grammar' of processions and masquerades.
There the poor had celebrated a mock funeral of the rich whose flesh
they pretended to eat on Mardi Gras, until the law and order party
had organized a massacre in retaliation, arraying themselves for the
ambush in carnival costume and carrying carnival torches.[17] The Roman
carnival in *Julius Caesar* follows a similar timetable and pattern through
the cannibalistic feast of Caesar's assassination and the mock-trial of
the conspirators at the funeral, to the counterrevolution of a revanchist
repression. In Shakespearean Rome, as in actual Romans, the symbolic
discourse of public festival is a system whose social significance will
be dictated by the strongest. Likewise, poems, plays, letters, music,
names, dreams, prophecies, clouds, storms, stars, entrails and flights
of birds are all discredited as 'idle ceremonies' (2.1.197) in *Julius Caesar*,
the random signifiers on which praxis enforces meaning. This is a
deconstructive carnival that leads ineluctably to the burlesque textuality
of Caesar's bloodstained 'vesture' as interpreted by Antony in the
Forum through its gaps and 'wounded' tears, and finally, when the
corpse is divested of even that last tattered shred of discursivity, to the
exposure of Caesar's naked 'will': the 'bleeding piece of earth' which
is metonymic of all desire and power (3.2.130–60). Twenty-seven times
in thirty lines the favourite Shakespearean phallic pun is repeated
through all its libidinous connotations as it is taken up by Antony and
passed around the crowd, to substantiate in a riot of polysemy that at
the point where the text and body fuse, discourse and power are one.
Caesar had offered his murderers wine on the Ides of March. Now his
carved meat becomes with cannibalistic literalism the carnival sacrament
of a festive fraternity of blood.

Power constructs its own discursivity in Shakespearean tragedy by
appropriating the radical subversivensss of carnival, and a text such
as *Julius Caesar* seems knowingly to mediate upon its participation in
this process of sublimation and control. Thus, Caesar's will, which is
his butchered flesh, is also by etymological extension his testament
– his will power disseminated through his signed and written text –
where the potency denied him in his sterile marriage and abortive reign
is regenerated from his posthumous stimulation of the desires of the
crowd he makes his heir. Where there's a will, in the modern state,
there is also a way for power to make its own, and Caesarism works
here through a system of license and surveillance that exactly parallels
the real dividing practices of Shakespearean London. Sequestered
in the suburb of the city, desire can henceforth be partitioned and
canalized in the interests of the governing group:

Antony
Moreover, he hath left you all his walks,
His private arbours, and new-planted orchards,
On this side Tiber: he hath left them you,
And to your heirs for ever: common pleasures,
To walk abroad and recreate yourselves.
Here was a Caesar! When comes such another?

Plebeian
Never, never! Come away, away!
We'll burn his body in the holy place,
And with the brands fire the traitor's houses.
Take up the body.

(3.2.249–58)

So the incendiary brands of carnival are transformed into instruments of counterrevolution (as in London the Corpus Christi and Midsummer cressets became the flambeaux for the Lord Mayor's Show and the stolen fire of Halloween illuminated the thanksgiving for Stuart deliverance from the Gunpowder Plot). Caesar's authoritarian paternalism deflects the *vox populi* towards the institution of the monarchy by the invigilation of the people's private desires. Likewise, the sexual licence of the Bankside funfair would prove the conduit through which power would recreate itself by the regulation of the public's common pleasures in the impending bourgeois age. The corpse exhibited by Antony stands in something of the same relation to the organization of modern subjectivity, therefore, as the exemplary cadaver in Rembrandt's picture of *The Anatomy Lesson of Dr. Tulp* discussed by Francis Barker. It is the material ground, the 'earth' (3.1.254), on which bourgeois ideology will proceed to write its own interpretation of society and human life, inscribing a discourse of reason and morality on a scene of lust and blood that 'else were a savage spectacle' (3.1.223). This is quite literally how Antony uses the body for demonstration, when he effaces his own discursive practice in the interpellation of the members of the crowd as obedient subjects of the revived monarchic state:

For I have neither wit, nor words, nor worth,
Action, nor utterance, nor the power of speech
To stir men's blood; I only speak right on.
I tell you that which you yourselves do know,
Show you sweet Caesar's wounds, poor poor/dumb mouths,
And bid them speak for me.

(3.2.223–8)

Like Tulp's dissection, Antony's anatomy lesson – to be repeated with the body of Brutus – reproduces the spectacular corporeality of the carnivalesque in the service of the new power of the disciplinary society, forcing the corpse to signify 'that which you yourselves do know' about what it is to say 'This was a man!' (5.5.75). And as Antony turns desire in the mob to authoritarian ends, this is also the manoeuvre of the Shakespearean text, which reworks the ceremonies of an older kind of ritual – 'to execute, to dismember, to eat' – not simply to erase them but, as Barker notes of Rembrandt's painting, 'to take them over, to appropriate the ancient vengeful motifs and to rearticulate them for its own new purposes.' Text and picture belong to a moment, that is to say, when the bourgeoisie still has need of the energies of 'the earlier pageant of sacramental violence,' and when its 'image fashions an aesthetic which is rationalistic, classical, realistic, but one to which the iconography of a previous mode of representation is not completely alien.' As Barker goes on to explain, 'if it continues to evoke the signs of a punitive corporeality,' bourgeois representation 'also aims to draw off and reorganise the charge of these potent residues, and to invest them, transformed,' in the name of the rational spirit of capitalism, 'which will soon free itself entirely from the old body, even if it trades at first on the mystique and the terror of that abandoned materiality.'[18] So Antony must yoke 'mischief' to his politics and 'let it work' for the restoration of the social status quo (3.2.262). By syphoning the subversiveness of popular festivity in the representation of a deflected and contained rebellion, the Shakespearean text anticipates the counterrevolution of the Cromwellian Commonwealth and faithfully enacts the coercive strategy of those subtle London masters who 'stir up servants at an act of rage' (2.1.176) the better to control them. Located on the threshold of revolutionary upheaval, *Julius Caesar* is the image of bourgeois ascendency as 'necessary, and not envious,' (2.1.178) separated from popular or sectarian movements, and the natural issue of 'a general honest thought' – as Antony claims over the body of Brutus – 'and common good to all' (5.5.71–2).

Julius Caesar is the representation of a world turned upside-down to be restored, where citizens' houses are set alight by the mob in order that property values should be upheld. The question that it seems to address in this paradoxical operation is the one which would become, according to Christopher Hill, the critical dilemma of the Commonwealth, posed eventually by a pamphleteer of 1660: 'Can you at once suppress the sectaries and keep out the King?'[19] Because it arises from a historical juncture when the English bourgeoisie was engaged in a reorganization of the absolutist state to effect this end, it is a text that discloses the materiality of power with self-important openness. In particular, this early Globe play reflects candidly on the process whereby hegemony is obtained through the control of discourse, a process in which the inauguration of the playhouse was itself a major intervention. Victory in *Julius Caesar* goes to those who administer and distribute the access to discourse, and the conspiritors lose possession of the initiative in the action the moment that they concede Antony permission to 'speak in the order of [the] funeral' (3.1.230–50). Inserting his own demagogic rhetoric into Brutus's idealistic scenario, Antony disrupts that order of discourse, rearranges the 'true rites and lawful ceremonies' (3.1.241) of the republic to facilitate his countercoup, and imposes his domination through the populist device of Caesar's will. Censorship, Barker insists, was 'a constitutive experience' in the seventeenth-century construction of both the bourgeois subject and the modern state, and one which predicated the very possibility of bourgeois enunciation.[20] This text proclaims that fact when Antony revises the clauses of the will to finance his army, cuts off Cicero's Greek irony with the orator's 'silver hairs' (2.1.144), and 'damns' his enemies 'with a spot' when 'their names are prick'd out' on his proscription list (4.1.1–10). The murder by the mob of the poet Cinna for his 'bad verses' (3.3.30) and mistaken name merely confirms what Cassius and Brutus learn to their cost, that power goes with those who command the materiality of signs (3.3.30–5). Tzvetan Todorov proposes that the Incas and Aztecs fell victim to the Spanish Conquistadors because of their inferior system of signification, defeated, he believes, by Cortez's capacity to decipher their semiotic conduct whilst baffling them with his own.[21] Likewise, the republicans fail in *Julius Caesar* when they lose control of signs. Quarrelling over the meaning of their correspondence and at cross-purposes in their reading of the 'signs of battle' (5.1.14–24). Brutus and Cassius become deaf even to Homer's textual warning when they hear *The Iliad* read (4.3.129–37), while the words of Caesar that the Romans record when they 'mark him and write his speeches in their books' (1.2.125) come back to haunt the assassins at the end in the form of the Ghost, which appears the instant Brutus finds 'the leaf turn'd down' in his book and opens it to read, presumably, the avenging text: '*Veni, vidi, vici*' (4.3.251–75). 'Words before blows' (5.1.27) is the battle-order in this play which rehearses the English Revolution by enacting the Gramscian doctrine that the iron fist is preceded by the velvet glove, and that power is first enthroned in pulpits, poetry and plays.

Carnival, *Julius Caesar* reminds us, was never a single, unitary discourse in the Renaissance, but a symbolic system over which continuous struggle to wrest its meaning was waged by competing ideologies. It is the pretense of the Shakespearean text, however, that the masquerade of false appearances comes to its end in bourgeois realism, as Antony closes the action and announces his domination when he discounts all 'objects, arts, and imitations' as 'out of use and stal'd by other men' (4.1.37–8), learning to separate the idleness of drama from the business of politics. Thus the rupture forced by holiday in history would be sealed during the course of the seventeenth century as the English bourgeoisie elided its own revolutionary past. To make this representation of tragic acquiescence possible, nonetheless, the playhouse had been made the bloody site of contestation between social groups. 'The Triumph of Lent' is what Peter Burke calls the seventeenth century suppression of the carnivalesque 'World Turned Upside Down.' It was a triumph achieved only after many eruptions into the Shakespearean space of festive rout, and to grasp the operation of the new theatre as an institution of division it is only necessary to recall those intrusions from outside the enclosure of the 'Wooden O': interruptions like the episodes of Shrewsbury in 1627 when the actors of the Globe were driven out of town in the middle of a performance by fairground revellers with flaming brands, or the one that recurred on Shrove Tuesday in the capital itself, according to reports, when players half-way through an 'excellent tragedy' were 'forc'd to undress and put off their tragic habits' by the holiday crowd, and made to 'conclude the day with *The Merry Milkmaids*. And unless this were done, and the popular humour satisfied (as sometimes it so fortun'd that the players were refractory), the benches, the tiles, the laths, the stones, oranges, apples, nuts, flew about most liberally; and as there were mechanics of all professions there upon these festivals, every one fell to his trade and dissolved the house in an instant, and that made the ruin of a stately fabric.'[22] The floor of the new playhouse was not yet quite an arena which the dominant ideology could call its own, and excluded or enclosed the festive melee still found the means on occasion to deconstruct – or transvalue – the sign system of the imposing 'house with the thatched roof'.

Notes

A version of this paper was given to the 1986 Higher Education Teachers of English Conference at the University of Sussex.

1. Quoted in T.S. Dorsch, ed., The Arden Shakespeare: *Julius Caesar* (London: Methuen, 1955), vii. All citations of *Julius Caesar* are to this edition and will be included parenthetically in the text.

2. E.K. Chambers, *The Elizabethan Stage* (Oxford: Oxford Univ. Press, 1923), 4:340–1 (Order of the Middlesex Sessions, October 1, 1612).

3. Francis Barker, *The Tremulous Private Body: Essays on Subjection* (London: Methuen, 1984), 18; The Arden Shakespeare: *Hamlet*, ed. Harold Jenkins (London: Methuen, 1982).

4. Christopher Hill, *Society and Puritanism in Pre-Revolutionary England* (Harmondsworth: Penguin, 1986), 163.

5. Thomas Nashe, *Pierce Penniless* in *The Unfortunate Traveller and other Works*, ed. J.B. Steane (Harmondsworth: Penguin, 1972), 114–15; Chambers, 4:307 (Privy Council Minute, July 25 1591); L.A. Govett, ed., *The King's Book of Sports* (London, 1890), 30.

6. Peter Burke, *Popular Culture in Early Modern Europe* (London: Temple Smith, 1978), 203.

7. Chambers, 1:264–5.

8. Peter Clark, *The European Crisis of the 1590s: essays in comparative history* (London: Allen and Unwin, 1985), 54.

9. Michel Foucault, 'The Order of Discourse,' trans. I. McLeod, in Robert Young, ed., *Untying the Text: A Post-Structuralist Reader* (London: Routledge, 1981), 52–3.

10. R.E. McGraw, *Encyclopaedia of Medical History* (London: Macmillan, 1985), 138.

11. A.L. Beier, *Masterless Men: The vagrancy problem in England, 1560–1640* (London: Methuen, 1985). For Platter's comment, see 164.

12. Foucault, *Discipline and Punish: The Birth of the Prison*, trans. A. Sheridan (Harmondsworth: Penguin, 1979), 221; Umberto Eco, 'The Frames of Comic Freedom,' in Thomas Sebeok, ed., *Carnival!* (New York: Mouton, 1984), 3. Mikhail Bakhtin's influential account of carnival is in *Rabelais and his World*, trans. H. Iswolsky (Bloomington: Indiana Univ. Press, 1984). See also Michael Bristol, *Carnival and Theatre* (London: Methuen, 1985); Chambers, 1:265.

13. Natalie Zemon Davis, 'The Reasons of Misrule,' in *Society and Culture in Early Modern France* (Stanford: Stanford Univ. Press, 1975).

14. Robert Herrick, *The Poems of Robert Herrick*, ed. L.C. Martin (Oxford: Oxford Univ. Press, 1965), 5. Hill, *The World Turned Upside Down: Radical Ideas During the English Revolution* (Harmondsworth: Penguin, 1975), 353–4.

15. Anne Barton, *Shakespeare and the Idea of the Play* (Harmondsworth: Penguin, 1967), 141.

16. Jonathan Dollimore, *Radical Tragedy: Religion, Ideology and Power in the Drama of Shakespeare and His Contemporaries* (Brighton: Harvester, 1984); Stephen Greenblatt. 'Invisible Bullets: Renaissance authority and its subversion, *Henry IV* and *Henry V*,' in Jonathan Dollimore and Alan Sinfield, eds., *Political Shakespeare: New Essays in Cultural Materialism* (Manchester, Manchester Univ. Press, 1985), 33; Cyril Tourneur, *The Revenger's Tragedy*, ed. R.A. Foakes (London, 1966), 5.1.181.

17. E. Le Roy Ladurie, *Carnival in Romans: A People's Uprising in Romans 1579–1580* (Harmondsworth: Penguin, 1981), 192–215; for cannibalistic symbolism see 173, 198.

18. Barker, 76

19. Hill, *The World Turned Upside Down*, 347.

20. Barker, 51.

21. Tzvetan Todorov, *The Conquest of America: The Question of The Other* (New York: Harper and Row, 1984).

22. E. Gayton, 'Festivous Notes Upon Don Quixote' (1654), in Chambers, 1:265.

3 'Fashion it Thus': *Julius Caesar* and the Politics of Theatrical Representation*

JOHN DRAKAKIS

John Drakakis emphasises here one of the central preoccupations of literary critics in recent decades: an engagement with the politics and paradigms of *representation*. Drakakis sees the re-presentation of images of political power within the world of the early modern theatre as being a precarious and ambiguous endeavour. This theatrical enterprise anxiously locates itself, Drakakis suggests, in a position which simultaneously affirms and exposes, courts and seeks to evade the mechanisms of state control. Drakakis's position is quite similar to that adopted by Jonathan Dollimore in *Radical Tragedy*, though Drakakis finally takes an altogether more sceptical view of the potentially subversive thrust of theatre in this period.

In David Zucker's 1988 film of *The Naked Gun*, a hapless Los Angeles Chief of Police, Lieutenant Frank Drebin, is warned by his relatively pacifist Mayoress employer to curb his propensity for violence. Drebin, himself an exaggerated post-modernist collocation of easily recognizable film texts, counters with a policy statement of his own sufficient to rival any pronouncement of Clint Eastwood's Dirty Harry:

Yes, well when I see five weirdos dressed in togas stabbing a guy in the middle of the park in full view of a hundred people, I shoot the bastards. That's my policy.

The response of his outraged employer is the embarrassed revelation that: 'That was a Shakespeare in the park production of *Julius Caesar* you moron. You killed five actors: good ones.' The choice of the assassination scene from *Julius Caesar* to illustrate the violence necessary to redress an alleged crime echoes parodically one of two familiar critical readings of this Shakespearian text. In Zucker's film the comic extolling of Caesarism through the wholly inept efficiency of a law enforcement officer unaware of his own representational status and also, at the same time, unable to distinguish other forms

---

*JOHN DRAKAKIS, ' "Fashion it Thus": *Julius Caesar* and the Politics of Theatrical Representation', *Shakespeare Survey* 44, pp. 65–73.

of representation, is reinforced by the reactionary nature of his task: the protection of a visiting English queen against the threat of assassination. The latter, ironically republican critical perspective is exemplified in Alex Cox's film *Walker* (1988) which utilizes a scene from *Julius Caesar* to explore, in the thinly veiled allegorical setting of nineteenth-century Nicaragua, the ironies and contradictions inherent in an imperialist project.[1]

The case of Lieutenant Drebin is not unlike that of Julius Caesar himself, who, according to Thomas Heywood, was so accomplished an 'actor' that on at least one occasion he was involuntarily taken in by the veracity of representation itself. In *An Apology for Actors* (1612), in an argument designed, astonishingly, to advance the cause of acting, Heywood relates the following incident:

> *Julius Caesar* himselfe for his pleasure became an Actor, being in shape, state, voyce, judgement, and all other occurrents, exterior and interior excellent. Amongst many other parts acted by him in person, it is recorded of him, that with generall applause in his owne Theater he played *Hercules Furens*, and amongst many other arguments of his compleatenesse, excellence, and extraordinary care in his action, it is thus reported of him: Being in the depth of a passion, one of his seruants (as his part then fell out) presenting *Lychas*, who before had from *Deianeira* brought him the poysoned shirt, dipt in the bloud of the Centaure, *Nessus*: he in the middest of his torture and fury, finding this *Lychas* hid in a remote corner (appoynted him to creep into of purpose), although he was, as our Tragedians vse, but seemingly to kill him by some false imagined wound, yet was *Caesar* so extremely carryed away with the violence of his practised fury, and by the perfect shape of the madnesse of *Hercules*, to which he fashioned all his actiue spirits, that he slew him dead at his foot, & after swoong him *terq; quaterqu;* (as the Poet sayes) about his head.[2]

This incident is not recorded, unfortunately, in North's translation of *Plutarch's Lives*, and it has all the hallmarks of an apocryphal story. Indeed, apart from Caesar's allegedly acting in a Senecan play, at least some forty years before the birth of Seneca, it is likely that Heywood confused two stories from Philemon Holland's translation of Suetonius' *The Historie of Twelve Caesars* (1606), conflating episodes from the lives of Julius Caesar and Nero.[3] For Heywood Julius Caesar forsakes his status as an historical personage and becomes an actor himself, a focus for a range of narratives invested with sufficient authority to underwrite the activities of other 'actors'. In short, Caesar is adapted for a particular purpose, endowed with what Roland Barthes might call 'a type of social *usage*',[4] accorded the status of a 'myth' which is then used to legitimize an institution whose preoccupation is the business of representation itself. As a mythical entity, the figure of Caesar consisted of material that, as Barthes would say, had *already* been worked on so as to make it suitable for communication.[5]

Some twelve years before the appearance of Heywood's *An Apology for Actors*, and in the newly built Globe Theatre, on 21 September 1599, the Lord Chamberlain's Men mounted a production of *The Tragedie of Julius Caesar*. A Swiss visitor, Dr Thomas Platter, saw the performance, and recorded that 'at the end of the play they danced together admirably and exceedingly gracefully, according to their custom, two in each group dressed in men's and two in women's apparel.'[6] *Julius Caesar* is hardly a play to set the feet tapping, and if, indeed, this was the play that was written, as Dover Wilson conjectured, 'expressly for the opening' of the Globe[7] then the dance about which Dr Platter enthused may have had more to recommend it than mere 'custom'. Indeed, in the light of a persistent outpouring of anti-theatrical sentiments throughout this period, combined with what Jonas Barish identified as 'a deep suspicion toward theatricality as a form of behaviour in the world',[8] such a gesture, in a newly opened theatre, may be interpreted as an act of flagrant political defiance.[9] This view receives some general reinforcement from Steven Mullaney's persuasive argument that the suburbs where the public theatres were situated constituted 'a geo-political domain that was crucial to the symbolic and material economy of the city . . . traditionally reserved for cultural phenomena that could not be contained within the strict or proper bounds of the community'.[10] Moreover, the potential for resistance derived from this contextualization of the theatre is reinforced by his suggestion that dramatic performance may be defined as 'a performance *of* the threshold, by which the horizon of community was made visible, the limits of definition, containment and control made manifest'.[11] In other words, the liminal position of the theatre, which is shared with other forms of festivity, far from simply ventriloquizing the discourses of political domination, engaged in forms of representation through which other, potentially subversive voices could be heard.

A useful model for this complex process might be Volosinov's reformulation of the Freudian opposition between the 'conscious' and the 'unconscious', as a conflict between 'behavioural ideology', which, he argues, is, in certain respects, 'more sensitive, more responsive, more excitable and livelier' and 'an ideology that has undergone formulation and become "official"'.[12] In an attempt to recuperate the Freudian unconscious for a political account of the relationship between the individual and society, Volosinov insists that what is repressed or censored represents a *conscious* expression of 'behavioural ideology' in so far as it expresses 'the most steadfast and the governing factors of class consciousness'.[13] More recently, Antony Easthope has challenged the notion of a 'political unconscious' as it emerges in the work of Pierre Macherey and Fredric Jameson, on the grounds that while the notion of 'class' as a means of positioning the individual 'is involuntary and acts against the individual's will . . . it is not *unconscious* or *repressed* in the psychoanalytic sense of these terms'.[14] For Volosinov, where forms of human behaviour which are not divorced from what he calls 'verbal ideological formulation', but which remain 'in contradiction with the official ideology', it is manifestly not the case that they 'must degenerate into indistinct inner speech and then die out', but rather that they 'might well engage in a struggle with the official ideology'.[15] It is the resultant maintenance of contact both with society and with communication that gives to certain forms of behavioural ideology their revolutionary potential. Volosinov grounds the motive for such a struggle on *'the economic being of the whole group'*, but he goes on to suggest that such motives develop within 'a small social milieu' before being driven into 'the underground – not the psychological underground of repressed complexes, but the salutary political underground'.[16] This is not to suggest that the Elizabethan public theatre was a fully conscious proponent of 'revolutionary ideology', but it does go some way to ascribing intention of a sort within a very complex social formation, while at the same time designating this emergent institution as responsive, excitable, and lively. Indeed, when we consider the timing of performances, the constraints of official censorship, the social heterogeneity and consequent volatility of public theatre audiences,[17] along with the desire for respectability amongst practitioners, and the attempts to secure influential patronage, it becomes clear that the liminal status of a theatre such as the Globe effectively guaranteed its relative 'openness' to the production of contradictory cultural meanings. In addition, Volosinov goes on to suggest that where there is discontinuity between behavioural and official ideologies, then the result is a radical decentring of the individual human subject; he argues:

> Motives under these conditions begin to fail, to lose their verbal countenance, and little by little really do turn into a 'foreign body' in the psyche. Whole sets of organic manifestations come, in this way, to be excluded from the zone of verbalized behaviour and may become *asocial*. Thereby the sphere of the 'animalian' in man enlarges.[18]

We see some evidence of this decentring, and of the crisis of representation which results from it, in Shakespeare's second tetralogy, and especially in *Henry V*, a play very close temporally and thematically to *Julius Caesar*, where theatrical production itself is something for which a choric apology is required as the precondition of a larger revisionary justification for authority.[19] For Henry V, like his father before him, authority resides primarily in those ritual representations through which class interests and force are articulated: the 'idol ceremony' which is defined, somewhat defensively, in terms of a rhetorical question which discloses the operations of ideology: 'Art thou aught else but place, degree, and form, / Creating awe and fear in other men?' (*Henry V*, 4.1.243–4). As Jonathan Dollimore and Alan Sinfield have cogently argued, at this point the king 'claims to be an effect of the structure which he seemed to guarantee',[20] but he also manipulates those symbols from which he seeks some temporary disengagement in order to elicit sympathy for what we might call, with the benefit of hindsight, 'the management interest'. Of course, the figure of the king is what Derrida, in another context, identifies as a 'central presence',[21] responsible for the ordering, extending, and multiplying of a range of signifiers. And it is precisely this presence, 'which has never been itself, has always already been exiled from itself into its own substitute',[22] which the decline and death of Richard II reinforces as what we might call an '*imaginary* signification'.[23] The difficulty for *Henry V* arises directly from the confrontation which takes place in the play between a central organizing signification charged with the task of reconstituting its authority, and the behavioural ideology which challenges, on the terrain of history itself, its efficacy as an instrument for restricting meaning. The relocation – which is also to some extent a dislocation – of this process in the setting of the beginnings of Imperial Rome, and the invocation of a narrative *differentially* constructed along the axis of an opposition between 'popular' and 'humanist' readings of the Caesarian myth, makes *The Tragedie of Julius Caesar* an exemplary text whose own 'ambivalence' is brought into constitutive alignment with the openness and instability of the theatre itself. Indeed, as I shall try to show, the play's concern is not with the *subject* of representation: that is, of rendering a hitherto inaccessible reality present whose ontological status is not in question; but rather with what Robert Weimann has identified as the 'difference within the act of representation' through which a struggle for 'material interests' is articulated.[24] Indeed, if the theatre deals in representations and metaphors it also has the capability to disclose the power that authority *invests* in them, sometimes in the very act of denying their efficacy.

As a number of commentators have shrewdly observed, *Julius Caesar* contains no king; that is, absent from the play is what Derrida calls 'a re-assuring certitude which is itself beyond the reach of play'.[25] Caesar's appropriation of the feast of Lupercal, historically and mythically a festival of origins, clearly has the effect of suppressing *difference*, although this ceremonial affirmation of presence is rendered ambivalent by the anti-theatrical puritanism of Flavius and Marullus who challenge this specific *use* of 'holiday'.[26] In his instruction to Marullus to 'Disrobe the images / If you do find them decked with ceremonies' (1.1.64–5), Flavius initiates a deconstruction of the very representations which are a constitutive element of Caesar's success. They are the signifying practices which position Caesar 'above the view of men' at the same time as they reinforce the social hierarchy by keeping 'us all in servile fearfulness' (1.1.74–5). The following scene firmly inscribes Caesar in the process of 'ceremony' both as a producer and an actor, of whom Antony can say: 'When Caesar says "Do this", it is perform'd' (1.2.12), and who insists upon a complete performance: 'Set on, and leave no ceremony out.' (1.2.13) By contrast, Brutus admits, 'I am not gamesom' (1.2.30), although this anti-festive expression is quickly belied by a tacit admission of consummate acting: 'If I have veiled my look, / I turn the trouble of my countenance / Merely upon myself' (1.2.39–41); and similarly, the Cassius who eschews ritual but articulates his political desires through its language is later affirmed by Caesar as an enemy of theatrical performance: 'He loves no plays' (1.2.204). But it is ironical that while one performance is taking place elsewhere, to which the audience is denied full access, Cassius proposes to Brutus a performance of another kind, deeply dependent upon the mechanics of representation. In an attempt to disclose his 'hidden worthiness' (1.2.59), Cassius constructs a 'self' for Brutus which the latter identifies as both dangerous and alien, and it is one which involves the exposure of the means through which the allegedly tyrannical image of Caesar is sustained. Ironically, the demythologizing of Caesar, which involves divesting his name of political resonance, is itself dependent upon a representation: 'I, your glass, / Will modestly discover to yourself / That of yourself which you yet know not of (1.2.70–2). Here the 'self' is not that ontologically stable '*Center* of my circling thought' of Sir John Davies's *Nosce Teipsum*,[27] but a fabrication that can be persuaded that it is fully the subject of its own actions:

> Men at some time were masters of their fates.
> The fault, dear Brutus, is not in our stars,
> But in ourselves, that we are underlings.

> (1.2.140–2)[28]

Indeed, it is characteristic of all the conspirators that they oppose 'truth' to a distinctly theatrical falsity, as evidenced in the opposition Casca sets up between Caesar the theatrical performer and himself as a 'true man': 'If the tag-rag people did not clap him and hiss him, according as he pleased and displeased them, as they use to do the players in the theatre, I am no true man.' (1.2.258–61). Also, it is not entirely inappropriate that Messala's eulogy over the body of Cassius at the end of the play should focus upon the ambivalence of representation itself: 'Why dost thou show to the apt thoughts of men / The things that are not?' (5.3.67–8). Indeed, in the play as a whole, one man's truth is another man's theatre. If, as Ernest Schanzer speculated, 'perhaps there is no real Caesar, that he merely exists as a set of images in other men's minds and his own',[29] then the same is doubly true of Brutus, a self fashioned in accordance with the demands of an ambivalent narrative which elicits, to use Schanzer's phrase, 'divided responses'.[30]

Cassius, the stage machiavel, whose metaphorical location in the play, despite protestations in principle to the contrary, is 'Pompey's Theatre' (1.3.152) – significantly, also, the place where Caesar's own death will be staged in accordance with the generic demands of *de casibus* tragedy – initiates here a theatrical process which resonates through the remainder of the play. Casca, plucked by the sleeve, will, like a metropolitan drama critic, 'after his sour fashion, tell you / What hath proceeded worthy note today' (1.2.181–2). Cassius himself will script the representations of an alternative theatre where language itself is an irreducibly material phenomenon, and where signifiers such as 'offence', 'virtue' and 'worthiness' will depend for their meanings upon the alchemical process produced by an appearance: 'that which would appear offence in us / His countenance, like richest alchemy, / Will change to virtue and to worthiness' (1.3.158–60). As a subject of this discourse, where the stakes are political supremacy, Brutus, to use Althusser's phrase, works by himself. Indeed, in a speech which, in part, echoes Marlowe's Machevil,[31] he fabricates a narrative which radically opposes personal obligation – the friendship and 'love' through which imperial politics articulate their hierarchical interests – against a republican view which justifies human intervention in the social order:

> But 'tis a common proof
> That lowliness is young ambition's ladder,
> Whereto the climber-upward turns his face;
> But when he once attains the upmost round,
> He then unto the ladder turns his back,
> Looks in the clouds, scorning the base degrees
> By which he did ascend. So Caesar may.
> Then lest he may, prevent. And since the quarrel
> Will bear no colour for the thing he is,
> Fashion it thus:

(2.1.21–30)

Brutus, like Cassius before him, conjures here a representation of a Caesar that the play never allows us to observe as anything other than a wholly fabricated identity, and as a consequence the action is pushed further into that liminal realm already occupied by the theatre itself.

Cassius and Casca's 'fashioning' of Brutus is an indispensable precondition for the success of the conspiracy, and Brutus's soliloquy at the beginning of Act 2 moves the action deeper into that liminal area where ideology and subjectivity intertwine. It is also the area where strategies for the controlling and contesting of meaning are formulated. There is very little in the play as a whole that does not generate alternative readings, whether it be public display, ritual sacrifice, or psychic phenomenon, and it is this hermeneutic instability, the consequence of the existence of two radically opposed forms of authority in Rome, that returns the analysis of motive and action to the space occupied by the theatre which can now claim both to produce *and* to interrogate ideologies. The theatre itself achieves this complex objective, to use Michael Holquist's formulation, through bending language 'to represent by representing languages';[32] and we can see precisely what is involved here in Brutus's response to Cassius's suggestion that Antony and Caesar should 'fall together' (2.1.161). In this debate, as elsewhere in the play, critics of the most liberal of persuasions have sided with Cassius,[33] but it is Brutus more than Cassius who grasps the importance of mediating the conspiracy through existing rituals and institutions.[34] Here representation accumulates a level of irony which discloses it as misrepresentation:

> Let's be sacrificers, but not butchers, Caius.
> We all stand up against the spirit of Caesar,
> And in the spirit of men there is no blood.
> O, that we then could come by Caesar's spirit,
> And not dismember Caesar! But, alas,
> Caesar must bleed for it.

(2.1.166–71)

Clearly, liberation from alleged tyranny cannot be permitted to result in absolute freedom for all. If so, authority and power are not worth having. Resistant though the conspirators are to the Caesarian control of institutions and meanings, they formulate a strategy of temporary release and restraint which parallels the *ideological* usage of festivity, extending the potential for containment to the affective power of tragic form itself. These concerns are concentrated with remarkable economy in Brutus's appeal to his fellow conspirators: 'And let our hearts, as subtle masters do, / Stir up their servants to an act of rage, / And after seem to chide 'em' (2.1.175–7). From this point on the talk is of 'fashioning', of manufacturing, and hence of historicizing, truth, and, inevitably, of theatrical representation. The fully fashioned Brutus will now undertake to 'fashion' Caius Ligarius (2.1.219), an assertion that may well have received an added irony in the original performance where it is thought that the parts of Cassius and Caius Ligarius may have been doubled.[35] Such a suggestion would give added ironical point to Cassius's own speculation in his soliloquy at 1.2.314–15: 'If I were Brutus now, and he were Cassius, / He should not humour me.' Also Cassius's bid to revive Roman self-presence with his exhortation to the conspirators to 'Show yourselves true Romans' (2.1.222) is expanded by the one character whose 'countenance' is endowed with transformative power: 'Let not our looks put on our purposes; / But bear it as our Roman actors do, / With untired spirits and formal constancy' (2.1.224–6). Here theatrical representation is neither illusion nor self-delusion, rather it is the ground upon which the symbols of authority are contested. It is no accident that Thomas Beard could refer to the conspirators as those who 'were actors in this tragedy',[36] or that William Fulbecke could refer to Brutus as 'chiefe actor in Caesars tragedie'.[37]

If the conspirators are exhorted to sustain a 'formal constancy', then the Caesar which the first two acts of the play reveals is as consummate a Roman actor as his adversaries. To recuperate the assassination as the *origin* of a theatrical tradition in which the tragic protagonist is the unwitting participant, as Cassius later does, is simultaneously to expose the discursive mechanisms, at the moment that it seeks to reinforce, the historical and material determinants, of political power: 'How many ages hence / Shall this our lofty scene be acted over / In states unborn and accents yet unknown!' (3.1.112–14). In an augmentation of the practice of scripting, Brutus urges his accomplices to: 'Let's all cry "Peace, freedom, and liberty"!' (3.1.111), but this is followed almost immediately by the entry of a 'servant' who produces, not the voice of a free subject, but that of his 'master' Antony which he proceeds to ventriloquize. In the following scene it is the plebeian voice, emanating from an onstage audience credited with a dutiful quiescence which the actual Globe audience was unlikely to have reflected, which, ironically, through a replication of conspiratorial locutions, confirms the continuity of the rhetoric and symbols of political power: 'Let him be Caesar', 'Caesar's better parts / Shall be crowned in Brutus.' (3.2.51–3). As in the later play *Coriolanus* the 'audience' is simultaneously empowered and disempowered, allotted a rôle from which it cannot escape. In the later play, where the Roman populace is given a more substantial critical voice, the *irony* of this position is laid open to question as the Citizens are obligated to support a patrician in whom they have little confidence:

We have power in ourselves to do it, but it is a power that we have no power to do. For if he show us his wounds and tell us his deeds, we are to put our tongues into those wounds and speak for them; so if he tell us his noble deeds we must also tell him our noble acceptance of them. Ingratitude is monstrous, and for the multitude to be ingrateful were to make a monster of the multitude, of the which we, being members, should bring ourselves to be monstrous members.

(*Coriolanus* 2.3.4–13)[38]

If this is so, then it is extremely doubtful whether such self-consciously theatrical allusions serve, as Anne Righter has argued, 'preeminently to glorify the stage'.[39] This representation of the workings of political power, irrespective of intention, discloses an unstable institution proceeding gingerly into a terrain fraught with considerable political danger. Cast in a subversive role, confronted with the demands of official censorship, but nevertheless seeking legitimation, the actual choice of dramatic material would have been crucial. In *Julius Caesar* the Chamberlain's Men could displace their own professional anxieties onto a narrative which, by virtue of its very ambivalence, offered a space for the exploration of the ideology which governs the exchange of representations which take place between society and theatre, centre and margins.

In a culture in which those who would oppose theatrical representation continued to insist upon the power that inheres in the theatrical image itself, *Julius Caesar* is not so much a celebration of theatre as an unmasking of the politics of representation per se. The play does not *express* meaning; rather, in its readings of Roman history it *produces* meanings. Moreover, in its shuttling between the generic requirements of *de casibus* tragedy, and the Senecan tragedy of revenge, historical possibilities are simultaneously disclosed and withdrawn, in such a way as to propose an alignment of enjoyment with danger and with resistance. In its vacillation between 'fate' and human agency as the origins of action, and hence of history itself, *Julius Caesar* enacts the precarious position of the Globe itself. This is not the Shakespeare that we have been encouraged to regard as 'profoundly moving, or spiritually restoring, or simply strangely enjoyable', as recently proposed by Professor Boris Ford;[40] this carefully tailored brand of anti-intellectual prophylactic consumerism demands a kind of passivity that refuses to contemplate, among other things, the popular significance of that unsettling carnivalesque dance that closed the Globe performance of *Julius Caesar*. It subscribes tacitly to a teleological conception of Art not too far removed from the advice proffered by the Arts Minister, Richard Luce, as part of an argument in support of the suppression of modern 'popular' theatre: 'You should accept the political and economic climate in which we now live and make the most of it. Such an attitude could bring surprisingly good results.'[41] Of course, as we know from our own media representations of a crisis which is much nearer to us than Renaissance readings of the origins of Imperial Rome, no gun is ever naked.

Notes

1. See Geoffrey Bullough, *Narrative and Dramatic Sources of Shakespeare*, 8 vols. (London and New York, 1977), vol. 5, pp. 58–211, for the full range of source material for *Julius Caesar*.

2. Thomas Heywood, *An Apology For Actors*, I.G., *A Refutation of The Apology For Actors, The English Stage: Attack and Defense 1577–1730* (New York and London, 1973), sig. E3v.

3. C. Suetonius Tranquillius, *The Historie of Twelve Caesars, Emperors of Rome*, trans. Philemon Holland (London, 1606), sigs. C2v–3, and sigs. R4–4V. See also Suetonius, *The Twelve Caesars*, trans. Robert Graves (Harmondsworth, 1957), pp. 26ff. and pp. 219ff.

4. Roland Barthes, *Mythologies*, trans. Annette Lavers (St Albans, Herts., 1973), p. 109.

5. Ibid., p. 110.

6. William Shakespeare, *Julius Caesar*, ed. A.R. Humphreys (Oxford and New York, 1984), p. 1.

7. William Shakespeare, *Julius Caesar*, ed. J. Dover Wilson (Cambridge, 1941), p. ix.

8. Jonas A. Barish, *The Antitheatrical Prejudice* (Berkeley, Los Angeles, and London, 1981), p. 133.

9. See John Drakakis, *The Plays of Shackerley Marmion (1603–39): A Critical Old-spelling Edition*, 2 vols. unpublished PhD thesis, University of Leeds (1988), vol. 1, pp. 494ff. for a full account of the controversial position of dancing during the late sixteenth and early seventeenth centuries.

10. Steven Mullaney, *The Place of The Stage: License, Play and Power in Renaissance England* (Chicago and London, 1988), p. 9.

11. Ibid., p. 31.

12. V.N. Volosinov, *Freudianism: A Marxist Critique*, trans. I. R. Titunik (New York, San Francisco and London, 1976), p. 88.

13. Ibid., p. 88.

14. Antony Easthope, *Poetry and Phantasy* (Cambridge and New York, 1989), pp. 36–7. For a fuller articulation of the debate to which Easthope responds, see Pierre Macherey, *A Theory of Literary Production*, trans. Geoffrey Wall (London, 1978), pp. 85ff., and Fredric Jameson, *The Political Unconscious: Narrative as a Socially Symbolic Act* (London, 1981), pp. 17–103.

15. Volosinov, *Freudianism*, pp. 89–90.

16. Ibid., p. 90.

17. Cf. Andrew Gurr. *Playgoing in Shakespeare's London* (Cambridge, 1987), pp. 51–7.

18. Volosinov, p. 89.

19. See John Drakakis, 'The Representations of Power in Shakespeare's Second Tetralogy', *Cosmos: The Yearbook of the Traditional Cosmology Society*, vol. 2 (1986), ed. Emily Lyle, pp. 111–35.

20. Jonathan Dollimore and Alan Sinfield, 'History and Ideology: the instance of *Henry V*', in John Drakakis, ed., *Alternative Shakespeares* (London, 1985), pp. 222–3.

21. Jacques Derrida, *Writing and Difference*, trans. Alan Bass (London, 1978), p. 280.

22. Ibid.

23. See Cornelius Castoriadis, *The Imaginary Institution of Society*, trans. Kathleen Blamey (Cambridge, 1987), pp. 146–56.

24. Robert Weimann, 'Towards a Literary Theory of Ideology: Mimesis, Representation, Authority', Jean E. Howard and Marion O'Connor, eds., *Shakespeare Reproduced: The Text in History and Ideology* (New York and London, 1987), p. 271.

25. Derrida, p. 279.

26. Cf. Richard Wilson, '"Is this a Holiday?": Shakespeare's Roman Carnival', *English Literary History*, 54, no. 1 (Spring, 1987), 31–44. See also Mark Rose, 'Conjuring Caesar: Ceremony, History, and Authority in 1599', *English Literary Renaissance*, 19, no. 3 (Autumn, 1989), 291–304. For a more general discussion of the anti-authoritarian notion of festivity, see also Mikhail Bakhtin. *Rabelais and His World*, trans. Helene Iswolsky (Cambridge, Massachusetts, and London, 1968), pp. 21ff., and Peter Burke, *Popular Culture in Early Modern Europe* (London, 1979), pp. 182ff.

27. Sir John Davies, *The Poems of Sir John Davies*, ed. Robert Kreuger (Oxford, 1975), pp. 182ff.

28. I have followed the reading of 1.140 in *William Shakespeare: The Complete Works*, ed. Stanley Wells, Gary Taylor, John Jowett, and William Montgomery (Oxford, 1986). However, the Folio reading of the line is: 'Men at sometime, are Masters of their Fates', and this is followed in A. R. Humphreys, ed., *Julius Caesar* (Oxford and New York, 1984), and T. S. Dorsch, ed., *Julius Caesar* (London, 1965). The use of the present tense of the verb lends greater immediacy to Cassius's machiavellian proposition to Brutus.

29. Ernest Schanzer, *The Problem Plays of Shakespeare* (London, 1963), p. 32.

30. Ibid., p. 6.

31. Cf. Christopher Marlowe, *The Jew of Malta*, ed. N. W. Bawcutt (Manchester, 1978), p. 63:

> Though some speak openly against my books,
> Yet will they read me, and thereby attain
> To Peter's chair; and when they cast me off
> Are poisoned by my climbing followers.

(Prologue: lines 10–13)

32. Michael Holquist, 'The Politics of Representation', in *Allegory and Reprsentation*, ed. Stephen Greenblatt (Baltimore and London, 1981), p. 169.

33. Cf. Irving Ribner, *Patterns in Shakespearian Tragedy* (London, 1969), p. 60. See also Ernst Honigmann, *Shakespeare: Seven Tragedies: The Dramatist's Manipulation of Response* (London, 1976), p. 50; Alexander Leggatt, *Shakespeare's Political Drama: The History Plays and The Roman Plays* (London, 1988), p. 144; and Vivian Thomas, *Shakespeare's Roman Worlds* (London, 1989), p. 76.

34. For a more negative view, see Robert S. Miola, *Shakespeare's Rome* (Cambridge, 1983), p. 93, where it is suggested that 'Brutus's words reveal the savagery of the impending Roman ritual; in addition they expose the self-delusion of the conspirators.'

35. A.R. Humphreys, ed., *Julius Caesar*, pp. 80–1. I am also grateful to Professor Gunther Walch for having drawn this possibility to my attention in his unpublished paper ' "Caesar did never wrong, but with just cause": Interrogative Dramatic Structure in *Julius Caesar*'.

36. Thomas Beard, *The Theatre of God's Judgements* (London, 1597), p. 249, *Short Title Catalogue* 1659.

37. William Fulbecke, *An Historicall Collection of the Continuall Factions, Tumults, and Massacres of the Romans and Italians* (London, 1601), p. 170. *Short Title Catalogue* 11412.

38. See John Drakakis, 'Writing The Body Politic: Subject, Discourse, and History in Shakespeare's *Coriolanus*', *Shakespeare Jahrbuch*, ed. Gunther Klotz (1992).

39. Anne Righter, *Shakespeare and The Idea of The Play* (Harmondsworth, 1967), p. 141.

40. Boris Ford, 'Bardbiz', *Letters: The London Review of Books*, vol. 12, no. 14 (2 August 1990).

41. John McGrath, *The Bone Won't Break: On Theatre and Hope in Hard Times* (London, 1990), p. 161.

4 Theaters of War: Caesar and the Vandals*
ALAN SINFIELD

Alan Sinfield's piece on *Julius Caesar* is taken from his book *Faultlines: Cultural Materialism and the Politics of Dissident Reading*, which seeks to formalise and enact some of the strategies of criticism first evolved by Sinfield and Jonathan Dollimore when they facilitated the emergence of Cultural Materialism. Sinfield exposes the fractures which run through literary texts – those places where a text's various ideological codes come into conflict with each other. The stress which Sinfield lays on the contemporary as well as the historical in his analysis of *Julius Caesar* is typical of the Cultural Materialist approach. Sinfield also attempts here to 'intervene' in the text – to restructure the narrative according to an alternative political agenda.

Playing the globe

'Soviet Gains in Armor/Antiarmor Shape US Master Plan'; 'Services Adapt Airborne EW to Cope with Missile Threats' – these are titles of feature articles in the February 1989 issue of *Armed Forces Journal International*. In this context the armaments executive who wants his 'news ahead of the pack' (the journal's target reader in its promotion) must have been surprised to see on page 73 a full-page picture purporting to represent the 'Globe Theatre.' It looks sepia, old, misty, low-tech (engraved), romantic, even sentimental; possibly the kind of print the executive might put on his office wall to show off his culture; a contrast with the business rather than a part of it.[1] However, the legend proclaims a connection: 'We helped protect the Globe in 1588.' Turning the page, the executive finds a more reassuring scene: a double spread showing a feast of modern weaponry, all very much in action.

Three panels in vivid color feature air, land, and sea operations; they are congested and overflow towards the right; the whole ensemble

*ALAN SINFIELD, *Faultlines: Cultural Materialism and the Politics of Dissident Reading* (Oxford: Clarendon, 1992), pp. 1–28.

points towards the fourth panel and the headline that transforms catachresis into sense. Of course, it is a *theater of war*; as the headline says, 'You might be surprised by the theaters we play.' But the connection is specific: 'Since Shakespeare's work played at the Globe Theatre in 1588, Royal Ordnance products have been in action in every major event of Britain's military history.' This is true: the Royal Ordnance Company is a British weapons manufacturer deriving from the royal munitions factory and store of earlier centuries; in Queen Elizabeth I's time, it had quarters in the Tower of London, a store in the Minories nearby, and an artillery yard beyond Bishopsgate. Royal Ordnance did not help protect the Globe Theatre in 1588 because the Globe was not built until 1599, but it did help defend English interests worldwide (for that is part of the pun) from the Spanish Armada. Through the centuries of the British Empire, Royal Ordnance contributed to killing innumerable people around the globe.

Nowadays the empire is not what it was, and there are not so many opportunities for Britain to fight with ships and planes, other than as a U.S. satellite. Perhaps that is partly why the Thatcher government privatized Royal Ordnance in 1987: it is no longer credible for the British state to maintain an organization to supply it with a system of modern weaponry.[2] So, in February 1989, Royal Ordnance found itself exposed fully to the chilly blasts of private enterprise; and hence the advertisement. The profit these days is mostly in selling to dictatorial regimes that sustain themselves through repressing their citizenry and menacing their neighbors. In 1989, a year before the Iraqi invasion of Kuwait and despite an ostensible arms embargo, Ordnance was among the exhibitors at the Baghdad arms fair. In that year, and with encouragement from the British government's Department of Trade and Industry, Ordnance supplied strips of explosives retardant, necessary to help propel large rockets, to a middleman who sent them to Iraq.[3] In 1991 British Aerospace, now Ordnance's parent company, reported a 62 percent rise in profits from weaponry and declared itself in a strong position to take advantage of the 'opportunities expected to emerge in the Middle East after the Gulf War.'[4]

Despite such opportunities, the weapons business is an uncertain one for a British manufacturing base enfeebled by a decade of Thatcherism and subject to international developments over which it has no influence (on shipments to Iraq, the Trade and Industry minister advised that 'if the political overtones of the Iraq/Iran conflict change, e.g. if the US becomes more supportive of one side than at present, then the current order may change').[5] Although the advertisement pictures ships and planes, the text indicates that Royal Ordnance is actually working on a sensibly unpretentious range of components, which it hopes to combine with the products of other firms. The special

pitch in the advertisement is collaborations with U.S. companies.
'Partners in Excellence,' it says, with British and U.S. flags side by side.
Ordnance may be a small company but it has tradition and excellence:
'After 400 years, Royal Ordnance still plays the Globe. All of it. Thanks
to partnerships born in tradition and designed for excellence.' And the
ultimate witness to those where Britain is concerned is Shakespeare.
The Globe is indeed famous all round the globe; it is the part of
English achievement that still flourishes; the best-known 'royal'
institution after the monarchy is the Royal Shakespeare Company.
For U.S. entrepreneurs, it may yet recall the power that blasted out a
worldwide empire, once including Iraq; once even North America.

So the military-industrial complex is not unrelated to cultural
power, at least in the mind of a copywriter (who probably majored
in English). Yet cultural and military-economic power are not simply
aligned. In fact, the advertiser's strategy of surprise is quite risky;
too much tradition is a dangerous thing. Knowledge of the Ordnance
in Elizabethan times would certainly disturb the target reader of the
advertisement. It was honeycombed with corruption – stores were
improperly sold off, balances put to private uses, and kickbacks
extracted from purveyors. An enquiry found losses from fraud
totaling as much as £100,000; the Clerk of the Ordnance had to repay
nearly £2,000. 'The defeat of the Armada might have been even more
conclusive,' E.K. Chambers observes, 'but for a shortage of ammunition
in the English ships.[6] It was no better when the Earl of Essex became
master in 1597 – he saw the office merely as a chance to gain control
of the military apparatus so that he could set up adventures like the
disastrous search for the Spanish treasure fleet in the Azores. Such a
tradition is dangerously close to the weapons procurement scandals
reported today; not the kind of thing of which Royal Ordnance wants
to remind, say, Lockheed or McDonnell Douglas.

However, the copywriter evidently intends to play upon a
disequilibrium – '*you might be surprised* that we design and manufacture
a complete range of weapon systems and sub-systems.' Notice the
spellings – 'theater of military operations,' but 'Globe Theatre': that's
tradition for you, they hang on to their quaint old way of writing (it
has to be an English major)! It is a surprising strategy, for the link with
Shakespeare and olden times does not suggest high-tech competence;
it risks the thought that the British army might still be equipped with
pikes and halberds, that British technology might be old-fashioned.

Furthermore, the kind of traditional excellence that is associated
with Shakespeare is widely regarded as transcending physical
conflict, technology, and politics. As John Fekete puts it, 'The central
problematic of the tradition is structured by questions of unity and
equilibrium, of order and stability. From the beginning, but increasingly

systematically, the tradition embraces the "whole" and structures a totality without struggle and historical movement.'[7] To many people, Shakespeare represents art and spiritual nobility, and they might well seem incompatible with the details of weapons procurement and killing all those people. This was not a problem of principle in Elizabethan times. William Painter was Clerk of the Ordnance from 1560 to 1594, and he was the compiler of *The Palace of Pleasure* (1566–67), a handy quarry of stories for English writers. For most of this period the Earl of Warwick was Master of the Ordnance, and he anticipated the revival of aristocratic patronage of music by employing Thomas Whythorne in 1556 (though they parted when the earl did not pay the promised annuity).[8] In 1585 Sir Philip Sidney became Joint Master with Warwick. High culture did not seem incompatible with weaponry (though in fact a piece of ordnance destroyed the Globe Theatre, which burned down after the firing of a cannon during a performance of *Henry VIII*; some of the smoldering wadding lodged in the thatched roof – probably after 375 years they have found ways of preventing that).

But today the Shakespeare connection is challenging. It could undermine, rather than validate, the ambitions of the weapons company. The potential gain from the advertiser's point of view, which makes this risk worthwhile, is *a legitimation of imperial enterprise*. For, as British cultural critics have shown, Shakespeare's achievement has been made to symbolize a supposed imperial English destiny to civilize the whole world. The Gulf, for instance; Thomas Carlyle declared: 'Even in Arabia, as I compute, Mahomet will have exhausted himself and become obsolete, while this Shakespeare . . . may still be young; – while this Shakespeare may still pretend to be a Priest of Mankind, of Arabia as of other places, for unlimited periods to come!' At the time of the Falklands/Malvinas expedition, G. Wilson Knight reiterated his belief in 'the Shakespearean vision' of 'the British Empire as a precursor, or prototype, of world-order.'[9] So Shakespeare's authority may be designed to work with distinctive subtlety in the mind of the company president – not at the point where he checks the figures on the most economical 'low signature and liquid propellants' (perhaps for Iraqi rockets), but in that weakened moment of dawn waking when he wonders *what it is all for*. Then the slogan glimmers through his consciousness: 'We helped protect the Globe in 1588' . . . and later that morning he signs the contract with Royal Ordnance – in order to keep the world free for the performance of Shakespeare.

[. . .]

It has become fashionable to begin by analyzing an obliquely relevant picture. Several of the preoccupations that have engaged me for a decade and more are broached in my opening. It is designed to

epitomize a way of apprehending the strategic organizations of texts –
both the modes by which they produce plausible stories and construct
subjectivities, and the faultlines and breaking points through which
they enable dissident reading. And it focuses institutions as well
as texts, anticipating study of the cultural apparatuses that arrange
writing and theater in early modern England and the modern world,
and of their relations with other institutions (such as the church) that
tend partly to legitimate state violence but may be bent partly to other
purposes. The unstable juxtaposition of cultural and military-industrial
discourses in my picture is typical of the uneven and changing
relations between economic, political, military, and cultural power. It
is the project of ideology to represent such relations as harmonious
and coherent, so effacing contradiction and conflict; and the project of
cultural materialists to draw attention to this. [. . .] Cultural materialism
seeks to discern the scope for dissident politics of class, race, gender,
and sexual orientation, both within texts and in their roles in cultures.

These are topics of some importance if 'freedom' is to be detached
from the ideologies that have appropriated it and to be more widely
actualized in human societies. Of course, power resides with the
collaborators and customers of Royal Ordnance, with their specialist
combat vehicles and lightweight howitzer developments. Even so,
weapons still depend on the authority to use them – the cannon
in *Henry VIII* was not fired in battle but to add symbolic weight to
the king's entrance. In many countries, at some time, the state and
the military have had to yield when they have lost sufficient popular
legitimation; conversely, in the 'Western democracies,' a major question
is how right-wing governments get installed through the ballot. The
conferral of cultural authority is a principal role of Shakespeare in our
societies: he may be made to underwrite state bellicosity, or perhaps to
say something different.

Julius Caesar: acting precedents

In summer 1988, thanks to the financial assistance of the National
Endowment for the Humanities, which no doubt was looking for
tradition and excellence, Jonathan Dollimore and I were fortunate
enough to be invited to the University of California at Santa Cruz to
talk about Shakespeare. The condition was that we address the plays
being performed in the theater there. I agreed to discuss *Julius Caesar*
– it was a set text when I was a student, so I thought I would
be all right. But coming back to the play, I found I didn't care for it
much. I tried identifying with the characters in the way traditionally

advised, but that hardly helped – senators and commanders, with
their triumphs, victories, enterprises, and ensigns, sound unpleasantly
like the brands of company cars supplied to Royal Ordnance middle
management. Usually, in Shakespeare, the common humanity of such
figures is supposed to shine through details of status, but I could
not see it; and anyway, as a cultural materialist I don't believe in
common humanity. However, as Catherine Belsey observes, *Julius
Caesar* does stage political structures alternative to absolutism, raising
questions of tyranny, sedition, and freedom that were difficult to
handle in English history plays, so the play should offer some scope
for political negotiation.[10] Like many Shakespearean plays, it is about
gaining legitimation for the exercise of state violence. The wars initiated
by powerful men – Pompey, Caesar, Brutus, Cassius, Antony, and
Octavius – frame the action, but in between the issue is how people
may be persuaded to accept rival authority claims.

Since the occasion was a theater festival, I went to the stage history.
This confirmed what I had expected (funny how often that happens
in literary study): that theater people through the centuries have got
Julius Caesar to make sense for them by adjusting, often violently,
what appears to be the tendency of the received text. Shakespeare is
a powerful cultural token, such that what you want to say has more
authority if it seems to come through him. That is how Shakespeare
comes to speak to people at different times: the plays have been
continuously reinterpreted in attempts to coopt the bard for this or that
worldview. This is not surprising or illegitimate; it is a key practice
through which cultural contest proceeds. In the eighteenth century,
people experienced very reasonable anxieties about the blatantly
unjust system of rule in Europe and North America, and *Julius Caesar*
was understood as addressing despotism and the rule of the gentry
through Parliament. Generally it was appropriated as a blast against
autocracy, with Brutus as the hero of patrician oligarchy and Caesar as
a ranting, strutting villain. Francis Gentleman believed in 1770 that the
play inculcates 'one of the noblest principles that actuates the human
mind, the love of national liberty.'[11] In fact, the text was cut, rewritten,
and extended to produce this reading. The most awkward incidents
were the killing of Cinna the Poet (3.3) and Octavius and Antony
deciding who shall be murdered (4.1): they seem to present particularly
discreditable consequences of the killing of Caesar, and hence were
usually omitted.[12] And since it seemed unfair and superstitious that
the noble and reasonable Brutus should be afflicted with Caesar's
Ghost, they cut that as well. Productions in the American colonies
shared the identification with the patricians – they thought they were
as civilized as the classical Romans (well, they had Roman institutions
like oligarchy and slavery). In the revolutionary period, *Julius Caesar*

figured the struggle against English domination; in 1770 the play
was advertised for the theater as 'The noble struggles for liberty by
that renowned patriot Marcus Brutus.' Abigail Adams wrote to her
husband John: 'There is a tide in the affairs of men' and sometimes
signed herself 'Portia'; Thomas Jefferson's commonplace book begins
with passages from the play. As president, George Washington is said
to have staged an amateur production of *Julius Caesar* in the garret
of his executive mansion in Philadelphia, with himself as Brutus.[13]
Conversely, in England, although the play had been popular as
alluding to British liberties, it was not performed at all from the time
of the American Revolution, through the French Revolution, until
well into the nineteenth century. The writer Mrs. Elizabeth Inchbald
explained in 1808 that it had been not 'advisable' to stage it:

> When men's thoughts are deeply engaged on public events,
> historical occurrences, of a similar kind, are only held proper for
> the contemplation of such minds as know how to distinguish, and
> to appreciate, the good and evil with which they abound. Such
> discriminating judges do not compose the whole audience of a
> playhouse; therefore, when the circumstances of certain periods
> make certain incidents of history most interesting, those are the very
> seasons to interdict their exhibition.[14]

Some of the less discriminating might have been inspired to stage their
own revolution. Later, speeches from *Julius Caesar* were valued in the
British Labor movement – the communist trades unionist Tom Mann
was still roaring out in old age: 'I had as lief not be as live to be / In
awe of such a thing as I myself.'[15]

For the centenary of U.S. independence in 1875–76, republican
sentiments were combined with the nineteenth-century enthusiasm for
spectacle. According to a contemporary record, the end of *Julius Caesar*
was elaborated with the funeral pyre of Brutus:

> The lights of the distant city glitter on the hillside, and the army,
> marshalled in the foreground, looks strange and weird with its many
> torches and the reflected lights on helmets, shields, and spears. In
> the centre of the stage is the funeral-pyre, which is presently lighted;
> and then, amid music, a wild confusion of lights and mysterious
> shadows, warlike ranks with banners and glittering arms, and a
> leaping blaze in the centre, the curtain falls.[16]

As many as four hundred extras were used (almost on the scale of
the battle scene in the Royal Ordnance advertisement; both reporters
and airmen present at the initial, euphoric bombing of Baghdad in

January 1991 said it was like fireworks on July 4). The idea may have been to recall the twelve-day funeral procession of Abraham Lincoln in 1865, some of it at night time 'in the flare of torches and gaslights,' with a guard of honor of prominent army officers and detachments from scores of regiments; in New York as the bells tolled midnight, 'a German chorus of some seventy voices commenced suddenly to sing the *Integer vitae*.' (At the rear in New York came a body of freed slaves, allowed to march after an appeal to the secretary of war, though it was feared they would provoke disorder.)[17] One opposition senator said it was all like 'the crafty skill of Mark Anthony in displaying to the Roman people the bloody mantle of Caesar,' but for many people Lincoln was the freedom-loving Brutus.[18] Or perhaps the idea was that Brutus's funeral would dispel other images of mass dedication to freedom: the demonstrations of farmers and workers in every part of the Union that marked the 'red scare' of 1873–78. Strikers, the unemployed, socialists, and eight-hour campaigners, inspired by the Paris Commune and energized by economic recession, rallied in their thousands. In very many cases, they were brutally assaulted by militia and police.[19]

Modern productions of *Julius Caesar* usually take it to be about the personal qualities and dilemmas of the patricians. This liberal approach works by centralizing Brutus as the intellectual tempted out of his study, where he has maintained a noble integrity, and into the corrupting public world. [. . .] For Orson Welles in 1937, the play was subtitled 'Death of a Dictator': it was about 'the eternal, impotent, ineffectual, fumbling liberal; the reformer who wants to do something about things but doesn't know how and gets it in the neck in the end.' Rather gleefully, Welles saw Brutus as 'the bourgeois intellectual, who, under a modern dictatorship would be the first to be put up against a wall and shot.' The received text was thoroughly reorganized to produce this reading. In the drama of liberal anguish, the death of Cinna the Poet suddenly becomes crucial, for the danger from the populace seems as great as that from the dictator. Welles played Cinna's murder to big effect, augmenting it with lines from *Coriolanus*, believing that it is the crude, insensitive people that cause fascism – 'the hoodlum element you find in any big city after a war, a mob that is without the stuff that makes them intelligently alive, a lynching mob, the kind of mob that gives you a Hitler or a Mussolini.'[20] The theme of liberal impotence surfaced also in the 1953 film directed by Joseph L. Mankiewicz, with cautiously unobtrusive reference to the confusion of the well-intentioned in the face of the McCarthyite House Un-American Activities Committee. Mankiewicz had been elected president of the Screen Directors' Guild in 1950 on a platform of resistance to requiring members to swear that they were not communists. While Mankiewicz was absent in Europe, however, the right-wing Cecil B. deMille put through a mandatory oath and suggested that Mankiewicz was a 'pinko,' a 'fellow traveller,' an unreliable intellectual. After caucus meetings distinctly like those of the Brutus-Cassius conspiracy, Mankiewicz managed to preserve his position – but he felt it necessary to require the loyalty oaths anyway.[21]

Another liberal version was offered by Minos Volanakis in his London Old Vic production in 1962: Brutus is 'the very embodiment of the ideals that fired the Renaissance and fostered modern liberalism,' Volonakis said, asserting that the project of the play is 'to examine and exhaust the possibility of salvation through politics.'[22] Michael Kahn, director of the Shakespeare Theater, Ontario, produced a comparable version at the time of the Nixon-McGovern presidential election of 1972. Kahn says he wanted to do *Julius Caesar* then because he sympathized with McGovern but thought Nixon would make a stronger president; and that this was like Brutus and Caesar. Thinking of the slaughter in the Vietnam War and recent assassinations, Kahn asked himself, somewhat ambitiously, 'Do you go out and bomb Hitler, do you kill Richard Nixon? . . . violence as a political act concerned me, and I continually faced my ambivalences about it.'[23] Despite his respect for Caesar/Nixon, Kahn's 'ambivalences' align him with his liberal Brutus; Kahn found politics 'an almost insoluble problem to deal with,' so in *Julius Caesar* 'everybody was right and everybody was wrong' (p. 76). This is the dominant attitude among modern humanities intellectuals. At the same time, usually, the private individual is validated as against nasty public politics. Trevor Nunn, at the Royal Shakespeare Company in 1972, found in *Julius Caesar* 'the theme of the disparity and friction between private and public. I mean private morality and public necessity.' And again: the play is about 'the requirements of a system of good government, of world politics as opposed to what it is that's rich and rare individually in people. Individuals are destroyed.'[24] Arthur Humphreys in his Oxford edition of the play admires the BBC/Time-Life version (1978) which 'went less for Romans or politicians than for human beings, caught in an impetuous action' (p. 71).

Such an interpretation plainly tends to discourage political engagement. To be sure, there is no system of government that will not require unremitting vigilance, and in many circumstances the cost of dissidence may be high. But it is not constructive to suggest that if you try to make the world better you will only sacrifice your integrity and probably make things worse. Nor is the individual outside politics. To the contrary, 'the individual' is an ideological concept, and the whole idea of anything being outside politics is a political idea tending to inhibit understanding and action. *Julius Caesar* in fact raises these questions, in that Brutus is not, of course, a humanistic intellectual in any modern sense, but a senator, a senior member of the governing elite. Insofar as he is also a philosopher, that is because intellectual concerns were not believed to be incompatible with government at the time of either Brutus or Shakespeare (consider Cicero and Francis Bacon). It is characteristic of our cultures, not theirs, to validate art and philosophy by denying their connection with political power (such that Shakespeare and Royal Ordnance now constitute a provocative juxtaposition).

Although the received text of *Julius Caesar* encourages liberal attention to the personal qualities of the patricians, it also allows us to see other factors in the political process. The action is a feast for the new historicist idea of power as display:[25] set pieces alternate with sudden histrionic appeals, especially to the plebeians, for Caesar's success has problematized the prevailing conventions of authority in the Roman state. At the start, the tribunes Flavius and Marullus are persuading the people not to celebrate Caesar's triumph; they remove his trophies from statues. 'Leave no ceremony out,' Caesar says (1.2.11), perhaps thinking to stage his coronation. He is the arch performer in the theater of power – the people 'clap him and hiss him, according as he pleas'd and displeas'd them, as they use to do the players in the theatre' (1.2.255–58). Brutus has a similarly theatrical notion of political activity: 'Let not our looks put on our purposes,' he tells his fellow conspirators, 'But bear it as our Roman actors do' (2.1.225–26). He assumes that popular support must be won by suitable representation, and he wants to manage the killing of Caesar such that 'appearing to the common eyes, / We shall be call'd purgers, not murderers' (2.1.179–80). Legitimacy in Rome depends on theatrical flare in public relations. The first move after the assassination must be to 'Run hence, proclaim, cry it about the streets' (3.1.79); hence the importance of the rival speeches of Brutus and Antony in the forum. The battle at Philippi is determined by the loyalties of the armies and the patricians' apprehensions about them. Octavius (a great patron of the arts) is to alter this pattern by suppressing popular rights and instituting an even more elaborate apparatus of theatrical representation, posing as a god in an imperial cult of personality. Such a sequence has occurred in many countries.

These aspects of the play enable us to glimpse a *Julius Caesar* with a different politics to those so far discussed, one that would center upon the relations between the people and those who scheme to gain their allegiance. The problem is how to bring it out, given that the received text seems mainly concerned with the patricians, with but slight, and slighting, role for the plebeians. One indication of the extent to which Shakespearean interpretation is not a quest for the true reading

but a historically located cultural convention, or rather bundle of
conventions, is the wider freedom that theater directors are customarily
allowed. Since my talk at Santa Cruz was to accompany a theater
festival, I thought I might commandeer some of the director's larger
license, releasing myself from the demand of literary criticism that lines
that seem to resist your reading must somehow be incorporated or
explained away. Inspired by the diverse renderings of *Julius Caesar* on
the stage, I felt emboldened to devise a reworking of my own.

[. . .]

An obvious strategy would be to undermine the status of the
patricians by making them appear analogous to stupid and corrupt
modern politicians. We might make the theatrical Caesar resemble
Ronald Reagan – who, after all, was identified by Gore Vidal as the
'acting president' and by Michael Rogin as *'Ronald Reagan,' The Movie.*
Both leaders have perplexed commentators by combining star-wars
fantasies of omnipotence with bumbling, forgetfulness, and superstition
that might or might not be strategic.[26] It would be important not to
suggest that others of the ruling elite are more honest or capable than
Caesar (that is the liberal move); they are parts of the same gang (they
all turn out to be superstitious). However, one drawback with such
a comparison between *Julius Caesar* and the modern political situation
lurks in the region of U.S.–U.K. power relations. For if imperial Rome
is the United States then Britain, as in Roman times, is a remote
outpost of empire; and hence a candidate, like Shakespearean Egypt,
for a tourist theme park where the imperial power can fantasize an
exotic other (for Alexandria read, say, Stratford).

[. . .]

Creative vandalism

The other drawback with such a version of *Julius Caesar* is that
ridiculing the governing elite, which of course has often been done,
maintains its centrality; in the modern equivalent, it maintains the
media fiction that Washington infighting is the necessary and adequate
site of political activity. To represent the potential of other forces in
the state, it will be necessary to engineer a radical shift in perspective.
Given the license of the theater director, I would move the plebeians
to the center, challenging directly the tendency of criticism to see them
as the eternal mob and the tribunes as rabble-rousers (even Annabel
Patterson, who argues for a positive representation of the citizens in

Coriolanus, sees them in this way).[27] The received text certainly licenses such a view. Casca finds Cassius persuasive when he blames the people for Caesar's dominance:

> And why should Caesar be a tyrant then?
> Poor man! I know he would not be a wolf,
> But that he sees the Romans are but sheep;
> He were no lion, were not Romans hinds.
> Those that with haste will make a mighty fire
> Begin it with weak straws. What trash is Rome,
> What rubbish, and what offal, when it serves
> For the base matter to illuminate
> So vile a thing as Caesar!
>
> (1.3.103–11)

Upper-class rule is necessary, it is suggested, because the people are likely to endorse tyranny. But 'the mob' is not an adequate concept with which to handle the roles of the plebeians, even in the received text. To be sure, some of them perpetrate unreasonable violence, but to a tiny extent in comparison with the patricians in their battles. The play in fact allows us to see that at other times the people are lively, independent, shrewd, and sensible.

The key figures are the tribunes, Marullus and Flavius. An attractive reading is to see the plebeians in the opening scene as unruly Bakhtinian revelers, the possessors of a traditional popular wisdom that is put down by the tribunes. Richard Wilson considers the tribunes' ordering the plebeians back to work in the light of Christopher Hill's thesis that puritans attacked popular festivities in order to control the emerging work force.[28] However, it is a mistake to abstract carnival from historical conditions, to regard it as an absolute political quality. As Wilson shows, it was not a single, unitary discourse, 'but a symbolic system over which continuous struggle to wrest its meaning was waged by competing ideologies'; the ceremonies are made to feed into Caesar's coronation and the carnivalesque 'becomes a model of authoritarian populism'. With this in mind, I would activate a fact that is widely overlooked, and that admittedly, is scarcely registered in the Shakespearan play – namely, that the tribunes, historically, were not 'ruling-class' spokesmen, but the chosen leaders of the plebeians.[29] Their election by open popular ballot was, at least in potential, a democratic feature of the republican polity, a major constitutional check upon patrician power. In 81 B.C. the dictator Sulla undermined the role of the tribunes when they 'revived the dormant sovranty of the People'; Pompey restored their rights in

70 B.C.[30] So in the opening scene of *Julius Caesar*, Marullus and Flavius are understandably dismayed by their constituents' enthusiasm for Caesar and remind them of their erstwhile support for Pompey. The subversive vitality of the Cobbler is very well, but if popular rights are to be defended, it has to be blended with analysis, organization, and strategy; party discipline has to be maintained. Machiavelli argues the need for plebeian leaders: as an 'excited crowd,' the populace may become 'cowardly and weak,' he says, so 'it should at once make one of its members a leader so that he may correct this defect, keep the populace united, and look to its defence; as did the Roman plebs, when, after the death of Virginia they quitted Rome and for safety's sake appointed twenty of their members as tribunes.' Machiavelli adds that in hundreds of years, the Roman populace 'did not make four elections of which it had to repent.'[31]

In *Julius Caesar*, the tribunes' political program is vastly superior to that generated among the ruling elite, for instead of plotting to murder Caesar, they exhort the people to act openly, constitutionally, and collectively against the alterations to the constitution proposed by Caesar's party. They urge them to display signs of their crafts, for class solidarity, and to organize a counter-demonstration against Caesar's triumph:

> Go, go, good countrymen, and for this fault
> Assemble all the poor men of your sort;
> Draw them to Tiber banks, and weep your tears
> Into the channel, till the lowest stream
> Do kiss the most exalted shores of all.
>
> (1.1.56–60)

That concluding image, of the popular demonstration flooding the political system, such that the 'lowest' people achieve a significant voice, proves optimistic, but the people do, in fact, exercise their influence against Caesar's undermining of traditional rights. Even through the snobbish and disdainful (funny) speech of Casca, it is clear that the plebeians cheer Caesar when he reluctantly *refuses* the crown offered him by Antony:

> He put it the third time by; and still as he refus'd it, the rabblement
> hooted, and clapp'd their chopt hands, and threw up their sweaty
> night-caps, and uttered such a deal of stinking breath because
> Caesar refus'd the crown, that it had, almost, choked Caesar; for he
> swounded, and fell down at it.
>
> (1.2.239–45)

Contrary to the idea implicit in some new historicist writing, the people are not easily fooled by the theater of state that the patricians clumsily improvise. Caesar is forced into improvisation and offers his throat for the cutting, perceiving that 'the common herd was glad he refus'd the crown' (1.2.260–64).

[. . .]

However, we hear shortly, 'Marullus and Flavius, for pulling scarfs off Caesar's images, are put to silence' (1.2.282–83). This is a move against the political power of the people – in North's Plutarch we read that in accusing 'the tribunes of the people,' Caesar 'spake also against the people, and called them Bruti and Cumani, to wit, beasts and fools.[32] Hereafter, the substance of the play, in my version, is the destruction of plebeian political institutions and consciousness. Deprived of their leaders, the people gradually become pawns and victims in the power struggle of the ruling elite. In the forum scene, they plan responsibly, at the start, to evaluate the speeches of Brutus and Antony:

First Plebeian
I will hear Brutus speak.
Second Plebeian
I will hear Cassius, and compare their reasons,
When severally we hear them rendered.

(3.2.8–10)

But they get manipulated. Not allowing the people a serious stake in the system turns a few of them into the louts who murder Cinna. The moral for us is that lower-class and other dissident political groupings should be strengthened to resist the encroachments of the governing elite. Most of the play therefore, in my version, is the agon of the tribunes: they suffer as the people are exploited. I would represent this by having Flavius and Marullus taken, when they are arrested, one to each side of the stage. There they would be detained for the rest of the action, being tortured by the patricians' officers – all, of course, in the usual Royal Shakespeare Company kinky black PVC, chains, and construction-site helmets. At moments of special frustration in the political process, the tormenters would intensify their activity so that the tribunes shriek out in pain. They are tortured, figuratively, by the destruction of plebeian institutions and consciousness.

[. . .]

Even so, reorienting the action so as to produce such a political slant will require some violence to the received text. I call it the New

Reductionism. But then in *The Wars of the Roses*, done for the Royal
Shakespeare Company in 1963, John Barton made three plays out
of just over half the lines of *Richard III* and the three parts of *Henry
VI*, together with 1,400 lines of his own.[33] My *Julius Caesar* could be
accomplished by the commoner and more discreet tactics usual in
the theater – namely, cutting patrician scenes (admittedly heavily)
so as to make prominent the incidents where the people feature,
and supplying 'business.' Reported events involving the plebeians
would be performed in mime, the battle scenes would show, not
the anguished integrity of the leaders, but the plight of the ordinary
soldiers (according to Plutarch thousands were slain), and the final
spectacle would be, not the funeral of Brutus, but Octavius and Antony
establishing authoritarian power in Rome. My ultimate precedent, of
course, is Shakespeare's political license with his sources. Plutarch, the
principal source for *Julius Caesar*, presents the plebeians and tribunes
much more respectfully, particularly in their rejection of Caesar's
monarchical aspirations; Shakespeare has slanted his representation,
producing a certain political effect. In *2 Henry VI*, comparably, the
revolutionary leader, Jack Cade, is changed from the 'young man
of goodly stature and pregnant wit,' a 'subtle captain,' 'sober in
communication' and 'wise in disputing,' described by Edward Hall,
the Tudor apologist (Cade must have had some competence, after all,
for he captures London). In Shakespeare's version Cade is cruel and
stupid, admitting his own dishonesty, viewed skeptically even by his
followers.[34] By thus altering his sources, Shakespeare produces one
story about disruptive lower-class people. My version of *Julius Caesar*
attempts to substitute an alternative.

My aim is simply this: to check the tendency of *Julius Caesar* to add
Shakespearean authority to reactionary discourses. Shakespearean
plays are powerful cultural tokens, places where meaning is established
and where it may be contested. The received text collaborates with
Caesar's dictatorial tendency by removing the tribunes from the action,
so allowing members of an audience to forget the principles that they
may represent. The tribunes are not quite Pierre Macherey's 'not-said,'
since they have appeared. But the putting of Marullus and Flavius to
silence constitutes them as a point at which the text falls silent, and a
point, therefore, at which its ideological project may be apprehended.
All stories comprise within themselves the ghosts of the alternative
stories they are trying to repress.[35] Holding the tribunes at each side
of the stage holds them and their political significance in view. It is
comparable to the way the received text keeps the idea of Caesar before
the audience by making his ghost appear.

[. . .]

The dream of Cinna the poet

Reorienting *Julius Caesar* by bringing minor characters into the
foreground and suppressing the principals might be attempted also
with the women. Robert Miola believes the 'Roman' demand that
Portia and Calphurnia conduct themselves like heroic men indicates
a culture that is 'strange, unnatural, inhuman, and doomed.' The
turning of Caesar from Calphurnia, Miola says, and 'of Portia from
herself and her womanhood, implicitly denies sexual identity, the
fundamental principle of procreation and healthy family life.'[36]
For those of us who want to deny those things, the play might
be reoriented to indicate the opposite: the indeterminacy of sexual
identities and the cultural organization of gender roles. Suppose some
of the senators were women?

The other figure who might be centralized is Cinna the Poet who,
after all, is a far more plausible ancestor of the modern humanities
intellectual than Brutus. 'I am Cinna the poet, I am Cinna the Poet,' he
says, 'not Cinna the conspirator' (3.3.29, 31) – hoping to save himself
by invoking just such a demarcation as characterizes present-day
assumptions about aesthetics and politics. But there is no safety in
withdrawal, Cinna gets caught in the crossfire. His brief appearance
and early death may seem to spoil my idea of making him a central
character; but that would not have stopped G. Wilson Knight. Luckily
there is a second poet in the text. He comes on in the quarrel scene
(4.3) and tells Brutus and Cassius to make friends; they mock him,
not welcoming the intrusion of the Globe Theatre upon their theater
of war. And there is Cicero, who surely means to encourage creative
vandalism in his only two cogent lines: 'But men may construe things,
after their fashion, / Clean from the purpose of the things themselves'
(1.3.34–35). To centralize humanities intellectuals I obviously have to
amalgamate these characters, so that the idea of them dominates the
action; and to do that I have to make the whole production surreal,
dreamlike. Luckily again, Cinna says he has this ominous dream:

> I dreamt to-night that I did feast with Caesar,
> And things unluckily charge my fantasy.
> I have no will to wander forth of doors
> Yet something leads me forth.

> (3.3.1–4)

This is the dream and the nightmare of modern intellectuals: that they
are invited to feast with Caesar, to become significant in government.
That is why they imagine themselves as Brutus (and, indeed, as
Hamlet). But the dream is fraught with anxiety about the consequences

of commitment. The second poet sustains the fantasy that he might contribute a transcendent insight to the generals' quarrel. Appealing to an ancient heroic culture in which poets were the keepers of the communal lore, he quotes Nestor's lines from the *Iliad*: 'Love, and be friends, as two such men should be; / For I have seen more years, I'm sure, than ye' (4.3.130–31). But Cassius and Brutus thrust him out.

In my version, *Julius Caesar* is the fantasy of Cinna as well as the agon of Flavius and Marullus. In fact the whole play is Cinna's dream, his tormented vision of a political reality that constructs, entices, and destroys him. It is the anxious fantasy of the Shakespearean intellectual, despised by the military-industrial complex and scapegoated by the people.[37] So, explicitly, I would have Cinna on stage at the start, he would fall asleep and dream *Julius Caesar*. 'I dreamt to-night that I did feast with Caesar,' he would say, 'And things unluckily charge my fantasy.' And these things would be the play, Cinna's play. This device is not altogether un-Shakespearean. Dreams of power inform the framing induction to *The Taming of the Shrew*: Christopher Sly, the tinker, is quite ready to cultivate the notion that he is a great lord, and the Lord, fresh from hunting, is happy to sponsor a fantasy of male power (the Petruchio-Katherina play). Indeed, it has been suggested that almost the whole performance is Sly's dream of a more powerful position in the social order.[38] I propose Cinna as such a creative dreamer – after all, he is a poet.

Such centering of Cinna's self-destructive ambitions may seem to be leading back towards the liberal notion, which I have rejected, that no productive political engagement is feasible for intellectuals. However, if Cinna dreams *Julius Caesar*, then at least, so to speak, he writes the play (if he does not figure very well in it, that is because he has timorously deferred to those senators and generals). Cultural producers, this suggests, cannot jump out of ideology, but they do have a certain distinctive power – an ideological power – to write some of the scripts. And that includes dramatists, copywriters, and literary critics. In the *Shrew*, the First Huntsman reassures the Lord that identity is socially constructed and within his control:

> My Lord, I warrant you we will play our part
> As he shall think by our true diligence
> He is no less than what we say he is.
>
> (Induction, 1.74)

I would argue that meaning is produced culturally, and that humanities intellectuals contribute to the contest to make some stories, some representations, more plausible than others. Our sense of who we are is of a piece with the ideas we have of proper authority and of the potential for dissidence. Brutus and Cassius kill themselves rather than be led in triumph through the streets of Rome (5.1.108–13); such a spectacle would contribute to the legitimacy of Antony and Octavius. As Walter Benjamin remarked, 'cultural treasures' are usually a principal feature of triumphal processions; it is our task to resist this parading, to prevent such 'documents of civilization' being coopted to enhance the plausibility of oppressive stories. What we make of Shakespeare is important politically because it affects what he makes of us. It is, we may say, a theater of war. My *Julius Caesar* follows Benjamin's recommendation that we regard cultural treasures with cautious detachment, brushing history 'against the grain.'[39]

The career of Cinna the Poet raises these issues; in my version he would manifest authorial power. So he would look like – well, you've guessed, he would look like 'Shakespeare,' the enigmatic bust with the noble forehead (though probably Shakespeare did not wander forth of doors during the Essex rebellion, and so lived to tell the tale). Yet also Cinna would merge, ultimately, with Caesar himself; their deaths are the same death, for there are cultural empires as well as geographical. And the backdrop would be 'the Globe Theatre,' romantic in appearance and still powerful after 400 years (thanks, it would say in the program, to sponsorship from Royal Ordnance). Shakespeare, as our cultures have produced him, has dreamt us; for centuries he has been a key imperial site where ideology is produced. As Cassius warns,

> How many ages hence
> Shall this our lofty scene be acted over,
> In states unborn and accents yet unknown!
>
> (3.1.111–13)

But in the long term, the emperors could not keep out the Vandals. We may challenge, perhaps in uncouth accents, the stories that Shakespeare is usually made to tell; we too may intervene among the contested scripts of our societies.

Notes

1. It is a sentimental derivative of Claes Jansz Visscher's long view of London; see Irwin Smith, *Shakespeare's Globe Playhouse* (London: Peter Owen, 1963), pp. 20–23. I am indebted to Susan Schweik for showing me the advertisement.

2. Robert Fraser and Michael Wilson, *Privatisation: The UK Experience and International Trends* (London: Longman, 1988), pp. 81–82.

3. In this, Ordnance was only typical – like Bimec, Thorn EMI, Wickman Bennett, Racal, Churchill, and many continental European companies. See 'How Minister Helped British Firms to Arm Saddam's Soldiers,' *Sunday Times*, December 2, 1990, p. 5. John Drakakis drew this article to my attention.

4. *Financial Times*, February 27, 1991, pp. 22, 23.

5. 'How Minister Helped British Firms,' p. 5.

6. E.K. Chambers, *Sir Henry Lee: An Elizabethan Portrait* (Oxford: Clarendon Press, 1936), pp. 121, 119–27; and see H.C. Tomlinson, *Guns and Government: The Ordnance Office under the Later Stuarts* (London: Royal Historical Society, 1979), pp. 1–6.

7. John Fekete, *The Critical Twilight* (London: Routledge, 1977), p. 195. See Jonathan Dollimore, *Radical Tragedy*, 2d ed. (Hemel Hempstead: Harvester Wheatsheaf, 1989), ch. 3.

8. *The Autobiography of Thomas Whythorne*, ed. James M. Osborn (Oxford: Clarendon Press, 1961), pp. xxviii–xxx, 83–86, 298–99.

9. Thomas Carlyle, *On Heroes, Hero-Worship and the Heroic in History* (London: James Frazer, 1841), p. 181; quoted by Malcolm Evans, *Signifying Nothing: Truth's True Contents in Shakespeare's Text*, 2nd ed. (Hemel Hempstead: Harvester Wheatsheaf, 1989), p. 88; and see pp. 86–108. Wilson Knight is quoted by Terence Hawkes, *That Shakespeherean Rag: Essays on a Critical Process* (London: Methuen, 1986), p. 68. See also Peter Widdowson, ed., *ReReading English* (London: Methuen, 1982); Graham Holderness, ed., *The Shakespeare Myth* (Manchester Univ. Press, 1988); Chris Baldick, *The Social Mission of English Criticism, 1848–1932* (Oxford Univ. Press, 1983); Ania Loomba, *Gender, Race, Renaissance Drama* (Manchester Univ. Press, 1989).

10. Catherine Belsey, *The Subject of Tragedy* (London: Methuen, 1985), pp. 101–3; see also id., 'Shakespeare and Film: A Question of Perspective,' *Literature/Film Quarterly* 11 (1983): 152–58. For the case against 'humanity,' see, e.g., John Drakakis, ed., *Alternative Shakespeares* (London: Methuen, 1985), p. 4.

11. Quoted by Arthur Humphreys, ed., *Julius Caesar* (Oxford: Clarendon Press, 1984), p. 52.

12. John Ripley, *'Julius Caesar' on Stage in England and America, 1599–1973* (Cambridge Univ. Press, 1980), pp. 23–24, 28, 147.

13. Ibid., p. 100; Alfred Van Rensselaer Westfall, *American Shakespearean Criticism, 1607–1865* (New York: H.W. Wilson, 1939), p. 221.

14. Ripley, *'Julius Caesar,'* p. 317.

15. Raphael Samuel, Ewan MacColl, and Stuart Cosgrove, *Theatres of the Left, 1880–1935* (London: Routledge, 1985), pp. 8–9; see also E.P. Thompson, *The Making of the English Working Class*, rev. ed. (Harmondsworth: Penguin Books, 1968), p. 809. *Julius Caesar* is quoted from the New Arden edition, ed. T.S. Dorsch (London: Methuen, 1955), 1.2.94–95.

16. Ripley, *'Julius Caesar,'* pp. 140, 332.

17. Ida M. Tarbell, *The Life of Abraham Lincoln* (New York: McClure, Phillips, 1908), 2:252–60. Tarbell's account is laced with implicit allusions to *Julius Caesar*, such as the tearing down of banners, speech-making, and crowd action against opponents; 3.2.135–39 is quoted (pp. 246–51).

18. David Donald, *Lincoln Reconsidered*, 2d ed. (New York: Knopf, 1965), p. 5; Michael Rogin, 'Ronald Reagan,' *The Movie* (Berkeley: Univ. of California Press, 1987), pp. 86–90, and illustrations 3.3, 3.4, 3.5. In 1939 *Julius Caesar* was found to have been the one most read in schools: see Esther Cloudman Dunn, *Shakespeare in America* (1939; New York: Benjamin Blom, 1968), pp. 219–20, 244.

19. Robert Justin Goldstein, *Political Repression in Modern America from 1870 to the Present* (Cambridge, Mass.: Schenkman, 1978), pp. 24–34.

20. Ripley, 'Julius Caesar,' p. 223.

21. See Victor S. Navasky, *Naming Names* (New York: Viking Press, 1980), pp. 179–81. For the idea and the reference I am indebted to Vivian Sobchack, who placed Mankiewicz's *Caesar* in this context in a talk at Santa Cruz in 1988. On the liberalism of this film, see Belsey, 'Shakespeare and Film.'

22. See Ripley, 'Julius Caesar,' p. 260. However, Glen Byam Shaw's 1957 Stratford production re-centred Caesar: see Roy Walker, 'Unto Caesar: A Review of Recent Productions,' *Shakespeare Survey* 11 (1958): 128–35.

23. Ralph Berry, *On Directing Shakespeare* (London: Croom Helm, 1977), pp. 75–81.

24. Interview with Trevor Nunn in Berry, *On Directing Shakespeare*, pp. 63–66; quotation from Nunn in Ripley, 'Julius Caesar,' p. 270. For further comparable productions, see Humphreys, ed., *Julius Caesar*, pp. 66–71; Martin Spevack, ed., *Julius Caesar* (Cambridge Univ. Press, 1988), p. 40.

25. See Jonathan Goldberg, *James I and the Politics of Literature* (Baltimore: Johns Hopkins Univ. Press, 1983), pp. 163–76.

26. The time set for the inauguration of President Reagan had to be changed when astrologers said it was unfavorable for him. See Garry Wills, *Reagan's America* (New York: Doubleday, 1987), pp. 299, 196–97.

27. See Ch. 8, below.

28. See Ch. 2, above. See Peter Stallybrass and Allon White, *The Politics and Poetics of Transgression* (London: Methuen, 1986), Introduction.

29. Here I disagree with David Margolies, 'Teaching the Handsaw to Fly: Shakespeare as a Hegemonic Instrument,' in Holderness, ed., *The Shakespeare Myth*, p. 44.

30. S.A. Cook, F.E. Adcock, and M.P. Charlesworth, eds., *The Cambridge Ancient History* (Cambridge Univ. Press, 1932), 9:291–93, 334–36.

31. Niccolò Machiavelli, *The Discourses* 1.57–58, ed. Bernard Crick (Harmondsworth: Penguin Books, 1974), pp. 251, 255.

32. Dorsch, ed., *Julius Caesar*, pp. 138–39.

33. See Sinfield, 'Royal Shakespeare,' in Jonathan Dollimore and Alan Sinfield, eds., *Political Shakespeare* (Manchester: Manchester Univ. Press; Ithaca, N.Y.: Cornell Univ. Press, 1985), p. 160.

34. See Richard Wilson's powerful article, ' "A mingled yarn": Shakespeare and the Cloth Workers,' *Literature and History* 12 (1986): 164–80, pp. 167–69; also my program note, 'History and Power,' for the Royal Shakespeare Company production of *The Plantagenets* (two reconstructed *Henry VI* plays plus *Richard III*), directed by Adrian Noble in 1988.

35. See Pierre Macherey, *A Theory of Literary Production*, trans. Geoffrey Wall (London: Routledge, 1978); also Jonathan Goldberg, 'Speculations: *Macbeth* and Source,' in Jean E. Howard and Marion F. O'Connor, eds., *Shakespeare Reproduced* (New York: Methuen, 1987), p. 247.

36. Robert S. Miola, *Shakespeare's Rome* (Cambridge Univ. Press, 1983), p. 96.

37. Richard Wilson points out that Jack Cade and his supporters are hostile to writing (' "A Mingled Yarn" ', p. 168).

38. See Ann Thompson's New Cambridge edition of Shakespeare, *The Taming of the Shrew* (Cambridge Univ. Press, 1984), pp. 35–36, and the Bogdanov interview in Holderness, ed., *The Shakespeare Myth*, p. 90.

39. Walter Benjamin, *Illuminations*, ed. Hannah Arendt, trans. Harry Zohn (Glasgow: Fontana/Collins, 1973), pp. 258–59.

5 *Antony and Cleopatra**

LEONARD TENNENHOUSE

This short piece on *Antony and Cleopatra* is taken from Leonard Tennenhouse's book *Power on Display*. In common with John Drakakis in his analysis of *Julius Caesar*, Tennenhouse in this book is deeply interested in the ways in which power is represented in the early modern period. He explores, for instance, the manner in which the various images of Queen Elizabeth were constructed and apprehended in the period. In this extract from the book, Tennenhouse examines the process of representing and perceiving the figure of another queen – Cleopatra – and he finds significance in the fact that Shakespeare provides here a *post*-Elizabethan image of female monarchy.

We might consider *Antony and Cleopatra* as both the easiest and the most difficult of Shakespeare's tragedies for us to read. The language of the play translates so well into modern cultural terms that more than one critic has read the play as if it were a Renaissance version of a modern romance on the order of *Wuthering Heights*. For this very reason, it proves most difficult to understand this play in relation to other Jacobean tragedies and the poetics of display which gave them their form. The sexual relationship between Antony and Cleopatra displaces the political struggles within the Roman empire to the point where sexuality – at least from a modern perspective – appears to transcend politics in the play. Even the most dedicated historical critic feels hard pressed to think otherwise and therefore to maintain his or her concern for the vicissitudes of state power in this play. But, I will argue, this temptation to say the play is about love rather than politics is a form of seduction which Shakespeare himself has built into *Anthony and Cleopatra*. He sees to it that his audience feels the seduction of a world independent of patriarchal power all the while knowing such a world is impossible. Where the modern reader feels the utopian attraction of a private world free of ideology, however, the early seventeenth-century theater-goer would have rejected it

---

*LEONARD TENNENHOUSE, *Power on Display: The Politics of Shakespeare's Genres* (London: Methuen, 1986), pp. 142–6.

because of the undesirable political features inherent in such a utopia.

Contrary to novelistic strategies, Shakespeare's drama sets up the possibility of detaching sexuality from politics only to demonstrate the preposterousness of thinking of the body this way. *Antony and Cleopatra* resembles *King Lear* in the respect that kinship and kingship constitute a single strategy for distributing political power and thus for understanding the operations of such power in the world. But if *Antony and Cleopatra* seems somehow more mythic in its presentation of this theme, it is because the play self-consciously interweaves the various themes of Jacobean culture and works through the same problematic terms of its most important categories – sexuality and politics. Like other assaults on the political body – the senate's willingness to overrule Desdemona's father, Lear's attempt to divide his kingdom among his daughters, or Lady Macbeth's usurpation of patriarchal prerogatives – Antony's profession of love flies in the face of political reality to threaten the most basic law of Renaissance culture:

> Let Rome in Tiber melt, and the wide arch
> Of the rang'd empire fall! Here is my space,
> Kingdoms are clay; our dungy earth alike
> Feeds beast as man; the nobleness of life
> Is to do thus [*embracing*] – when such a mutual pair
> And such a twain can do't, in which I bind,
> [On] pain of punishment, the world to weet
> We stand up peerless.
>
> (I.i.33–40)

In making this statement, Antony obviously calls for a complete separation of love from nationalism, but his claim for the legitimacy of this relationship ultimately requires much more in the way of a cultural transformation than this. In his affection for, or his dotage on the Egyptian queen – depending on whose view one adopts – nobleness springs neither from aristocratic birth nor from the metaphysics of blood. It is engendered by the queen's embrace. Their relationship, in short, requires nothing less than a semiotic apocalypse. The basis of meaning itself – and with it the mating and mismating of terms – will henceforth be decided according to nature rather than the distinctions culture makes between nations or even between east and west. Any Jacobean audience would, I think, have recognized instantly the nature of the delusion. Antony can not actually separate politics from sexuality in this speech or for that matter anywhere else in the play. The very desire to have sovereignty over one's sexual relations and therefore to construct a private world within the public domain is an inherently political act. The play clearly demonstrates that by desiring a Cleopatra rather than a Fulvia or an Octavia, Antony does not remove himself from political history. Rather, the consequences of his desire change the course of history itself.

In the Elizabethan plays, union with the aristocratic female was always a political act. In fact, desire for the female and desire for political power could not be distinguished one from the other. But in Jacobean drama the iconic bond between the aristocratic female and the body politic is broken. No longer conceived as a legitimate means for access to membership in the corporate body, the aristocratic female has the potential to pollute. Nowhere is this clearer than with Cleopatra. Using her, Shakespeare undertakes his most thorough revision of that figure of the autochthonous female which had uses so central to Elizabethan representations of power. Cleopatra is Egypt. As such, however, she embodies everything that is not English according to the nationalism which developed under Elizabeth as well as to the British nationalism later fostered by James. It is perhaps difficult for us to see Cleopatra as such a threat to the political body. She contrasts Egyptian fecundity, luxury and hedonism to Rome's penury, harshness and self denial. The fact is, however, that no matter how well we romanticize her, Shakespeare has represented her in much the same terms Bakhtin uses to identify the grotesque – or popular – body in Renaissance culture. Shakespeare clearly endows her with all the features of carnival. These define her as the ultimate subject and object of illicit desire as Enobarbus's well known description suggests,

> Age cannot wither her, nor custom stale
> Her infinite variety. Other women cloy
> The appetites they feed, but she makes hungry
> Where most she satisfies; for vilest things
> Become themselves in her, that the holy priests
> Bless her when she is riggish.

> (II.ii.234–9)

A body that incorporates the basest things represents the very antithesis of aristocratic power. It is that which threatens to pollute the aristocratic community. Egypt's queen thus resembles other Jacobean females who in desiring or being desired become a source of pollution. That such a sexual threat poses a threat to the political body is repeated in several different variations. His sexual bond to Cleopatra strips Antony of his military judgement, deprives him of prowess in battle, and deceives him into committing suicide.

Unlike this Jacobean rendering, Elizabethan versions of the Antony and Cleopatra story, like the sources for *King Lear*, represent the threat to the body politic in terms of division and inversion. *The Tragedie of Antonie* (1595), the Countess of Pembroke's translation of Garnier's play, begins with the following, 'After the overthrowe of Brutus and Cassius, the libertie of Rome being now utterly oppressed, and the Empire settled in the hands of Octavius Caesar and Marcus Antonius . . . .'[1] In Daniel's *The Tragedie of Cleopatra* (1599), the action begins after Antony has committed suicide. Tragic consequences develop, then, from competition for political supremacy. In his version of this story, however, Shakespeare makes certain that the threat to Rome comes from an external rather than internal source. This is the first condition for the staging of pollution and its resolution, the scene of punishment. First Labienus with Parthian troops attacks Roman garrisons on the Asian border, and then Pompey attacks Rome's 'borders maritime' in the Mediterranean. In both cases, the play makes it quite clear that Rome is thus besieged because Antony has been, in Caesar's words, 'rioting in Alexandria.' For one thing, Pompey readily agrees to a truce when he hears that Antony has returned to Rome. For another, we see that the Roman world can tolerate division; even competition between Antony and Caesar is not in itself a bad thing. As long as they can exchange women as Caesar and Antony do, these powerful men remain part of a common political body. Even when Caesar seizes Lepidus or breaks the treaty with Pompey, he does not really endanger the nation. In a word, all serious threats to Rome stem from Antony's alliance with Cleopatra.

To so locate the source of political disorder is to represent such disorder as pollution. Why else would Shakespeare dwell on the danger of the offspring of Antony and Cleopatra. As Caesar explains to his friends Maecenas and Agrippa, Antony's mismating with Egypt has engendered another illegitimate aristocracy whose blood will contend for legitimate authority over Rome:

> I' th' market-place, on a tribunal silver'd,
> Cleopatra and himself in chairs of gold
> Were publicly enthron'd. At the feet sat
> Caesarion, whom they call my father's son,
> And all the unlawful issue that their lust
> Since then hath made between them. Unto her
> He gave the stablishment of Egypt, made her
> Of lower Syria, Cyprus, Lydia,
> Absolute queen.

> *Maec.*
> This in the public eye?

Caes.
I' th' common show-place, where they exercise.
His sons [he there] proclaim'd the [kings] of kings . . .

(III.vi.3–13)

To his sister, Caesar more bluntly describes the danger Antony's alliance with Cleopatra poses: 'He hath given his empire / Up to a whore' (III.vi.66–7).

In destroying Antony and Cleopatra, Shakespeare accomplishes two things. First he relocates the sources of legitimate authority in Rome. Secondly, he establishes the figure of uncompromising male power over that of the autochthonous female. Shakespeare not only illegitimizes this figure of power by linking it to that of the grotesque body, he also subjects that body of the other to ritual purification. Shakespeare gives Cleopatra the entire last act to gather up the features associated with illegitimate authority. Having denied her the privilege of committing suicide in the Roman manner, he dresses her as Queen of Egypt, surrounds her with her eunuch and ladies in waiting, and then kills her off with an Egyptian viper. This elaborate scene of punishment purges the world of all that is not Roman. In this manner of delivering the world over to patriarchy, however, Shakespeare makes it very clear that a whole way of figuring out power has been rendered obsolete. One might call his play Shakespeare's elegy for the signs and symbols which legitimized Elizabethan power. Of these, the single most important figure was that of the desiring and desired woman, her body valued for its ornamental surface, her feet rooted deep in a kingdom.

Note

1. *Narrative and Dramatic Sources of Shakespeare*, ed. Geoffrey Bullough (New York: Columbia Univ. Press, 1966), V. 358.

6 Making Defect Perfection*

JANET ADELMAN

Janet Adelman is a feminist critic whose approach to literary analysis is deeply indebted to psychoanalytic paradigms. This extract is taken from her book *Suffocating Mothers*, which explores images of maternity and nurturance in the works of Shakespeare. Her concern here, however, is less with constructions of the figure of the mother or of the female generally, than it is with the construction of alternative images of masculinity within the play generally and specifically within the figure of Antony. Adelman sees Cleopatra as facilitating the evocation of a new image of Antony's masculinity – an image predicated on her own 'imaginative fecundity'. She explores both the fragility of this image and its relevance to Shakespeare himself as a dramatist. Adelman's discussion of *Antony and Cleopatra* follows on from a discussion of *Timon of Athens*.

In *Antony and Cleopatra*, scarcity is the sign of the state from which the female has been excised: there are virtually no women in Rome, there is no natural abundance. In effect, Caesar and his Romans have claimed scarcity as their own, institutionalizing it and making it the basis of their male selfhood, as though they could divorce themselves from subjection to the unreliable female and the problematics of her generativity by willfully embracing a condition of limited resources, in which measure is the means to success and any excess counts as waste. Thus localized as the emotional landscape of masculine selfhood in Rome, scarcity becomes the domain of its competing siblings, the rival brothers who cannot stall together in the whole world because the whole world is not large enough for them; no longer the mother's fault, hunger, rivalry, and the incompletion of the male self now seem intrinsic to the all-male society that has attempted to divorce itself from her.

---

*JANET ADELMAN, *Suffocating Mothers: Fantasies of Maternal Origin in Shakespeare's Plays*, Hamlet *to* The Tempest (New York: Routledge, Chapman and Hall, 1992), pp. 176–92.

Bounty and scarcity continue to be the key terms in *Antony and Cleopatra*, as they are in *Timon*, but in *Antony and Cleopatra*, Shakespeare succeeds in transvaluing them and hence in transfiguring their relation to male selfhood. *Antony and Cleopatra* is ostentatiously framed by its two memorializing portraits of Antony, Caesar's in act 1 and Cleopatra's in act 5. Caesar's locates Antony in the Timonesque landscape of absolute deprivation, where he must browse on the bark of trees and eat strange flesh to survive; and it figures his heroic masculinity as his capacity to survive in this wintry landscape. Cleopatra's locates him in a landscape of immense abundance with no winter in it; and it figures his heroic masculinity as his capacity to participate in the bounty of its self-renewing autumn. If Timon is driven from his fantasy of bounty to a landscape of absolute scarcity and is made to acknowledge that landscape as his psychic home, Antony begins in Caesar's landscape of scarcity but then finds himself in Cleopatra's bounty. And what is at stake in this trajectory is the relocation and reconstruction of heroic masculinity.[1]

The contest between Caesar and Cleopatra, Rome and Egypt, is in part a contest between male scarcity and female bounty as the defining site of Antony's heroic masculinity. Longing for that heroic masculinity is, I think, at the center of the play. Though Enobarbus's great set-piece on Cleopatra at Cydnus would seem to create Cleopatra as the play's ultimate unattainable erotic object, Antony himself is the primary absent object of desire for all the major characters. Both Caesar and Cleopatra fill up the gap his absence makes by imagining him present, addressing him in the second person as though he were there, both at the beginning and at the end of the play (1.4.55–56, 1.5.27; 5.1.35, 5.2.286, 311);[2] and Enobarbus dies, speaking to him (4.9.18–23). No one is more keenly aware of his absence than Antony himself, who watches his status as 'Antony' dissolve and become as indistinct as water is in water (4.14.11); his peculiar pain turns in part on his awareness of himself as the standard against which his own loss of heroic masculinity must be measured. Even when he is on stage, that is, his presence is suffused with a sense of absence or loss; except in his triumphant land battle, his heroic grandeur is always constructed retrospectively, in his – and its – absence.

In the figure of Antony and the complex longing that surrounds him, Shakespeare restages the loss of idealized masculinity that had initiated *Hamlet*; and in his recovery of Antony through Cleopatra's dream of bounty, Shakespeare brings that masculinity back to life. This recovery seems to me momentous in Shakespeare's career: through it, Shakespeare in effect undoes the conditions that have defined tragic masculinity since Old Hamlet's death. In the tragedies that follow from *Hamlet*, heroic masculinity has been constructed defensively, by a rigid separation from the dangerous female within and without; founded in the region of scarcity, the self-protective and niggardly manliness of Macbeth or Coriolanus illustrates the impasse at the end of this defensive construction. By locating Antony's heroic manhood within Cleopatra's vision of him, Shakespeare attempts in effect to imagine his way beyond this impasse, recovering the generous masculinity of Old Hamlet in Antony by realigning it with its female source. In effect, Shakespeare returns masculinity to its point of origin, the maternal body; and without denying the potentially devastating effects of that return – indeed, the play is full of references to Cleopatra's emasculating effect on Antony – he rewrites that body as the source of male bounty. This rewriting is only tenuously achieved, but it nonetheless seems to me at the center of *Antony and Cleopatra*; and it is, I think, deeply bound up with Shakespeare's own recovery of theatrical play and hence with his move beyond tragedy and toward the manifold recoveries of *The Winter's Tale*.

From the beginning, Caesar is the spokesman for the realm of scarcity and the masculinity constructed on its model. His first words constitute Egyptian excess as an effeminizing threat to that masculinity:

> From Alexandria
> This is the news: he fishes, drinks, and wastes
> The lamps of night in revel; is not more manlike
> Than Cleopatra.
>
> (1.4.3–6)

According to Caesar's distinctly Roman economy of the self, plenty constitutes self-waste, compromising the stringent self-withholding that is his ideal. Satiety itself is suspect: Caesar imagines Antony's sexual exploits as a kind of voluptuous over-feeding in which bodily fullness becomes its own punishment ('If he fill'd / His vacancy with his voluptuousness, / Full surfeits, and the dryness of his bones / Call on him for't' [1.4.25–28]). And if fullness compromises a fragile Roman masculinity, emptiness guarantees it; womanly when he feasts with – and on – Cleopatra, voluptuously filling his vacancy, Caesar's Antony can be manly only when he is starving:

> Antony,
> Leave thy lascivious wassails. When thou once
> Was beaten from Modena, where thou slew'st
> Hirtius and Pansa, consuls, at thy heel
> Did famine follow, whom thou fought'st against,
> Though daintily brought up, with patience more
> Than savages could suffer. Thou didst drink

The stale of horses, and the gilded puddle
Which beasts would cough at: thy palate then did deign
The roughest berry, on the rudest hedge;
Yea, like the stag, when snow the pasture sheets,
The barks of trees thou browsed. On the Alps
It is reported thou didst eat strange flesh,
Which some did die to look on: and all this—
It wounds thine honor that I speak it now—
Was borne so like a soldier, that thy cheek
So much as lank'd not.

(1.4.55–71)

This is a landscape of absolute deprivation, at the furthest possible remove from the emasculating excess Caesar associates with Egypt; as such, it – rather than the battlefield Philo evokes in the play's opening lines – serves as the test of Antony's heroic masculinity. Scarcity is the ground of masculine selfhood, as Caesar defines it: Antony proves himself the equal of the preeminently masculine stag when he survives the bleak winter of famine. As in *Coriolanus*, the hungry self is the manly self; not-eating permits the fantasy of entire self-sufficiency, the escape from the body and its effeminizing need.

The mixture of awe, longing, and envy in Caesar's reconstruction of the heroic Antony is unmistakable; and it seems to me to position Caesar in effect as a son in relation to the legendary father who constitutes the standard of masculinity. Caesar's need for such a figure rests in complex ways on his imagined relation with his own father, Julius Caesar, and on Antony's role in the oedipal dynamic between them. Inadvertently or not, Shakespeare rewrites history to make the fathers of both Caesar and Pompey Cleopatra's lovers.[3] Both Pompey and Caesar display a prurient interest in Antony's sexual life with Cleopatra; Antony himself asks Caesar, 'My being in Egypt, / Caesar, what was't to you?' (2.2.35–36). What, indeed? For a generation of Romans that has successfully excised the female – in which there are no wives, in which mothers are apparently necessary only for the production of illegitimate children in Egypt – Egypt is the only place of sexual concourse, Cleopatra the only mother there is. For these unwomaned sons, she carries the taint of the whore-mother, site of the father's contamination; and through his liaison with her, Antony restages that contamination, becoming the focus both of longing for the father who might be exempt from woman and of disgust at the father who is not.[4]

Caesar's one oblique reference to his father in fact locates him precisely in Antony's position, condemning Rome by fathering illegitimate Egyptian issue:[5]

Contemning Rome he has done all this, and more
In Alexandria: here's the manner of't:
I' the market-place, on a tribunal silver'd,
Cleopatra and himself in chairs of gold
Were publicly enthron'd: at the feet sat
Caesarion, whom they call my father's son,
And all the unlawful issue that their lust
Since then hath made between them.

(3.6.1–8)

And although other Romans are tolerant of Julius Caesar's liaison with Cleopatra – they in fact mythologize its details, as though creating a barroom legend – Caesar himself seems distinctly uncomfortable with it. His reference to Caesarion linguistically undoes his father's paternity of him, reducing it to the status of a rumor, as though he would undo the sign of his father's liaison with Cleopatra altogether if he could. For insofar as his father effortlessly brings together aspects of selfhood that Caesar works to keep separate – kissing Cleopatra's hand while musing on taking kingdoms in (3.13.82–85) – he destabilizes the distinctions through which Caesar has constructed his own niggardly masculinity; always already contaminated by Egypt, he can be of no service to his son in Rome.

In the intensity of its longing, Caesar's encomium of Antony seems to me to serve the function of recuperating the damaged image of paternal masculinity, in effect re-inventing the father-figure Caesar needs as the basis for his own stringent masculinity: if 'Julius Caesar / Grew fat with feasting' in Egypt (2.6.64–65), at least this father-figure starves honorably. And his honorable starvation indicates his separation from the effeminizing realm of women and bodily need: this father could do without the nurturance everywhere associated with Egypt and Cleopatra, in effect do without maternal provision altogether; surviving the landscape of maternal deprivation – the spatial projection of Lady Macbeth's or Volumnia's withholding – Antony demonstrates his invulnerability to the female, thus over-mastering what over-mastered Julius Caesar. His masculinity is so secure that he can survive even the most dangerous sorts of feeding:

> On the Alps
> It is reported thous didst eat strange flesh,
> Which some did die to look on.

(1.4.66–8)

These are mysterious lines, and deliberately so: Shakespeare's lack of specificity – especially compared with Plutarch's much more matter-of-fact reference to 'such beasts, as never men tasted of their flesh before'[6] – invokes the presence of the bizarre, even the tabooed. What is this strange flesh that some did die to look on? Cleopatra will soon recall that Pompey 'would stand and make his eyes grow in my brow, / There would he anchor his aspect, and die / With looking on his life' (1.5.32–34); she herself is the locus of visual desire and visual danger in the play, as well as the locus of dangerous feeding. Caesar's 'strange flesh' leads back to Antony's 'Egyptian dish,' the 'ordinary' wherein he 'pays his heart / For what his eyes eat only' (2.6.123, 2.2.225–26). And the condensation of eating, looking, and dying in Caesar's image suggests what is at stake in Antony's heroic oral exemption: he can survive not only maternal deprivation but the danger inherent in maternal flesh itself. Caesar's deadly 'strange flesh' seems to me to invoke the taboo against that flesh, returning us to the realm of infantile fantasy where looking and devouring the mother's body coalesce, and where both are punishable by death. Antony's importance for Caesar – and for the fantasy the play articulates through him – lies in his capacity to survive this death: to survive the confrontation not only with maternal deprivation but with the maternal body, the other/mother that is Egypt.

Midway between the generation of the fathers and the generation of the sons, the idealized Antony can serve as the repository of Roman masculinity, in effect recuperating the heroic father lost in Julius Caesar. But this is an inherently unstable position for Antony to occupy: by stressing Caesar's youth and Antony's age,[7] Shakespeare structures their relationship oedipally, making it resonate with the son's contest against the father he must idealize, possess, and, above all, subdue. From Caesar's first entrance, denying that he hates his 'great competitor' (1.4.3), Shakespeare has insisted on the mix of awe and rivalry in Caesar's attitude toward Antony; and in fact Caesar does everything he can to undermine – not to recuperate – Antony's past heroism and seems positively gleeful when he can report the disgusting details of his captivity by Egypt. For like the oedipal father, Antony is the measure of Caesar's own stature: 'When such a spacious mirror's set before him, / He needs must see himself' (5.1.34–35). And this rivalrous identification with Antony is dangerous to Caesar: in so spacious a mirror, how can he not see himself diminished? The impetus toward idealization that makes Antony the legendary father is consequently counterbalanced by the contrary impetus to cut him down to size: Caesar uses Antony simultaneously to recuperate the father destroyed in Julius Caesar and to master his prodigious presence, basing his own potency on that mastery.

The need to subdue Antony's magical presence – in effect to reduce him from an idealized father to an equal rival/brother – seems to me to govern Caesar's pursuit of Antony throughout. It is, I think,

the impetus behind Caesar's initial gleeful relishing of the details of
Antony's degradation: in his account, the effeminized Antony restages
Julius Caesar's Egyptian revels in a diminished form, serving not as
a spacious mirror but as a monitory image that confirms Caesar's
own superiority. As a virtual case study in self-loss, this diminished
paternal image rationalizes Caesar's self-withholding, his determination
to possess himself and everything around him: xenophobia toward
his father's Egypt, hatred of its bodily processes and their attendant
wastes, fear of the gender transformations that they entail – all these
become definitive of his new-style Roman masculinity, dependent
on the news from Alexandria to shore up its sense of itself. And
in relation to this Antony, Caesar can constitute himself not as an
awestruck son but as a righteous father, chiding him 'as we rate boys'
(1.4.31). We can see the operation of the same impetus at the end,
in the speech with which Caesar responds to the news of Antony's
death. He begins by acknowledging Antony's stature as a legendary
figure equivalent to Julius Caesar and entitled to the same portents that
heralded his death:[8]

> The breaking of so great a thing should make
> A greater crack. The round world
> Should have shook lions into civil streets,
> And citizens to their dens.

(5.1.14–17)

But within a few lines, he has obliquely made the claim to equal stature
(only 'a moiety' – half – the world lay in Antony's name [5.1.19]; the
rest is Caesar's); and as he continues, he carries the reduction of the
spacious mirror even further:

> O Antony,
> I have follow'd thee to this, but we do launch
> Diseases in our bodies. I must perforce
> Have shown to thee such a declining day,
> Or look on thine: we could not stall together,
> In the whole world. But yet let me lament
> With tears as sovereign as the blood of hearts,
> That thou my brother, my competitor,
> In top of all design; my mate in empire,
> Friend and companion in the front of war,
> The arm of mine own body, and the heart
> Where mine his thoughts did kindle; – that our stars,
> Unreconciliable, should divide
> Our equalness to this.

(5.1.35–48)

Even 'moiety' turns out not to be enough: the brother-competitor must be rewritten first as a disease, and finally as a diminished part of Caesar's own gigantic body, Caesar – not the stars – has divided their 'equalness' to this.

'We could not stall together, in the whole world': the scarcity that is the landscape of Antony's Roman masculinity proves also to be the landscape of male bonds in Rome, where there is never enough to go around, where even the whole world is too small. And if the famine had not existed, Caesar would have had to invent it: only its psychic landscape could justify his version of Roman selfhood and the ruthless competition through which he defines himself. Moreover, Shakespeare's presentation of Caesar's relation to Antony is less the exploration of an individual psyche than of an entire society: in this preeminently patriarchal city, rivalry itself is a hand-me-down from father to son.[9] And Cleopatra turns out to be oddly inessential to this father-son story: in his final version of Antony's story, Caesar never mentions her. If we read the play backwards from his response to Antony's death, then the official Roman line – that Antony was destroyed by Cleopatra's entrapment – begins to look like a cover-up: if Cleopatra had not been there, Caesar's Rome would have had to invent her too. With or without the existence of Cleopatra, Rome could not be the memorializing site of Antony's heroic masculinity: in the scarcity that rules its emotional economy, it must first establish, and then destroy, its legendary fathers.

Very shortly after Caesar cuts Antony down to size in the service of establishing his own gigantic stature, Cleopatra dreams her Emperor Antony, reconstructing him as the colossus of her abundant imagination. Claiming the right to Antony's memory, she in effect reinserts herself into the story from which she has just been occluded; furthermore, she makes herself – and not Caesar – the repository of his heroic masculinity. In thus giving Cleopatra the last word, Shakespeare robs Caesar of his 'triumph,' his attempt to arrange how these events will be remembered; in effect, she displaces his play with her own. And through this gesture, Shakespeare revises both the gender and the site of memory: although Shakespeare's own play is based on the historical record and concerned throughout with the judgments of history, memory in it is no longer purely the province of male history, which must subdue its objects, dismembering in order to remember; it now becomes the province of female desire, which 'kiss[es] / The honour'd gashes whole' (4.8.10–11).

Cleopatra's monumental recreation of Antony seems to me the great generative act of the play; and it is unprecedented in Plutarch – or at least in Plutarch's 'Life of Marcus Antonius.' But it does have a precedent, I think, in another probable Plutarchian source

for the play: Plutarch's 'Of Isis and Osiris.'[10] If in 'The Life' – and
in one Roman version of Antony's story in *Antony and Cleopatra* –
the woman figures the destruction of a great man, in 'Of Isis and
Osiris' she is the agent of salvation; by inserting elements of 'Of
Isis and Osiris' into the more monovocal 'Life,' Shakespeare opens
up interpretative possibility,[11] rewriting the female as the potential
site of both generation and regeneration. As in *Antony and Cleopatra*,
the loss and recovery of a charismatic male figure is at the center
of Plutarch's Egyptian regeneration myth; like Antony, Osiris is the
absence over which male and female rivals contend.[12] Typhon, Osiris's
brother-rival, repeatedly pursues Osiris to his death, first locking him
into a chest and throwing him into the sea, then cutting his body into
fourteen parts and scattering them widely; Isis, Osiris's sister-wife,
repeatedly performs the work of revival, first retrieving Osiris from
the chest, then gathering up the scattered body parts and building
memorials to them. This configuration of male rivalry and a saving
female presence seems to me teasingly similar to *Antony and Cleopatra*;
in both, the male dismembers while the female remembers. Caesar in
effect holds Typhon's place as the male destroyer in Shakespeare's
text; his attempt to reduce Antony to an arm of his own body or to a
disease that must be launched bears the traces of Typhon's persistent
attempt to dismember Osiris. And if Caesar is Typhon to Antony's
Osiris, Cleopatra takes on the role along with the 'habiliments' of the
goddess Isis (3.6.17), 'wandring heere and there, gathering together the
dismembered pieces' of Osiris (p. 1309), restoring the memory and the
sacramental generative potential of the scattered hero. When Typhon
cuts off Osiris's 'privy member' and feeds it to the fishes, Isis makes
and consecrates a 'counterfeit one, called Phallus' (p. 1294); when
Caesar virtually dismembers – and disremembers – Antony, making
him into the arm of his own gigantic body, Cleopatra restores his
potent image in her dream-vision of him. Like Isis, Cleopatra finds and
restores, memorializes and consecrates Antony's male identity: in the
womblike receptive space of her female memory, suffused with sexual
longing, he can live again.[13]

Shakespeare achieves his refiguration of female generativity in
Cleopatra partly by aligning her with Plutarch's Isis for whom
generativity is her sign of divinity; his Isis

is the feminine part of nature, apt to receive all generation, upon
which occasion called she is by Plato, the nurse and Pandeches,
that is to say, capable of all: yea, and the common sort name her
Myrionymus, which is as much as to say, as having an infinite
number of names, for that she receiveth all formes and shapes.
(p. 1310)

Cleopatra's 'infinite variety' seems to me to have its source in Isis Pandeches; in her particolored nature, she replicates Isis's own multitudinousness:

> Moreover the habilliments of Isis, be of different tinctures and colours: for her whole power consisteth and is emploied in matter which receiveth all formes, and becommeth all maner of things, to wit, light, darknesse, day, night, fire, water, life, death, beginning, end. (p. 1318)

Like Isis – and unlike the more decorous Cleopatra of the 'Life' – Shakespeare's Cleopatra is at home in the realm of becoming: 'every thing becomes' her (1.1.49), as she becomes everything; even 'vilest things / Become themselves in her' (2.2.238–39). And like Isis, she acquires her restorative power from that realm: if Isis restores Osiris by immersing him in generation, Cleopatra would 'quicken with kissing' (4.15.39).[14]

Transferred from the divine to the human plane in Cleopatra, Isis's restorative gesture will necessarily be incomplete and equivocal; Cleopatra herself reminds us that she does not have a goddess's power, that 'wishers were ever fools' (4.15.33, 37). Nonetheless, the model of Isis may have partly enabled the opening out of trust in the female that leads Shakespeare toward *The Winter's Tale*: although Cleopatra cannot literally kiss the honored gashes whole, she can restore Antony's presence through her generative memory, assuaging his loss. From the beginning, her erotic longing has been the memorializing site of Antony's heroic masculinity: immediately after Caesar has located Antony's glory firmly in the past, in the landscape of starvation, Cleopatra recreates him as 'the arm / And burgonet of men' (1.5.23–24), conflating him with Mars; when Mardian evokes 'What Vensus did with Mars,' Cleopatra answers, 'O Charmian, / Where think'st thou he is now?' (1.5.18–19). Antony's manhood is alive and well in her erotic recreation of him. And the play does not encourage us to dismiss this recreation merely as foolish wishing: Antony's one moment of represented martial heroism – his victorious land battle, greatly expanded from Plutarch's account[15] – issues from and returns to Cleopatra and to the specifically erotic energy she gives him.

Preparation for that battle begins on the familiar territory of the morning-after scenes in *Romeo and Juliet* and *Troilus and Cressida*, where the man arises, apparently feeling depleted by the sexual encounter and ready to reaffirm his manhood in the world outside the bed, while the woman tries to keep him with her; like Juliet's 'Wilt thou be

gone?' (3.5.1) or Cressida's 'Prithee, tarry' (4.2.15), Cleopatra's 'Sleep
a little' (4.4.1) initially seems to register the dangerous pull toward
dissolution in the female. But in a wonderful transformation of this
motif, Cleopatra helps harden her man for that world, making him
'a man of steel' (4.4.33); as she becomes not only 'the armourer of
[his] heart' but the armorer of his body, 'a squire / More tight at this'
than Eros (4.4.7, 14–15), she demonstrates in effect that Venus can
arm as well as disarm Mars. For Shakespeare's other martial heroes –
Troilus, Macbeth, Coriolanus – manliness means radical disavowal of
the female; but Antony is never more manly than when he is armed
by Cleopatra. Armed by her, he fights as well as ever in his idealized
Roman past; and he returns his victory to her in language that
suggests how fully he acknowledges her as the point of origin of his
masculinity:

> O thou day o' the world,
> Chain mine arm'd neck, leap thou, attire and all,
> Through proof of harness to my heart, and there
> Ride on the pants triumphing!

(4.8.13–16)

The enormous energy of these lines comes in part from the way in
which they transform Roman threat into Egyptian triumph: images of
entrapment and servitude are revised as boundary permeation itself
becomes an expression of deep erotic delight. Despite the Roman
conviction that Cleopatra has weakened Antony – a conviction that he
himself sometimes shares – the entire sequence from 4.4 to 4.8 enfolds
his martial heroism within her embrace.

These moments prepare us for the impassioned act of memory
through which Cleopatra recreates her Emperor Antony in the last
act. For that act comes in the most literal way from what Cleopatra
herself has earlier called 'the memory of my womb' (3.13.163), her own
sexualized desire for what is absent. In her phrase, the sheltering space
of female memory becomes one with the nurturant space of the womb
itself: in context, 'the memory of my womb' refers periphrastically
to her children, as though they were what her womb remembered, as
though they were made by its memorializing powers. Early in the
play, Cleopatra imagines herself pregnant with the 'idleness' Antony
suspects her of (''Tis sweating labour, / To bear such idleness so near
the heart / As Cleopatra this' [1.3.93–95]. Mardian's later report
of her pseudo-death makes her pregnant not with idleness – the
womb-wishes the Soothsayer senses in Charmian (1.2.37) – but with
Antony's name:

> . . . in the midst a tearing groan did break
> The name of Antony; it was divided
> Between her heart, and lips: she render'd life
> Thy name so buried in her.

(4.14.31–34)

Given the frequency with which women rendered up their lives with their babies buried in them, it is hard not to hear in this pseudo-death the echo of an abortive birth; and of course the Romans would be happy to see Cleopatra's body as the burial ground of Antony's noble name. But Cleopatra's monumental recreation of Antony rewrites this abortive birth: in the protected female space of her own monument, the memory of her womb can at last bring Antony forth whole and undivided, rendering him life.

This is obviously an equivocal image, capable of multiple readings; the return to maternal origins is never unproblematic in Shakespeare. In casting Cleopatra as Plutarch's 'mother of the world' (p. 1304) and bringing Antony to rest in her monument, Shakespeare evokes all the ambivalence of the mother-infant bond.[16] Antony has already told us that Cleopatra's 'bosom was [his] crownet, [his] chief end' (4.12.27): through Cleopatra's final image, the end of the play returns him to Cleopatra's maternal body, the resting place from which he will no longer stray. In Cleopatra's final words, he becomes one with the asp, the baby at her breast, as she carries them both toward death ('O Antony! Nay, I will take thee too. / What should I stay—' [5.2.311–12]). Insofar as the play ends, with the fantasy of a mutual sleep that undoes boundaries, it fulfills the dangerous desire at the heart of masculine selfhood, the dream of reunion with the maternal matrix. And fulfillment of this dangerous dream seems to require no less than all: Antony can be cured only with a wound (4.14.78).

And the play insists on the danger: for the male self in Rome, individuated selfhood is simultaneous with masculinity; both mark the self as distinct from the mother, not-female. The affiliation of 'masculine' Rome with the solid and bounded, 'feminine' Egypt with the fluid,[17] registers this simultaneity: from the Roman point of view, the melting of the boundaries of the self is necessarily its effeminization, its pull back toward that matrix. Hence, for example, Enobarbus's worry that dissolving into tears will make him a woman (4.2.36) or Antony's rewriting his self-dissolution as the loss of his sword when he sees the eunuch Mardian (4.14.23): for individuated masculinity as it is defined in Rome, castration is the price of merger, and death its promised satisfaction. Like most of the men in Shakespeare's tragedies, Caesar builds his masculinity on this threat: in attenuated form, he is the exemplar of defensive masculinity; and

he demonstrates the dead end to which it leads. For the whole of
his masculine selfhood as he defines it depends on his denial of
the female, its reduction to the manageable proportions of his sister
Octavia. From his first description of Antony in Egypt, he makes it
plain that the female could only contaminate the male; from his point
of view, there would be only one way to read the image of Antony
dressed in Cleopatra's clothing. In his construction of masculinity,
he belongs in the company of Richard III, Troilus, Lear, Macbeth,
Coriolanus – all those Shakespearean men who fear contamination from
the mother within. And the Typhon who is his avatar provides the
founding metaphor for this relation to the maternal: Plutarch tells us
that Rhea 'brought forth Typhon, but he came not at the just time nor
at the right place, but brake thorow his mothers side and issued forth
at the wound' (p. 1292).[18] Plutarch's account of Typhon's birth figures
aggressive escape from the maternal body as the founding gesture of
his male selfhood; as a radical metaphor for differentiation from the
originary maternal matrix, Typhon's birth could serve as the model for
all of Shakespeare's would-be Caesarian sons.[19]

These sons define themselves by their differentiation from that
dangerous matrix; but Antony has allowed himself to be pulled back
toward it from the start. From his first entrance, he knows that his love
will require of him not only the dissolution of his Roman selfhood, but
the dissolution of all such firm boundaries: the command that would
undo his Roman selfhood – 'Let Rome in Tiber melt!' (1.1.33) – follows
from his claim that love is by nature unbounded ('There's beggary
in the love that can be reckon'd' [1.1.15]). The love he seeks will
necessarily entail the dissolving of the self into dangerous and fecund
waters – into the Nile, if not the Tiber. Antony resists this pull for
much of the play: from 1.2 until 4.14, he occupies himself in shoring
up the boundaries of his masculine selfhood as Rome defines it. But
the concealed accents of desire are audible even in his most plangent
grieving for the dissolution of this self:

Ant.
Eros, thou yet behold'st me?

Eros
Ay, noble lord.

Ant.
Sometime we see a cloud that's dragonish,
A vapour sometime, like a bear, or lion,
A tower'd citadel, a pendent rock,

A forked mountain, or blue promontory
With trees upon't, that nod unto the world,
And mock our eyes with air. Thou hast seen these signs,
They are black vesper's pageants.

Eros
Ay, my lord.

Ant.
That which is now a horse, even with a thought
The rack dislimns, and makes it indistinct
As water is in water.

Eros
It does, my lord.

Ant.
My good knave Eros, now thy captain is
Even such a body: here I am Antony,
Yet cannot hold this visible shape, my knave,

(4.14.1–14)

No longer Herculean in his response to catastrophe, Antony
contemplates his own dissolution with a quiet melancholy, letting go of
his defining rage.[20] The very images of prominent manhood – dragon,
bear, lion, citadel, rock, mountain, promontory, trees – now dissolve
before his eyes, as though they had been illusory all along, merely
temporary shapes wrested from vapor; in comparing himself to them,
Antony acknowledges that he himself has mimicked the shapes of
masculine identity only to dislimn, revealing his watery foundation.

As Antony imagines himself becoming indistinct as water is
in water, he embraces the desire to lay it all down, to let go of
the Roman selfhood maintained by such rigid vigilance. For the
masculinity of the sword – the masculine selfhood that defines itself
by rigid differentiation from the female – has increasingly seemed too
constraining for Antony's fluid desires. And so he greets Mardian's
news that Cleopatra is dead with an odd sense of acquiescence and
relief, as though he can at last stop struggling to bear the armor of a
selfhood that has always been too heavy, too encasing:

Unarm, Eros, the long day's task is done,
And we must sleep. . . .
                    Off, pluck off,
The seven-fold shield of Ajax cannot keep
The battery from my heart. O, cleave, my sides!

Heart, once be stronger than they continent,
Crack thy frail case! Apace, Eros, apace!
No more a soldier: bruised pieces, go,
You have been nobly born.

(4.14.35–43)

Othello bids farewell to his military occupation (3.3.353–63) only with
intense pain, as the sign of his loss of honor and of the heroic selfhood
he had invested in Desdemona; but Antony gives up his bruised
pieces willingly, as though he has finally gotten what he has wanted
all along. His armor and his body coalesce as he lets both go, for both
now seem to confine the desire that would overflow their boundaries.
'Unarm, Eros, the long day's task is done, / And we must sleep': the
langorousness of the language itself suggests the wished-for dissolution
of the self into the unbounded state of sleep ('lie down and stray no
farther' [4.14.47]) and the dream of unbounded fusion with Cleopatra.[21]

Shakespeare is acutely aware of the danger of this letting go; the
play's repeated images of unmanning do not let us forget what is
at stake. Nonetheless, in giving up the boundaries of his selfhood,
Antony can be recreated in and through his merger with Cleopatra;
and in her re-creation of him, the play reaches toward a new kind of
masculinity. If Caesar's masculinity is founded on differentiation from
the female – and on the psychic scarcity that is the consequence of
that differentiation – Antony's is finally founded on incorporation of
the female: in Cleopatra's vision of him, his bounty flows from him
as though it were an attribute of his own body. In his capacity to give
without being used up, he replicates the female economy of breast
milk, self-renewing in its abundance; leaving behind Caesar's male
economy of limited resources, he becomes like Cleopatra, feeding and
renewing the appetite in an endless cycle of gratification and desire,
making hungry where most he satisfies. Shakespeare begins the play
by giving us an Antony whose compromised manhood allows him to
be mistaken for Cleopatra (1.2.76); he ends it by giving us an Antony
whose manhood rests on his return to her as the source of his own
bounty.

Insofar as the memory of Cleopatra's womb becomes the nurturant
space that holds the fullness of Antony's masculine bounty, insofar
as she herself becomes the model and the source for that bounty,
Antony and Cleopatra is Shakespeare's most strenuous attempt within
the tragedies to redefine the relationship of masculinity to the maternal,
hence to redefine tragic masculinity itself. Through her, Shakespeare
allows himself to imagine a fully masculine selfhood that can overflow
its own rigid boundaries, a masculinity become enormous in its
capacity to share in the female mystery of an endlessly regenerating

source of supply, growing the more it is reaped. But this imaginative
act is hedged around with conditions. It is, first of all, deeply
retrospective, as much a lament for a dream that is irrevocably gone
as a recreation of it in the present. In fact, both of the protagonists
must die in order for it to be safe: death is not only the image but
also the detoxifying agent of merger and of the masculine selfhood
achieved through its means.[22] And Cleopatra must, in particular, die
for the right reason: she can become the repository of Antony's new
masculinity only insofar as she is willing to die specifically for him,
simultaneously validating their love and her vision of him. Throughout,
she has been presented almost entirely in relation to Antony: although
she is allowed far more dramatic force than Shakespeare's other tragic
women – we more frequently see matters from her point of view,
and the fourth act 'female interlude'[23] in which the other women
characteristically register their helplessness and self-abandonment is
strikingly relocated to the fifth act, where it becomes potent enough
to outwit Caesar and to redefine the tragedy in its own terms –
the arena of her subjectivity and power has nonetheless been very
carefully circumscribed.[24] Her queenship is largely implicit, her subjects
invisible; she is one with her feminized kingdom as though it were
her body, not her domain. Political power is reserved for the men;
Cleopatra's royalty in the end consists of dying well. The entire drama
is played out within the context of Caesar's final conquest of Egypt and
the establishment of patriarchal rule there.[25] The serious threats to this
rule – the Gonerils, Lady Macbeths, Volumnias – are in effect banished
from this play; they make a brief cameo appearance under the guise of
Fulvia and then are chased off the stage, as though Shakespeare could
allow himself to re-imagine a masculinity founded on incorporation of
the maternal only by first exorcising their destabilizing power.

But despite all these circumscriptions and qualifications,
Shakespeare's imaginative achievement in this play seems to me
extraordinary – and extraordinarily liberating. For one fragile moment,
Shakespeare is able to imagine the possibility of a maternal space that
is neither suffocating nor deforming; now, the memory of Cleopatra's
womb becomes the site of her – and his – imaginative power to
restore the heroic male whose loss has haunted Shakespeare's plays
at least since *Hamlet*, which begins with a mother's sexualized failure
to remember right. And unlike *Lear*, where maternal space can be
imagined as protective only insofar as it is relentlessly separated from
sexuality, here the nurturing female space is profoundly allied with
generative process: Antony does not need to remake Cleopatra as the
virgin mother in order to rest on her kind nursery. The old images of
generation undergo transvaluation in *Antony and Cleopatra*: Hamlet's
sun breeding maggots (2.2.181), Othello's 'slime / That sticks on filthy

deeds' (5.2.149–50), have become Antony's potentiating 'fire / That quickens Nilus' slime' (1.3.68–69). The nightmare vision of female sexuality that initiates the tragedies and problem plays has its place in *Antony and Cleopatra*, but that place is partial:[26] the violent language of sexual loathing familiar from *Troilus and Cressida* – language of venereal disease, of fragmentation and spoiled food – makes a muted appearance in Roman accusations of Cleopatra (3.10.11; 3.13.117) but is finally dissolved as Cleopatra becomes a source of wholeness.[27] Through her, the baby cast violently away from Lady Macbeth's breast is restored to nurturance in the end and the witchcraft of *Macbeth* is recuperated in Cleopatra's enchantment, which makes defect perfection (2.2.231).

In thus realigning masculinity with the maternal, Shakespeare is able to see his way beyond the either/or of *Macbeth* and *Coriolanus*, and beyond the end-stopped genre of tragedy. The whole of *Antony and Cleopatra* overflows the measure; in its interpretative openness,[28] its expansive playfulness, its imaginative abundance, it seems to me to lead directly to *The Winter's Tale*, where trust in female process similarly bursts the boundaries of the tragic form. Identified with Cleopatra in his longing for Antony, Shakespeare in effect locates the recuperative power of his own art in the female space of her monument, making her imaginative fecundity the model for his own; and in his imaginative alliance with her, he is able to recuperate theater itself, rewriting its dangerous affiliation with the female in *Macbeth* and *Coriolanus*. In Caesar's theater of history – an extension of Malcolm's stripped-down and anti-theatrical theater, where there would be no room for illusion, where even Cleopatra would merely be boyed (5.2.219) – there is no space left for play; but in the spacious theater of Cleopatra's monument, we are given leave to play till doomsday.

Notes

1. It is by now a truism to say that a new kind of masculinity is represented in Antony; Eugene M. Waith's 'Manhood and Valor in Two Shakespearean Tragedies' (*English Literary History* 17 [1950]: 268–73), Robert Ornstein's 'The Ethic of the Imagination: Love and Art in "Antony and Cleopatra"' (*Later Shakespeare*, Stratford-upon-Avon Studies 8 [London: Edward Arnold, 1966], pp. 36–37), and R.J. Dorius's little-known 'Shakespeare's Dramatic Nodes and *Antony and Cleopatra*' (*Literatur als Kritik des Lebens* [Heidelberg: Quelle & Meyer, 1975], pp. 91–93) seem to me the best early statements of the theme. One name for this new masculinity is 'androgyny,' as Dorius hints; see, for example, Raymond B. Waddington ('Antony and Cleopatra: "What Venus did with Mars,"' *Shakespeare Studies* 2 [1963]: 223). Anne Barton (' "Nature's Piece 'Gainst Fancy,"' [Unpublished PhD, Bedford College,

University of London, 1973, pp. 39–40), James J. Greene ('*Antony and Cleopatra*: The Birth and Death of Androgyny,' *University of Hartford Studies in Literature* 19 [1987]: 25–44), and especially Erickson (*Patriarchal Structures*, pp. 131–34). But see Carol Thomas Neely's powerful argument that the lovers enlarge, but do not exchange or transcend, gender roles (*Broken Nuptials in Shakespeare's Plays* [New Haven, Conn.: Yale University Press, 1985], pp. 137–39, 150). Both sides in this debate seem to me right: insofar as Shakespeare grounds this new masculinity in acceptance of and relation to the female, he allows it to take on some of the qualities characteristically called female and hence to become, relatively speaking, 'androgynous'; but insofar as Shakespeare claims that Antony is no less 'manly' for this redefinition, he shores up (by enlarging) the category of manliness.

2. Caesar enters the play ambiguously announcing (by denying) his hatred of Antony; but his longing for Antony – reflected both in his obsessive focus on Antony and in the accents of betrayal that often accompany his criticism – seems to me the deepest unacknowledged current of feeling in the play. This longing is implicitly eroticized as he gives his sister – 'a great part of myself' – to Antony in marriage, with the ambiguous injunction that he 'use me well in't' (3.2.24–25). When he imagines the reception Octavia should have had as Antony's wife and his own sister – 'The trees by the way / Should have borne men, and expectation fainted / Longing for what it had not' (3.6.46–48) – the intense phallic giddiness of his language seems to me directed as much toward the Antony whom he reaches through Octavia as toward Octavia herself.

3. In Cleopatra's account, her lover is 'great Pompey' (1.5.31); in Antony's, he is (historically) Pompey the Great's son, Gnaeus Pompey (3.13.118). Ridley notes that Cleopatra's 'epithet is misleading' (Arden *Antony and Cleopatra*, p. 42); but it seems to me nearly irresisitible for an audience accustomed to associating Cleopatra with legendary masculine presences. Her other grand lover, Julius Caesar, is Octavius Caesar's father only by adoption; but Octavius Caesar refers to him as 'father' in his one oblique reference to him here (3.6.6), although he never does so in *Julius Caesar*.

4. Pompey in fact makes his own phallic potency depend on his capacity to wrest Antony away from this woman: if Antony returns to Rome, Pompey will 'rear / The higher our opinion, that our stirring / Can from the lap of Egypt's widow pluck / The ne'er-lust-wearied Antony' (2.1.35–38). Like Pompey's Caesar's contest with Cleopatra for possession of Antony has overtones of the negative oedipal complex, in which the father – rather than the mother – is both the object of desire and the measure of masculine success.

5. In fact, the ambiguity introduced by 'since then' nearly succeeds in fusing Julius Caesar and Antony in their illicit paternity: the phrase simultaneously assigns Caesarion's paternity to Antony, not Julius Caesar (he is the first of the unlawful issue Antony and Cleopatra have since then made between them) and assigns paternity of all the other unlawful issue (since Caesarion) to Julius Caesar.

6. Geoffrey Bullough, *Narrative and Dramatic Sources of Shakespeare* (New York) Columbia Univ. Press, 1966), vol. 5, pp. 267–68.

7. See Janet Adelman, *The Common Liar: An Essay on Antony and Cleopatra* (New Haven: Yale Univ. Press, 1973), pp. 137–39, for a more extended discussion of Antony's position between the generations of father and son.

8. See *Julius Caesar*, 1.3.3–4, 20, 75; many members of Shakespeare's audience would probably have noted the allusion.

9. Pompey models this dangerous inheritance in miniature. The quarrel he inherits from his father first seems to make a man of him (the people 'throw / Pompey the Great, and all his dignities / Upon his son, who high in name and power, / Higher than both in blood and life, stands up / For the main soldier' [1.2.185–89]); but it finally leads to his destruction when he proves too small for his father's role (2.6.82–83).

10. 'Of Isis and Osiris' was published in London in 1603, in Philemon Holland's translation of the *Moralia*; critics frequently assume that Shakespeare consulted it while working on *Antony and Cleopatra*, often without making explicit the basis for this assumption. See for example, Harold Fisch, '"Antony and Cleopatra": The Limits of Mythology,' *Shakespeare Survey* 23 [1970]: 61; Frank Kermode, *The Riverside Shakespeare*, ed. G. Blakemore Evans [Boston: Houghton Mifflin Company, 1974], p. 1345; and Walter R. Coppedge, 'The Joy of the Worm: Dying in *Antony and Cleopatra*,' *Renaissance Papers* [1988]: 41–50). The fullest accounts of Shakespeare's possible indebtedness to Plutarch's essay are those of Michael Lloyd ('Cleopatra as Isis,' *Shakespeare Survey* 12 [1959]: 91–94) and Barbara Bono (*Literary Transvaluation: From Vergilian Epic to Shakespearean Tragicomedy* [Berkeley: University of California Press, 1984], pp. 199–213), both of which seem to me more suggestive than conclusive. My own sense of Shakespeare's indebtedness to this essay turns specifically on Shakespeare's use of 'habiliments' to describe Cleopatra's clothing when she is dressed as Isis (3.6.17). The word is unusual in Shakespeare, occurring only five times in its various forms. In the comparable passage in the *Life*, North's Plutarch uses 'apparell': 'Now for Cleopatra, she did not onely weare at that time (but at all other times els when she came abroad) the apparell of the goddess Isis, and so gave audience unto all her subjects' (Bullough, *Narrative and Dramatic Sources*, vol. 5, p. 291). But in 'Of Isis and Osiris,' Holland's Plutarch uses 'habilliments' specifically to refer to the clothing of Isis: 'the habilliments of Isis, be of different tinctures and colours' (*The Philosophie, commonlie called The Morals*, trans. Philemon Holland [London, 1603], p. 1318). Since Shakespeare otherwise follows the passage in the *Life* quite closely, his use of 'habiliments' seems to me strong evidence that he consulted 'Of Isis and Osiris' while writing *Antony and Cleopatra*.

11. *Antony and Cleopatra* is a notoriously 'open' text; I have written elsewhere of the degree to which the play sets contrary interpretative possibilities side by side (*The common Liar*, esp. pp. 14–52, 99–171). 'Of Isis and Osiris' is similarly full of contradictory interpretations of its central story.

12. Curiously indeterminate in Plutarch's text, Osiris shifts his meaning according to the company he keeps: construed, for example, as the generative moon in relation to Typhon as destructively hot sun (p. 1304), he becomes the sun 'as the visible matter of a spirituall and intellectuall substance' in relation to Isis's female moon (p. 1308); construed as the principle of generative moisture in relation to Typhon's destructive heat (p. 1300), he becomes the Platonic Idea in relation to Isis's moist and receptive matter (p. 1310). If in the myth Isis and Typhon vie for

possession of Osiris's body, in Plutarch's text they vie in effect for interpretative control over his significance; and in this they resemble Caesar and Cleopatra, each of whom imagines an Emperor Antony, each of whom wants to establish his meaning only in relation to his or her own story.

13. Although neither Wheeler's *Shakespeare's Development and the Problem Comedies* [Berkeley, Cal.: University of California Press, 1981] nor Madelon Gohlke's '"I wooed thee with my sword": Shakespeare's Tragic Paradigms' (in *Representing Shakespeare*) contains full accounts of *Antony and Cleopatra*, both works have been (as always) seminal for my own; see, for example, Wheeler's reference to Antony, 'reborn through the fertile womb of [Cleopatra's] imagination' (p. 201) and Gohlke's to Cleopatra's 'conception' of Antony (p. 179).

14. In Plutarch's neo-platonic myth, Isis (receptive matter) restores Osiris (the Platonic Idea) by immersing him in the generative world: 'dying and being buried [the Ideas] doe many times revive and rise againe fresh by the means of generations' (p. 1311). Plutarch generally valorizes the generative realm as the site of immanence and regeneration; he reports that Isis once cut Jupiter's legs apart when they had grown together, 'which fable giveth us covertly thus to understand, that the understanding and reason of God in it selfe going invisibly, and after an unseene maner, proceedeth to generation by the meanes of motion' (p. 1312). Critics who comment on Cleopatra's resemblance to Isis generally do so on the basis of her immersion in the generative world, noting especialy her association with Isis's 'motion' (Lloyd, 'Cleopatra as Isis,' p. 91), with her moon (Waddington, 'Antony and Cleopatra,' p. 216; Kermode, 'Introduction,' pp. 1345–46; and with her variability and multitudinous garments (Colie, 'The Significance of Style,' p. 74). But for Coppedge ('The Joy of the Worm,' pp. 49–50), Fisch ('Antony and Cleopatra,' p. 63), and Bono (*Literary Transvaluation*, pp. 5, 209–13), the resemblance rests also on Cleopatra's final transcendence of the natural world. Bono in fact sees Plutarch's resolution of the contradictory naturalistic interpretations of the myth into the One of neo-platonic interpretation as analogous to both Isis's and Cleopatra's turning from the many to the one (pp. 204, 211–13). But in my reading of Plutarch, Isis's role in the neo-platonic interpretation rests on her continued identification with the generative realm – as does Cleopatra's role in the play.

15. Bullough, *Narrative and Dramatic Sources*, vol. 5, p. 307; see Neely's fine discussion of Shakespeare's version of this battle and its aftermath (*Broken Nuptials*, pp. 146–47).

16. Stephen A. Shapiro finds ambivalence of all kinds characteristic of the play ('The Varying Shore of the World: Ambivalence in *Antony and Cleopatra*,' *Modern Language Quarterly* 27 [1966]: 18–32). There has been very little full-scale psychoanalytic work done on *Antony and Cleopatra*, perhaps because Antony's emasculation is so transparent that it does not need much explication (but see Janis Krohn's explication of it: 'The Dangers of Love in *Antony and Cleopatra*,' *The International Review of Psychoanalysis* 13 [1986]: 89–96) or because the play's relatively high valuation of the lovers' deadly union does not fit well with psychoanalysis's usual negative stance toward

such matters. The classic (and to my mind, still the richest) psychoanalytic account of the play is Constance Brown Kuriyama's reading of the interplay between its oedipal and preoedipal components ('The Mother of the World: A Psychoanalytic Interpretation of Shakespeare's *Antony and Cleopatra*,' *English Literary Renaissance* 7 [1977]: 324–51).

17. This set of affiliations is by now commonplace; see, for example, Ornstein ('The Ethic of the Imagination,' p. 36), Adelman (*Common Liar*, pp. 127–31, 147–49), Michael Payne ('Erotic Irony and Polarity in *Antony and Cleopatra*,' *Shakespeare Quarterly* 24 [1973]: 266–69), Dorius ('Shakespeare's Dramatic Modes,' p. 93), Kuriyama ('The Mother of the World,' p. 338), and Susan Snyder ('Patterns of Motion in "Antony and Cleopatra,"' *Shakespeare Survey* 33 [1980]: 115–21). For these critics, and many others, Antony's turn toward a more 'fluid' way of being is at least as positive as it is negative.

18. By contrast, Osiris seems to be in no hurry to leave Rhea's womb: Plutarch reports that 'Isis and Osiris were in love in their mothers bellie before they were borne, and lay together secretly and by stealth' (p. 1292), perhaps elliptically signaling the extent to which generative harmony rests on a benign relationship to the maternal matrix.

19. Does Caesar's name locate him in the company of these sons? Although *OED* lists the first occurrence of *caesarian* as an obstetrical term in English in 1615, the term may well have been creeping toward common usage ten years earlier; it was first used in France in an obstetrical handbook in 1581 (Rousset's *Traité nouveau de l'hysterotomie ou Enfantement Caesarienne*, cited in J.H. Young, *The History of Caesarian Section* [London: H.K. Lewis, 1944], pp. 4, 23) and became commonplace in obstetrical literature thereafter. The obstetrical procedure itself, by whatever name, had a long association with the Caesars. Pliny the Elder thought that the first of the Caesars was so named because he had been cut from his mother's uterus ('Scipio Africanus prior natus, primusque Caesareum, a caeso matris utero dictus,' *The Natural History*, bk. 7, chap. 9, cited in Young, pp. 2–3). Partly because Pliny's formulation allowed for a certain amount of confusion, a long (and unhistorical) tradition had Julius Caesar born by caesarian section (see J. Paul Pundel, *Histoire de L'Opération Caesarienne* [Brussels: Presses Academiques Européennes, 1969], pp. 15–39, *passim*); in one Arabic manuscript, even Octavius Caesar was born by caesarian (Pundel, p. 40). Pliny attributed particular good fortune to caesarian children, whose mothers invariably died at their birth; does his attitude stand behind Macduff and the full-fortuned Caesar?

20. See Eugene M. Waith's classic discussion of Antony's Herculean age (*The Herculean Hero in Marlowe, Chapman, Shakespeare and Dryden* [New York: Columbia University Press, 1962], pp. 115–21).

21. That this mutual sleep is also imaged as orgasm – 'I come, my queen' (4.14.50); 'Husband, I come' (5.2.286) – suggests the deeply oral valence of genital sexuality in the play (see Kuriyama, 'The Mother of the World,' pp. 342–43; Roberta Hooks, 'Shakespeare's *Antony and Cleopatra*: Power and Submission,' *American Imago* 44 (1987), p. 37). Though the play initially celebrates phallic sexuality in Julius Caesar's ploughing (2.2.228), Antony's seedsman scattering his grain (2.7.21–22), and especially Cleopatra's cheerfully vulgar 'Ram thou thy fruitful tidings in mine ears' (2.5.24), the aim of that sexuality is boundary dissolution; the play ends in a *Liebestod*

that celebrates merger through Cleopatra's final image of the baby at her breast. As Kay Stockholder notes, the 'love-death fantasy . . . retains erotic fulfillment without taint from the world, the flesh, or sexuality' (*Dream Works: Lovers and Families in Shakespeare's Plays* (Toronto: University of Toronto Press, 1987), p. 166); in effect, death replaces genital sexuality as the imagined means to fusion, for the audience as well as for the lovers. Philo has early on invited our voyeurism ('Look, where they come' [1.1.10]), but the play thwarts it until the last scene; instead of the sexually climatic moment Philo invites us to see, we are given repeated near-misses. In fact, by locating the great central scene of reunion only within Caesar's report of it (3.6.1–19, 65–67), Shakespeare puts us in Caesar's position, as one of the conspicuously excluded parties: only the mutual death of the lovers answers our desire to witness their union.

22. In effect, death becomes the safe solvent of masculine identity, enabling the fantasy of fusion that proved so dangerous for Troilus; see especially Neely's account of the ways in which 'death renders female sexuality benign' (*Broken Nuptials*, p. 161).

23. I am thinking of such moments as Ophelia's mad scene and drowning (reported by Gertrude), Desdemona's willow song and conversation with Emilia, and Lady Macbeth's sleep-walking, each of which shows its protagonist in a state at once intimate and self-alienated, stabilizing our image of her and allowing us to say farewell as we move on to the hero's tragedy.

24. L.T. Fitz argues strenuously and wittily that Cleopatra is a tragic hero in her own right and sees the signs of sexism in the refusal to recognize her full subjectivity ('Egyptian Queens and Male Reviewers: Sexist Attitudes in *Antony and Cleopatra* Criticism,' *Shakespeare Quarterly* 28 [1977]: esp. 307–14). While I agree that criticism has tended to grant Cleopatra much less subjectivity than Shakespeare does, I nonetheless find, with Linda Bamber, that she lacks the full privileges of the Self in comparison with Antony (*Comic Women, Tragic Men: A Study of Gender and Genre in Shakespeare* [Stanford, Calif.: Stanford University Press, 1982], esp. pp. 55–59, 66–69).

25. The dwindling into patriarchy of Cleopatra's realm is in part anticipated by Charmian's final placing of her as 'a princess / Descended of so many royal kings' (5.2.325–26); until that moment, she had seemed – virtually alone of Shakespeare's women – to be *sui generis*.

26. Many critics note that Shakespeare revalues sexuality in *Antony and Cleopatra*; see, for example, Ornstein's account of Shakespeare's shift from a masculine to a feminine perspective on sexuality ('The Ethic of the Imagination,' pp. 34–35) and Erickson's fine account of the ways in which the dark lady of the sonnets is reclaimed in Cleopatra (*Patriarchal Structures*, pp. 125–27). As far as I know, the longest and most serious account of this revaluation is Brent Cohen's wonderful meditation on sexuality in *Antony and Cleopatra* in his unpublished Ph.D. dissertation, 'Sexuality and Tragedy in *Othello* and *Anthony and Cleopatra*' (University of California, Berkeley, 1981).

27. Through its dramatic structure, the play encourages our participation in this fatansy of wholeness. The play is from the beginning obsessed with gaps, absences, lacks (the word *lack* and its variants occur seven times), defects,

fragmentation. And its dramatic structure plays out this fragmentation in its violent wrenchings from place to place, its numerous short scenes. Particularly after the bustle of act 4, we (like Antony) long for a resting place; and we are given such a place in the luxurious last scene, where we (again like Antony) can come to rest in Cleopatra's monument. In this way, as in many others, *Antony and Cleopatra* undoes *Troilus and Cressida*: Troilus is punished for investing wholeness in Cressida, and the audience is made to undergo his punishment as the play becomes increasingly fragmented; but we and Antony are gathered up together in the recreative maternal space of Cleopatra's imagination.

28. The interpretative openness of *Antony and Cleopatra* is particularly striking if it is measured in relation to the plays around it: *Macbeth* and *Coriolanus* both attempt to restrict interpretative possibilities for their audiences sharply in the end, as they narrow the options for their protagonists. Is it purely coincidental that these are also the plays most deeply and explicitly suspicious of female power? Near the beginning of 'Of Isis and Osiris,' Plutarch suggestively associates the inaccessibility of truth (and hence instability of interpretation) with the female body: fables are veils for truth, but what is under Isis's veil remains a mystery ('I am all that which hath beane, which is, and which shall be, and never any man yet was able to drawe open my vaile' [p. 1291]). Perhaps Shakespeare's acceptance of difference – including interpretative difference – in *Antony and Cleopatra* turns in part on his new tolerance for the mystery of what lies beneath the veil, in effect his new capacity to trust in the female other.

7 Antony and Cleopatra (c.1607): Virtus under Erasure*

JONATHAN DOLLIMORE

This short piece is taken from Jonathan Dollimore's *Radical Tragedy*. Like Janet Adelman, Dollimore is concerned here with the way in which identity is constituted. Where Adelman focuses on how masculine identity is constructed, Dollimore turns his attention here to what he outlines as a shift in the period in the way in which 'honour' is constituted and martial prowess is perceived. This shift, in Dollimore's view, serves to expose what Alan Sinfield would characterise as a 'faultline' in the ideological codes which are embodied in the figure of Antony. For Dollimore, the opening up of this faultline serves finally to destroy Antony.

In Jonson's *Seganus*, Silius, about to take his own life in order to escape the persecution of Tiberius, tells the latter: 'The means that makes your greatness, must not come/In mention of it' (III. 311–12). He is of course exposing a strategy of power familiar to the period: first there occurs an effacement of the material conditions of its possibility, second, a claim for its transcendent origin, one ostensibly legitimating it and putting it beyond question – hence Tiberius' invocation only moments before of 'the Capitol,/. . . all our Gods . . . the dear Republic,/Our sacred Laws, and just authority/ (III. 216–18). In *Sejanus* this is transparent enough. In other plays – the representation of power is more complex in that we are shown how the ideology in question constitutes not only the authority of those in power but their very identity.

Staged in a period in which there occurred the unprecedented decline of the power, military and political, of the titular aristocracy, *Antony and Cleopatra* and *Coriolanus*, like *Sejanus* before them, substantiate the contention that "tis place,/Not blood, discerns the noble, and the base' (*Sejanus*, V. i. 11–12). Historical shifts in power together with the recognition, or at least a more public acknowledgement of, its actual operations, lead to the erasure of older

*JONATHAN DOLLIMORE, *Radical Tragedy: Religion, Ideology and Power in the Drama of Shakespeare and his Contemporaries* (Brighton: Harvester Wheatsheaf, 1984), pp. 204–17.

notions of honour and *virtus*. Both plays effect a sceptical interrogation of martial ideology and in doing so foreground the complex social and political relations which hitherto it tended to occlude.

In his study of English drama in the seventeenth century C.L. Barber detects a significant decline in the presence of honour as a martial ideal and he is surely right to interpret this as due to changes in the nature and occupations of the aristocracy during that period. These included the professionalising of warfare and the increasing efficiency of state armies. The effect of such changes was that by the end of the seventeenth century there was considerably less scope for personal military initiative and military glory; honour becomes an informal personal code with an extremely attenuated social dimension (*The Idea of Honour in the English Drama 1591–1700*, (Göteborg, 1957), pp. 269–79).

More recently, and even more significantly for the present study, Mervyn James has explored in depth the changing conceptions of honour between 1485 and 1642; most striking is his conclusion that there occurred 'a change of emphasis, apparent by the early seventeenth century . . . [involving] . . . the emergence of a "civil" society in which the monopoly both of honour and violence by the state was asserted' (*English Politics and the Concept of Honour 1485–1642* (Oxford: Past & Present Society, 1978) p. 2).[1]

Such are the changes which activate a contradiction latent in martial ideology and embodied in two of Shakespeare's protagonists, Antony and Coriolanus. From one perspective – becoming but not yet residual – they appear innately superior and essentially autonomous, their power independent of the political context in which it finds expression. In short they possess that *virtus* which enables each, in Coriolanus's words, to 'stand/As if a man were author of himself' (V. iii. 35–6). 'As if': even as these plays reveal the ideological scope of that belief they disclose the alternative emergent perspective, one according to which Antony and Coriolanus are nothing more than their reputation, an ideological effect of powers antecedent to and independent of them. Even as each experiences himself as the origin and embodiment of power, he is revealed to be its instrument and effect – its instrument because, first and foremost, its effect. Bacon brilliantly focusses this contradiction in his essay on martial glory: 'It was prettily devised of Æsop: *The fly sate upon the axle-tree of the chariot wheel, and said, What a dust do I raise!*' (*Esays*, p. 158). Throughout Bacon's essay there is a dryly severe insistence on that fact which martial ideology cannot internally accommodate: 'opinion brings on substance' (p. 158). Such is the condition of Antony and Coriolanus, and increasingly so: as they transgress the power structure which constitutes them both their political and personal identities – inextricably bound together if not identical – disintegrate.

Virtus and History

Antony and Cleopatra anticipates the dawn of a new age of imperialist consolidation:

The time of universal peace is near.
Prove this a prosp'rous day, the three nook'd world
Shall bear the olive freely

(IV. vi. 5–7)

Prior to such moments heroic *virtus* may appear to be identical with the dominant material forces and relations of power. But this is never actually so: they were only ever coterminous and there is always the risk that a new historical conjuncture will throw them into misalignment. This is what happens in *Antony and Cleopatra*; Antony, originally identified in terms of both *virtus* and these dominant forces and relations, is destroyed by their emerging disjunction.

In an important book Eugene Waith has argued that 'Antony's reassertion of his heroic self in the latter part of the play is entirely personal. What he reasserts is individual integrity . . . Heroism rather than heroic achievement becomes the important thing' (*The Herculean Hero*, (London: Chatto & Windus, 1962), p. 118). On this view Antony privately reconstitutes his 'heroic self' despite or maybe even because of being defeated by circumstances beyond his control. I want to argue that the reverse is true: heroism of Antony's kind can never be 'entirely personal' (as indeed Bacon insisted) nor separated from either 'heroic achievement' or the forces and relations of power which confer its meaning.

The reader persuaded by the Romantic reading of this play is likely to insist that I'm missing the point – that what I've proposed is at best only true of the world in which Antony and Cleopatra live, a world transcended by their love, a love which 'translineates man (sic) to divine likeness' (G. Wilson Knight, *The Imperial Theme* (London: Methuen, 1965), p. 217). It is not anti-Romantic moralism which leads me to see this view as wholly untenable. In fact I want to argue for an interpretation of the play which refuses the usual critical divide whereby it is either 'a tragedy of lyrical inspiration, justifying love by presenting it as triumphant over death, or . . . a remorseless exposure of human frailties, a presentation of spiritual possibilities 'dissipated through a senseless surrender to passion' (Traversi, *An Approach to Shakespeare*, II (London: Hollis & Carter, 1968), p. 208). Nor do I discount the Romantic reading by wilfully disregarding the play's captivating poetry: it is, indeed, on occasions rapturously expressive of desire. But the language of desire, far from transcending the power relations which structure this society, is wholly in-formed by them.

As a preliminary instance of this, consider the nature of Antony's belated 'desire' for Fulvia, expressed at news of her death and not so dissimilar to this ambivalent desire for Cleopatra (as the sudden shift of attention from the one to the other suggests):

> Thus did I desire it:
> What our contempts doth often hurl from us
> We wish it ours again; the present pleasure,
> By revolution low'ring, does become
> The opposite of itself. She's good, being gone;
> The hand could pluck her back that shov'd her on.
> I must from this enchanting queen break off.
>
> (I. ii. 119–25)

True, the language of the final scenes is very different from this, but there too we are never allowed to forget that the moments of sublimity are conditional upon absence, nostalgic contemplation upon the fact that the other is irrevocably gone. As for present love, it is never any the less conditioned by the imperatives of power than the arranged marriage between Antony and Octavia.

Virtus and *Realpolitik* (1)

In *Antony and Cleopatra* those with power make history yet only in accord with the contingencies of the existing historical moment – in Antony's words: 'the strong necessity of time' (I. iii. 42). If this sounds fatalistic, in context it is quite clear that Antony is not capitulating to 'Time' as such but engaging in *realpolitik*, real power relations. His capacity for policy is in fact considerable; not only, and most obviously, is there the arranged marriage with Octavia, but also those remarks of his which conclude the alliance with Lepidus and Caesar against Pompey:

> [Pompey] hath laid strange courtesies and great
> Of late upon me. I must thank him only,
> Lest my remembrance suffer ill report;
> At heel of that, defy him.
>
> (II. ii. 159–62)

In fact, the suggestion of fatalism in Antony's reference to time is itself strategic, an evasive displacing of responsibility for his impending

departure from Cleopatra. As such it is parallelled later by Caesar when
he tells the distraught Octavia,

> Be you not troubled with the time, which drives
> O'er your content these strong necessities,
> But let determin'd things to destiny
> Hold unbewail'd their way.

> (III. vi. 82–5)

The cause of her distress is divided allegiance between brother and
husband (Caesar and Antony) who are now warring with each other.
Caesar's response comes especially ill from one scarcely less responsible
for her conflict than Antony; her marriage to the latter was after all
dictated by his political will: 'The *power* of Caesar, and/His *power* unto
Octavia' (II. ii. 147–8; my italics). 'Time' and 'destiny' mystify power by
eclipsing its operation and effect, and Caesar knows this; compare the
exchange on Pompey's galley – *Anthony*: 'Be a child o' th' time./*Caesar*:
Possess it, I'll make answer' (II. vii. 98–9). Caesar, in this respect, is
reminiscent of Machiavelli's Prince; he is inscrutable and possessed
of an identity which becomes less fixed, less identifiable as his power
increases. Antony by contrast is defined in terms of omnipotence (the
more so, paradoxically, as his power diminishes): the 'man of men' (I.
iv. 72), the 'lord of lords' (IV. iii. 16).

In both *Antony and Cleopatra* and *Coriolanus* the sense of *virtus* (virtue)
is close to 'valour', as in 'valour is the chiefest virtue' (*Coriolanus*, II. ii.
82), but with the additional and crucial connotations of self-sufficiency
and autonomous power, as in 'Trust to thy *single virtue*; for thy
soldiers/. . . have . . ./Took their discharge' (*King Lear*, V. iii. 104–6).
The essentialist connotations of 'virtue' are also clearly brought out
in a passage from *Troilus and Cressida*: 'what hath mass or matter
by itself/Lies rich in virtue and unmingled'. In *Antony and Cleopatra*
this idea of self-sufficiency is intensified to such an extent that it
suggests a transcendent autonomy; thus Cleopatra calls Antony 'lord
of lords!/O *infinite virtue*, com'st thou smiling from/The world's great
snare uncaught?' (IV. viii. 16–18). Coriolanus is similarly described as
proud, 'even to the altitude of his virtue' (II. i. 38). Against this is a
counter-discourse, one denying that virtue is the source and ethical
legitimation of power and suggesting instead that the reverse is true
– in the words of Macro in *Sejanus*, 'A prince's power makes all his
actions virtue' (III. 717). At the beginning of Act III for example Silius
urges Ventidius further to consolidate his recent successes in war, so
winning even greater gratitude from Antony. Ventidius replies that,
although 'Caesar and Antony have ever won/More in their officer
than person' (III. i. 16–17), an officer of theirs who makes the fact too

apparent will lose, not gain favour. It is an exchange which nicely illustrates the way power is a function not of the 'person' (l. 17) but of 'place' (l. 12), and that the criterion for reward is not intrinsic to the 'performance' (l. 27) but again, relative to one's placing in the power structure (cf. *Sejanus*, III. 302–5: 'all best turns/With doubtful princes, turn deep injuries/In estimation, when they greater rise,/Than can be answered').[2]

Later in the same act Antony challenges Caesar to single combat (III. xiii. 20–8). It is an attempt to dissociate Caesar's power from his individual virtue. Enobarbus, amazed at the stupidity of this, testifies to the reality Antony is trying, increasingly, to deny:

> men's judgements are
> A parcel of their fortunes, and things outward
> Do draw the inward quality after them,
> To suffer all alike.

> (III. xiii. 31–4)

In Enobarbus' eyes, Antony's attempt to affirm a self-sufficient identity confirms *exactly the opposite*. Correspondingly, Caesar scorns Antony's challenge with a simple but devastating repudiation of its essentialist premise: because 'twenty times of better fortune' than Antony, he is, correspondingly, 'twenty men to one' (IV. ii. 3–4).

As effective power slips from Antony he becomes obsessed with reasserting his sense of himself as (in his dying words): 'the greatest prince o' th' world,/The noblest' (IV. xx. 54–5). The contradiction inherent in this is clear; it is indeed as Canidius remarks: 'his whole action grows/Not in the power on't' (III. vii. 68–9). Antony's conception of his omnipotence narrows in proportion to the obsessiveness of his wish to reassert it; eventually it centres on the sexual anxiety – an assertion of sexual prowess – which has characterised his relationship with both Cleopatra and Caesar from the outset. He several times dwells on the youthfulness of Caesar in comparison with his own age (eg. at III. xiii. 20, IV. xii. 48) and is generally preoccupied with lost youthfulness (eg. at III. xiii. 192; IV, iv 26; IV. viii. 22). During the battle scenes of Acts III and IV he keeps reminding Cleopatra of his prowess – militaristic and sexual: 'I will appear in blood' (II. xiii. 174); 'There's sap in't yet! The next time I do fight,/I'll make death love me' (III. xiii. 192–3); and:

> leap thou, attire and all,
> Through proof of harness to my heart, and there
> Ride on the pants triumphing.

> (IV. viii. 14–16)

All this, including the challenge to single combat with Caesar, becomes an obsessive attempt on the part of an ageing warrior (the 'old ruffian' – IV. i. 4) to reassert his virility, not only to Cleopatra but also to Caesar, his principal male competitor. Correspondingly, his willingness to risk everything by fighting on Caesar's terms (III. vii) has much more to do with reckless overcompensation for his own experienced powerlessness, his fear of impotence, than the largesse of a noble soul. His increasing ambivalence towards Cleopatra further bespeaks that insecurity (eg. at III, xii and IV. xii). When servants refuse to obey him he remarks 'Authority melts from me' – but insists nevertheless 'I am/Antony yet' (III. xiii. 92–3): even as he is attempting to deny it Antony is acknowledging that identity is crucially dependent upon power. Moments later even he cannot help remarking the difference between 'what I am' and 'what . . . I was' (III. xiii. 142–3).

It is only when the last vestiges of his power are gone that the myth of heroic omnipotence exhausts itself, even for him. In place of his essentialist fixedness, 'the firm Roman', the 'man of steel' he once felt himself to be (I. iv. 43; IV. iv. 35), Antony now experiences himself in extreme dissolution:

> That which is now a horse, even with a thought
> The rack dislimns, and makes it indistinct
> As water is in water . . .
> > Eros, now thy captain is
> Even such a body: here I am Antony,
> Yet cannot hold this visible shape

> (IV. iv. 9–14)

Virtus, divorced from the power structure, has left to it only the assertion of a negative, inverted autonomy: 'there is left us/Ourselves to end ourselves' (IV. xiv. 21–2). And in an image which effectively expresses the contradiction Antony has been living out, energy is felt to feed back on itself: 'Now all labour/Mars what it does; yea, very force entangles/Itself with strength' (IV. xix. 47–9). Appropriately to this, he resolves on suicide only to bungle the attempt. The bathos of this stresses, uncynically, the extent of his demise. In the next scene it is compounded by Cleopatra's refusal to leave the monument to kiss the dying Antony lest she be taken by Caesar. Antony, even as he is trying to transcend defeat by avowing a tragic dignity in death, suffers the indignity of being dragged up the monument.

There is bathos too of course in Caesar's abruptly concluded encomium:

Hear me, good friends—
Enter an Egyptian
But I will tell you at some meeter season.
The business of this man looks out of him

(V. i. 48–50)

The question of Caesar's sincerity here is beside the point; this is, after all, an encomium, and to mistake it for a spontaneous expression of grief will lead us to miss seeing that even in the few moments he speaks Caesar has laid the foundation for an 'official' history of Antony. First we are reminded that Caesar *is* – albeit regrettably – the victor. He then vindicates himself and so consolidates that victory by confessing to a humanising grief at the death of his 'brother' (though note the carefully placed suggestion of Antony's inferiority: 'the *arm* of mine own body'). Caesar further vindicates himself by fatalising events with the by now familiar appeal to necessity, in this case 'our stars,/Unreconcilable'. Earlier Caesar had told Octavia that 'The ostentation of our love . . . left unshown,/Is often left unlov'd' (III. vi. 52–3). Such is the rationale of his encomium, a strategic expression of 'love' in the service of power. The bathos of these episodes makes for an insistent cancelling of the potentially sublime in favour of the political realities which the sublime struggles to eclipse or transcend. Actually, bathos has accompanied Antony throughout, from the very first speech of the play, the last three lines of which are especially revealing (Philo is speaking of Antony):

Take but good note, and you shall see in him
The triple pillar of all the world transform'd
Into a strumpet's fool. Behold and see.

(I. i. 11–13)

The cadence of 'triple pillar of all the world' arches outward and upward, exactly evoking transcendent aspiration; 'transformed' at the line end promises apotheosis; we get instead the jarringly discrepant 'strumpet's fool'. Cynical, perhaps, but Philo's final terse injunction – 'Behold and see' – has prologue-like authority and foresight.

After Antony's death the myth of autonomous *virtus* is shown as finally obsolescent; disentangled now from the prevailing power structure, it survives as legend. Unwittingly Cleopatra's dream about Antony helps relegate him to this realm of the legendary, especially in its use of imagery which is both Herculean and statuesque: 'His legs bestrid the ocean; his reared arm/Crested the world' (V. ii. 82–3). Cleopatra asks Dolabella if such a man ever existed or might exist; he answers: 'Gentle Madam, no'. Cleopatra vehemently reproaches him only to qualify instantly her own certainty – 'But if there be nor ever were one such' – thereby, in the hesitant syntax, perhaps confirming the doubts which prompted the original question.

His legs bestrid the ocean: in dream, in death, Antony becomes at last larger than life; but in valediction is there not also invoked an image of the commemorative statue, that material embodiment of a discourse which, like Caesar's encomium, skilfully overlays (without ever quite obscuring) obsolescence with respect?

Honour and Policy

If the contradiction which constitutes Antony's identity can be seen as a consequence of a wider conflict between the residual/dominant and the emergent power relations, so too can the strange relationship set up in the play between honour and policy. Pompey's reply to Menas' offer to murder the triumvirs while they are celebrating on board his (Pompey's) galley is a case in point:

> Ah, this thou shouldst have done,
> And not have spoke on't. In me 'tis villainy:
> In thee't had been good service. Thou must know
> 'Tis not my profit that does lead mine honour:
> Mine honour, it. Repent that e'er thy tongue
> Hath so betray'd thine act. Being done unknown,
> I should have found it afterwards well done,
> But must condemn it now.

> (II. vii. 73–80)

Here honour is insisted upon yet divorced from ethics and consequences; the same act is 'villainy' or 'service' depending on who performs it; ignorance of intent to murder is sufficient condition for approving the murder after the event.

Elsewhere in the play we see these inconsistencies resolved in favour of policy; now honour pretends to integrity – to be thought to possess it is enough. Once again it is a kind of political strategy which takes us back to Machiavelli's *The Prince*. Antony tells Octavia: 'If I lose mine honour/I lose myself' (III. iv. 22–3). Octavia has of course been coerced into marriage with Antony to heal the rift (now reopened) between him and Caesar, her brother. So, for Antony to speak to her of honour seems hypocritical at least; when, however, Antony goes further and presents himself as the injured party ready nevertheless to forego his revenge in order to indulge Octavia's request that she be *allowed* to act as mediator – 'But, as you requested/Yourself shall go between's' (III. iv. 24–5) – the honour in question is shown to be just another strategy in his continuing exploitation of this woman.

When Thidias is persuading Cleopatra to betray Antony and capitulate to Caesar, honour is now a face-saving strategy for *both* sides; because she 'embraced' Antony through fear, says Caesar, he construes the scar upon her honour as 'constrained blemishes,/Not as deserv'd'. Cleopatra quickly concurs: 'He [Caesar] is a god, and knows/What is most right. Mine honour was not yielded,/But conquer'd merely' (III. xiii. 59–62).

In Enobarbus we see how policy aligns positively with realism and judgement. He, like Philo at the outset of the play, Ventidius in III. i. and the soldier in III. vii, who urges Antony not to fight at sea, occupies a role in relation to power very familiar in Jacobean tragedy: he possesses an astuteness characteristic of those removed from, yet involved with and dependent upon – often for their very lives – the centre of power; his is the voice of policy not in the service of aggrandisement so much as a desire for survival. So, for example, we see in III. vi. Enobarbus attempting to dissuade Cleopatra from participating in the war and Antony from fighting on Caesar's terms. Failing in the attempt, Enobarbus leaves Antony's command but is struck with remorse almost immediately. Since he left without his 'chests and treasure' (IV. v.8) we are, perhaps, to presume that material gain of this kind was not his motive. Enobarbus, like Antony, comes to embody a contradiction; the speech of his beginning 'Mine honesty and I begin to square' (III. xiii. 41) suggests as much, and it becomes clear that he has left his master in the name of the 'judgement' which the latter has abdicated but which is integral still to his, Enobarbus', identity as a soldier. Yet equally integral to that identity is the loyalty which he has betrayed.

The extent of people's dependence upon the powerful is something the play never allows us to forget. Cleopatra's beating of the messenger in II. v. is only the most obvious reminder; a subtler and perhaps more effective one comes at the end of the play when Cleopatra attempts to conceal half her wealth from Caesar. In the presence of Caesar she commands Seleucus, her 'treasurer', to confirm that she has surrendered all; 'speak the truth, Seleucus' she demands and, unfortunately for her he does, revealing that she has kept back as much as she has declared. Cleopatra has ordered him 'Upon his *peril*' (V. ii. 142) to speak the truth (ie. lie) while he, with an eye to Caesar, replies that he would rather seal his lips 'than to my *peril*/Speak that which is not'. Here, truth itself is in the service of survival. Cleopatra, outraged, finds this unforgivable; for servants to shift allegiance is, in her eyes (those of a ruler) 'base' treachery (V. ii. 156). The play however, in that ironic repetition of 'peril' (my italics) invites an alternative perspective: such a shift is merely a strategy of survival necessitated precisely by rulers like her.[3] Yet doubly ironic is the fact that while Seleucus is described as a 'slave, of no more trust/Than love that's hir'd' (V. ii. 153–4) her own deceit is approved by Caesar as the 'wisdom' (V. ii. 149) appropriate to one in her position. Elsewhere Caesar speaks in passing of the 'much tall youth' (II. vi. 7) that will perish in the event of war; Octavia speaks of the consequence of war between Caesar and Antony being as if 'the world should cleave, and that slain men/Should solder up the [rift]' (III. iv. 31–2; cf. III. xiii. 180–1; IV. xii. 41–2; IV. xiv. 17–8). It is a simple yet important truth, one which the essentialist rhetoric is never quite allowed to efface: to kiss away kingdoms is to kiss away also the lives of thousands.

Sexuality and Power

Those around Antony and Cleopatra see their love in terms of power; languages of possession, subjugation and conspicuous wealth abound in descriptions of the people. More importantly, Antony and Cleopatra actually experience themselves in the same terms. Antony sends Alexas to Cleopatra with the promise that he will 'piece/Her opulent throne with kingdoms. All the East/(Say thou) shall call her mistress' (I. v. 45–7). Later Caesar describes the ceremony whereby that promise was honoured, a ceremony aiming for an unprecedented *public* display both of wealth and power: 'Cleopatra and himself in chairs of gold/Were publicly enthron'd'; Antony gives to Cleopatra the stablishment of Egypt and makes her 'Absolute Queen' of Syria, Cyprus and Lydia. 'This in the public eye?' inquires Maecenas; 'I' th' common showplace' confirms Caesar (III. vi. 4–12). Cleopatra for her part sends twenty separate messengers to Antony. On his return from Egypt Enobarbus confirms the rumour that eight wild boars were served at a breakfast of only twelve people, adding: 'This was but as a fly by an eagle: we had much more monstrous matter of feast, which *worthily deserved noting*' (II. ii. 185, my italics).

Right from the outset we are told that power is internal to the relationship itself: Philo tells us that Antony has been subjugated by Cleopatra (I. i. 1–9) while Enobarbus tells Agrippa that Cleopatra has 'pursed up' (ie. pocketed, taken possession of) Antony's heart (II. ii. 190). As if in a discussion of political strategy, Cleopatra asks Charmian which tactics she should adopt in order to manipulate Antony most effectively. Charmian advocates a policy of complete capitulation; Cleopatra replies: 'Thou teachest like a fool – the way

to lose him!' (I. iii. 10). Antony enters and Cleopatra tells him: 'I have
no power upon you', only then to cast him in the role of treacherous
subject: 'O, never was there queen/So mightily betrayed. Yet at the
first/I saw the treasons planted' (I. iii. 23–6). Whatever the precise sense
of Cleopatra's famous lines at the end of this scene – 'O my oblivion
is a very Antony,/And I am all forgotten' – there is no doubt that they
continue the idea of a power struggle: her extinction is coterminous
with his triumph.

Attempting to atone for his departure, Antony pledges himself as
Cleopatra's 'soldier-servant, making peace or war/As thou affects' (I.
iii. 70). This is just one of many exchanges which shows how their
sexuality is rooted in a fantasy transfer of power from the public to the
private sphere, from the battlefield to the bed. In II. v. Cleopatra recalls
with merriment a night of revelry when she subjugated Antony and
then engaged in cross-dressing with him, putting 'my tires and mantles
on him, whilst/I wore his sword Phillipan' (II. v. 22–3). Inseparable
from the playful reversal of sexual roles is her appropriation of his
power, military and sexual, symbolised phallically of course in the
sword. Later Antony takes up the sword-power motif in a bitter
reproach of Cleopatra for her power over him; here he sees her as his
'conqueror' (III. xi. 66, and compare IV. xiv. 22–3). Another aspect of
the power-sexuality conjunction is suggested in the shamelessly phallic
imagery which the lovers use: 'Ram thou thy fruitful tidings in mine
ears,/That long time have been barren' (II. v. 24–5), although again
Cleopatra delights in reversing the roles (as at II. v. 10–15).

Here then is another aspect of the contradiction which defines
Antony: his sexuality is informed by the very power relations
which he, ambivalently, is prepared to sacrifice for sexual freedom;
correspondingly, the heroic *virtus* which he wants to reaffirm in and
through Cleopatra is in fact almost entirely a function of the power
structure which he, again ambivalently, is prepared to sacrifice for her.

Ecstasy there is in this play but not the kind that constitutes a
self-sufficient moment above history; if *Antony and Cleopatra* celebrates
anything it is not the love which transcends power but the sexual
infatuation which foregrounds it. That infatuation is complex: ecstatic,
obsessive, dangerous. Of all the possible kinds of sexual encounter,
infatuation is perhaps the most susceptible to power – not just because
typically it stems from and intensifies an insecurity which often
generates possessiveness and its corollary, betrayal, but because it
legitimates a free play of self-destructive desire. In Antony's case it is a
desire which attends and compensates for the loss of power, a desire
at once ecstatic and masochistic and playing itself out in the wake of
history, the dust of the chariot wheel.

Notes

1. See also Lawrence Stone, *The Crisis of the Aristocracy* (Oxford: Clarendon Press, 1965), pp. 239–40, 265–7; Ruth Kelso, *The Doctrine of the English Gentleman in the Sixteenth Century* (Chicago: University of Illinois, *Studies in Langauge and Literature*, Vol. 14, No. 1, 2, 1929), p. 11ff.
2. Machiavelli concurs: 'it is impossible that the suspicion aroused in a prince after the victory of one of his generals should not be increased by any arrogance in manner or speech displayed by the man himself' (*Discourses*, p. 181).
3. In North's Plutarch, Shakespeare's source, we are told that Cleopatra engineered this 'scene' in order to deceive Caesar into thinking she intends to live (*Antony and Cleopatra*, ed. Ridley (Harmondsworth: Penguin, 1983), p. 276). It is difficult to infer this from the play, but even if we are inclined to see her anger as feigned, it still presupposes the point being made here, namely that a double standard works for master and servant.

8 'Speak, speak!': The Popular Voice and the Jacobean State*

ANNABEL PATTERSON

Annabel Patterson's analysis of *Coriolanus* is taken from her book *Shakespeare and the Popular Voice*. This book has much in common with Jonathan Dollimore's *Radical Tragedy*, in that both works attempt to locate a radical, oppositional voice within early modern writing. Seen in the context of this project, *Coriolanus* is a particularly interesting and challenging text, in that it has, over the centuries, held considerable attractions for those professing extreme right-wing political views (Terry Hawkes details this aspect of the play's history in his essay in this collection). Patterson seeks to recontextualise *Coriolanus* by foregrounding the events which preceded the writing and staging of the play. In particular, she stresses the significance of the Midlands Rising of 1607. In the light of these events, Patterson sees Shakespeare, in writing the play, as participating in a larger debate about the nature and structure of political systems and the place and role of the 'commons' within the state.

Whereas in *King Lear* Shakespeare had moved from a posture of social questioning to one of social criticism and even of meliorism *within* the general frame of a constitutional monarchy, in *Coriolanus*, thanks to the incentive of the Midlands Rising of 1607 and what followed, he had evidently followed his own enquiry considerably further. If, as Machiavelli had argued, the patricians were forced by effective popular protest to 'grant the populace a share in the government', such an adjustment in the power reiations of the Jacobean state was not, however unlikely, inconceivable; and to dramaticize its occurrence in antiquity made the process of conceiving it visible and accessible to others. In *Coriolanus*, for the first time, Shakespeare's audience is invited to contemplate an alternative political system; and, more significantly still, to experience an entire dramatic action devoted to these questions: who shall speak for the commons; what power should

*ANNABEL PATTERSON, *Shakespeare and the Poular Voice* (Oxford: Basil Blackwell, 1989), pp. 127–46.

the common people have in the system; to what extent is common power compatible with national safety?

Further, Shakespeare returned to that aspect of populism that was most germane to his own role as a popular dramatist – how shall the voice of the people be heard? – with a new and daring focus. The play's second line, with its doubled invitation and exhortation, 'Speak, speak', for the first time allows the people to speak *for themselves* as a political entity, with legitimate grievances, and with a considerable degree of political self-consciousness. Most significantly, the play's center, both in terms of plot and structure, consists in two scenes (for which neither Plutarch nor Livy provided a mandate) in which Coriolanus's achievement of the consulate is made dependent upon the popular voice as a constitutional entitlement. In these two pivotal scenes the word 'voice' is repeated 28 times, almost in mockery of the dramatist's knowledge that an audience's attention is ensured by repetition. As Coriolanus himself puts it, 'Your voices: for your voices I have fought; watched for your voices; for your voices bear of wounds two dozen odd; . . . for your voices have done many things; some less, some more; your voices: Indeed I would be consul' (2:3:125–36). In *Coriolanus*, in other words, the popular has become unmistakably identified with popular power, expressed in part through tribunal representation, but also, a much more threatening concept, through the franchise. The voices are also votes.

[. . .]

In *Julius Caesar* the carpenter and the cobbler are dismissed in the opening scene as 'idle Creatures' who have mistaken a 'labouring day' for a holiday, and whose transfer from Pompey of the popularity that now makes Caesar such a threat is merely castigated, without further analysis.[1] In the opening scenes of *Coriolanus*, the people are introduced rather as 'mutinous Citizens', who are allowed to speak for themselves; and in so doing present a critique of precisely those assumptions (what James C. Scott calls 'official platitudes') that, in *Julius Caesar* permitted that easy, contemptuous dismissal. It is all the more disturbing, therefore, to see how often the dismissal is *transferred* by modern readers from *Julius Caesar* to *Coriolanus* and assumed, moreover, to be Shakespeare's own position. As early as 1710, Charles Gildon reproached Shakespeare for intending to 'flatter Arbitrary Power' by representing 'the Commons of Rome, as if they were the Rabble of an Irish village';[2] as late as 1964 Günter Grass defined *Coriolanus* as this 'bothersome play' in which Rome's plebeians, 'like London's artisans, are cowardly rats and ignorant dogs'.[3] Yet the evidence for this position (which is, of course, the view of Coriolanus himself) consists solely in the fact that the plebeians twice change their minds about him, the first time under the influence of the tribunes, who incite them to reverse his election as consul, the second under the influence of fear at the news of the Volscian invasion. That Coriolanus is twice persuaded to change *his* mind by his mother, the first time to modify his scorn of the plebeians until they have granted him the consulship, the second time to spare his city, is somehow not subject to the same stigma. One can only assume that Gildon and Grass and everyone in between who shared their view have been, for whatever reason, unable to focus on what Shakespeare actually wrote.

Take, for example, the term and concept 'multitude'. As a numerical sign, it points to the play's most important contrast – that between the many and the one. The plebeians' plurality is registered by their ordinal numbering, and marked by their anonymity, whereas Coriolanus's singularity is marked by his commitment to a *name* as the sign of personal identity and worth, and by Shakespeare's complete omission of the other consul. (To retain a balance of power, the consulate was always double.) But in Shakespeare's culture, as Christopher Hill has shown, the most common term for the many was 'multitude', whose function, especially when governed by 'many-headed', was to imply irrational action by the lower classes.[4] What has many heads can have no single agenda, the composite phrase implied, defying the linguistic logic that ordains that any collective noun must be, in effect, oxymoronic, the many as the one. In the anonymous *Histriomastix Or, The Player Whipt* (1610) a stage direction brings on 'a sort of Russetings and Mechanichalls (Fury leading them) and crying confusedly, Liberty, Liberty, Liberty' (F3v), who are immediately defined as 'this common beast the multitude . . . in a rebellious land,' (F4r). In *Coriolanus*, by contrast, the citizens themselves are aware that this terminology is invidious, and that Coriolanus has made it so: 'for once we stood up about the corn, he himself stuck not to call us the many-headed multitude' (2:3:15).[5] So says the First Citizen, who knows that 'to make us no better thought of, a little help [from ideology] will serve'. And the Third Citizen develops his insight into a self-mocking observation:

We have been called so of many; not that our heads are some brown, some black, some abram, some bald, but that our wits are so diversely colored. And truly I think, if all our wits were to issue out of one skull, they would fly east, west, north, south, and their consent of one direct way should be at once to all the points of the compass.

(2:3:18–25)

It would be possible to read this passage (humorlessly) as confirming the hegemony's rating. It is also possible to recognize the shape of one of the most intractable questions of political theory; in Hobbes's terms (as restated by Foucault), 'the problem of the distillation of a single will – or rather, the constitution of a unitary, singular body animated by the spirit of sovereignty – from the particular wills of a multiplicity of individuals.'[6] It is significant that both Hobbes and Foucault imagined this problem as a giant body, whose troubled shape appears also, of course, in the opening fable of *Coriolanus*. But in the central scenes where the citizens are preparing themselves to vote Coriolanus the consulship and assessing their qualifications to do so, it appears that Shakespeare has not only framed the question of the general will but also its partial solution. The negative implications of 'multitude' are to be countered, first, by the intimations of majoritarianism ('the greater part carries it', 2:3:42), and second, by individualism: 'We are not to stay all together, but to come by him where he stands, by ones, by twos, and by threes. He's to make his requests by particulars; *wherein every one of us has a single honor, in giving him our own voices with our own tongues*' (2:3:44–9). In the ratifying act of democracy, giving one's voice, casting one's vote, the paradox is reversed and the many become singularly one. Coriolanus, naturally, believes that there is no general will, but rather a 'general ignorance' (3:1:146), and that therefore the voice of the people can be silenced by depriving them of official representation, by cutting out 'the tongues o' th' common mouth' (3:1:22), the tribunes.

This is to make the same mistake as many of Shakespeare's critics, many of whom have identified, consciously or unconsciously, with Coriolanus. (Coriolanus is no more reliable a teacher of political theory than is Theseus on the subject of poetics.) It is also the same *kind* of error as that which claims *Henry VI, Part 2* as an antidemocratic document on the grounds that Jack Cade is represented as a vicious and self-contradictory hypocrite. The presence of Brutus and Sicinius as 'the tongues o' th' common mouth' is proof, rather, of Shakespeare's continued interest in the problem of who shall speak for the people, who here, evidently, require no ventriloquizers because they are not dummies. There is, however, a parody of spokesmanship by Coriolanus himself, reporting on the opening protest against the dearth, which even he calls a petition:

> They said they were an-hungry, sigh'd forth proverbs—
> That hunger broke stone walls; that dogs must eat;
> That meat was made for mouths; that the gods sent not
> Corn for the rich men only. With these shreds
> They vented their complainings . . .

(1:1:205–208)

By recalling his own use of the 'they say' formula in *Henry VI, Part 2*, Shakespeare warns us against taking at face value the ventriloquist's account, which is here manifestly reductive, reproducing only the 'shreds' of the popular tradition of protest. As for the tribunes themselves, they fully deserve the *moral* opprobium that has been heaped upon them; they are evidently no more genuinely popular leaders than Cade. It is they, not the plebeians, who are the 'tawdry petits bourgeois' of Günter Grass's condemnation, elected officials who exploit their position, despise their constituents, and (reversing the ventriloquist model) put into the people's mouths a more violent message than, left to themselves, would have been forthcoming:

> Assemble presently the people hither:
> And when they hear me say, 'It shall be so
> I'th' right and strength o' the commons,' be it either
> For death, for fine, or banishment, then let them,
> If I say fine, cry 'Fine,' if death, cry 'Death.'
>
> And when such time they have begun to cry,
> Let them not cease, but with a din confus'd
> Enforce the present execution.

> (3:3:12–21)

But before we too smugly assume that by making the tribunes unacceptable Shakespeare was warning his nation against classical republicanism, we ought to perceive that modern democracies are riddled with such types, that electoral politics depend on the manipulation of the electorate, and that the tribunes represent, in particular, a noxious form of the left-wing intellectual's dilemma – that leadership, coming from above, is difficult to distinguish from exploitation.

But the point that Shakespeare apparently wished to make was that Rome's plebeians, though they needed the tribunes as a structural device, were not the pathetic nonentities, aimless and inarticulate, with 'thick tongues', that readers from Gildon to Grass have thought they saw. They themselves have the 'gift of gab' that Grass, in rewriting the story at Brecht's expense, attributed solely to 'the Boss', playwright, director, left-wing intellectual.[7] This claim connects with E.P. Thompson's work in recuperating the signs of self-consciously political strategy in working-class protest movements, particularly the 'food riot', so-called in order to denote its participants as sub-rational.[8] Here I wish to focus on Thompson's brilliant phrase for the theory he rejects, the 'spasmodic' economic history that sees in food-centered protests only 'rebellions of the belly'. For it really was no coincidence

that Shakespeare began *Coriolanus* with a commoners' protest against
a shortage of grain, a focus which, as has often been observed, he
achieved by rewriting the history he received from Plutarch and Livy,
and condensing two uprisings into one. The result of this condensation
was to bring out the deepest social implications of the famous Belly
fable told by Menenius Agrippa, which in Plutarch was applied to an
uprising that did not have hunger as its cause, and so was severed
from its own truth. As Agrippa tells it, he faces not a rebellion *of* the
belly, but a rebellion against the Belly by the members of the body
politic. But, as almost all modern commentators have had to admit, the
famous fable is 'inept'.[9] It does not *apply*. It is manifestly the citizens
whose stomachs are grumbling. If the second line of the play ('Speak,
speak') introduces the theme of popular expression itself, the third
line connects that theme to its primal content, hunger. 'You are all
resolved,' says the First Citizen, 'rather to die than famish?' And the
response is indeed 'Resolved, resolved'.

But Shakespeare, having identified the undeniably physical content
of the citizens' motivation, does not leave them, in the terms that
Thompson deplored, clapping their hands spasmodically upon their
stomachs. On the contrary, they proceed to discuss the political
economy, not without wit, and not without considerable social
perspective:

> We are accounted poor citizens, the patricians good. What authority
> surfeits on would relieve us. If they would yield us but the
> superfluity while it were wholesome, we might guess they relieved
> us humanely; but they think we are too dear, the leanness that
> afflicts us, the object of our misery, is as an inventory to particularize
> their abundance; our sufferance is a gain to them. Let us revenge this
> with our pikes ere we become rakes. For the gods know I speak this
> in hunger for bread, not in thirst for revenge.
>
> (1:1:15–25)

For all of its anti-poetic protocols, one could hardly find elsewhere
in Shakespeare a passage that more rewards a careful exegesis. The
pun on 'rakes' (both the symbol of emaciation and a reminder that
this is an agricultural problem) is only the last and weakest in a
chain of polysemantics that includes the irony of 'they think we are
too dear', the two meanings of 'sufferance' (both pain and pain's
passive endurance) and the deep truth that perceives a society's moral
vocabulary ('We are accounted poor citizens, the patricians good') as
the ideological form of economic difference. But beyond this deep wit
and salty desperation lie practical and theoretical insights, fortifying
what might otherwise have remained at the discursive level of *Hamlet*'s

levelling gravedigger. There is food going to waste in the community
that could have been used, 'while it were wholesome', to relieve the
famine. 'Superfluity' recalls Lear's unfulfilled promise on the heath
to 'shake the superflux' to relieve 'houseless heads and unfed sides'
(3:4:35, 30).[10] And the reason for this waste, the first Citizen discerns,
is that the patricians *need* the dearth as a physical demonstration of
the reality of their own wealth, of economic difference. 'The leanness
that afflicts us . . . is *as an inventory* to particularize their abundance.'
Extreme indigence in others is the bottom line in the symbolic
computing of personal net worth. So it comes as no surprise that
Menenius Agrippa, before he proceeds to the Belly fable, asserts the
impossibility of any change in the system:

> For your wants,
> Your suffering in this dearth, you may as well
> Strike at the heaven with your staves as lift them
> Against the Roman state, whose course will on
> The way it takes, cracking ten thousand curbs
> Of more strong link asunder than can ever
> Appear in your impediment. For the dearth,
> The gods, not the patricians, make it, and
> Your knees to them (not arms) must help . . .
>   and you slander
> The helms o' th' state, who care for you like fathers.
>
>   (1:1:67–78)

But if these are hegemony's biggest guns (protest will fail, the gods and
the state are at once identical, benevolent, and impervious to change),
the plebeians are not deceived. They know the difference between
eternal laws and local legislation, and that the latter not only permits
change but has recently enacted it to their own disadvantage:

> Care for us! True, indeed. They ne'er cared for us yet. Suffer us to
> famish, and their storehouses crammed with grain; make edicts
> for usury, to support usurers; repeal daily any wholesome act
> established against the rich, and provide more piercing statutes daily
> to chain up and restrain the poor . . . and there's all the love they
> bear us.
>
>   (1:1:80–6)

And those who assume that the plebeians are pacified, as they were
in Plutarch, by Menenius Agrippa's fable, have patently ignored the
fact that they agree to listen, *provided* he does 'not think to fob off our
disgrace with a tale' (1:1:92–3). Even while it is in the telling, their

'petition' for formal representation, as Coriolanus himself reports, is being granted by the Senate.

The entire episode, complete with Agrippa's fable, finds its modern analogy in the late nineteenth century, when Marx himself entered an early challenge to the 'laws' of classical economic theory, and specifically to the principle of fixity in real wages in relation to the gross national product. In *Value, Price and Profit*, written in 1865 and first published in 1898, Marx addressed himself to the 'Citizens' of Europe in the context of an 'epidemic of strikes', to argue against John Weston for the legitimacy and efficacy of group protests in support of higher wages; and his argument was intended to show that wage levels were not fixed by absolute economic laws, but rather by 'the *mere will* of the capitalist, or the limits of his avarice'. 'It is,' wrote Marx, 'an arbitrary limit. There is nothing necessary in it. It may be changed *by* the will of the capitalist, and may, therefore, be changed *against* his will'; and he proceeded to translate macroeconomic concepts back to their primal and most human origins – food and its distribution:

> Citizen Weston illustrated his theory by telling you that when a bowl contains a certain quantity of soup, to be eaten by a certain number of persons, an increase in the broadness of the spoons would not produce an increase in the amount of soup. He must allow me to find this illustration rather spoony. It reminded me somewhat of the simile employed by Melenius Agrippa. When the Roman plebeians struck against the Roman patricians, the patrician Agrippa told them that the patrician belly fed the plebeian members of the body politic. Agrippa failed to show that you feed the members of one man by filling the belly of another.[11]

According to Allan Bloom, it was not until after Hobbes and Locke that we became capable (like Marx) of penetrating such 'myths of rulership' as the Belly fable, with its underlying notion of an organicist society joined for the common good.[12] According to Günter Grass, who rewrote the Belly fable yet again, this 'nonsense hallowed by tradition' was not only effective against Shakespeare's plebeians, it was still operative in modern East Germany. 'The barbs of progress cannot pierce its hide.'[13] Against them both, I aver that Shakespeare had not only pierced the fable's hide, he permitted his plebeians to do so as well; and one of the reasons for their insight was the Midlands Rising of 1607.

'No part of common powre?': The Midlands Rising

It has long been taken for granted that Shakespeare's decision to
stage the Coriolanus story, and to begin it with a food protest, was
motivated in part by the Midlands Rising. But after this historical
reference has been pressed into the service of our exercises in dating
the plays, it is usually abandoned, as one of 'those cobwebs of
topical allusion' which, as Fredric Jameson put it, 'the ahistorical and
formalising reader attempts desperately to brush away'.[14] And when,
as by E.C. Pettet, the connection between play and event has been
taken seriously, the result has been, not surprisingly, controlled by the
tradition of Shakespeare's innate conservatism. Thus Pettet concluded
that the play 'reflects the natural reactions of a man of substance to a
recent mob rising in his country',[15] the Coleridgean position (including
the derogatory 'mob') on Shakespeare's social attitudes, exaggerated
in this instance, it is assumed, by the self-interest of an increasingly
prosperous property owner. I have already demonstrated that these
assumptions must now be abandoned. But the Midlands Rising itself
now needs to be reinterpreted, and freed from constraints imposed on
its meaning by modern historians. In the wake of E.P. Thompson's
attractive but misleading thesis, some revisionist historians have
produced an account of the Rising that renders it politically innocuous:
that is to say, a conservative and ritual social action that is closer to
an 'extreme form of petitioning'[16] than a real threat to the system.
Derek Hirst's account may be taken as typical:

> The attitude of the authorities also helps to explain why popular
> disturbances were more akin to demonstrations than violent
> outbursts. The government balanced denunciation of disorder with a
> surprising understanding . . . Thus, after the Midland Rising of 1607
> against aggressive landlordism in the arable plain, the council issued
> wholesale pardons to the rioters while fining several landowners
> in star chamber . . . The behaviour of the poor in the few times
> of trouble is equally instructive. Whether in agrarian or food riot,
> the pattern of popular unrest manifests general acceptance of a
> patriarchal scheme of authority. Protesters invariably first approached
> the neighboring magistrate to complain about what they saw as
> antisocial activity, whether by landlords or food traders. Only if
> rebuffed did the poor act for themselves, and even they never
> challenged the social order, nor attacked the rich as rich.[17]

In fact contemporary records of the Rising do not themselves
support the revisionist account. It is true that the government
proceeded against notorious enclosers;[18] and it is also clear that the
Rising had certain ritual components, since it began, significantly,

on the eve of May Day, 1607, reminding us that festive practices and
inversion rituals, suppressed by Puritan-minded local authorities,
still functioned as symbols of popular solidarity. It began, too, in
Northamptonshire, whose people had three years earlier petitioned the
House of Commons to intervene against 'depopulation and excessive
conversion of tillage into pasture' and early involved Warwickshire
(Shakespeare's own county) whose self-named 'Diggers . . . from
Hampton Field' had petitioned the king against 'these devouring
encroachers'.[19] Yet it quickly ceased to be a local extension of those
earlier petitions, and by its rapid spread to other counties began to
take on the appearance of an organized rebellion. The rioters were
identified as 'levellers' and 'diggers', not, writes David Underdown,
'yet with the revolutionary connotations that the terms acquired forty
years later, but it was not an unthinkably long step from levelling
fences to levelling social distinctions.' And he cites a written challenge
thrown into a Northampton church during the Rising, entitled 'The
Poor Man's Friend and the Gentleman's Plague'.[20] But from the
government's perspective, the chief concern was the *spread* of the
disturbance, reaching Warwickshire and Leicestershire by late May,
and even after the Northampton rising had been put down in June,
spreading to Lincolnshire, Derbyshire, Worcestershire, Oxfordshire and
Bedfordshire, with the last two counties, moreover, involved in *revivals*
of previously suppressed disturbances.[21]

On 29 May, the Privy Council issued orders to local sheriffs and
justices of the peace to disperse any anti-enclosure gatherings. The
following day, King James issued a proclamation in his inimitably
querulous and self-righteous style, complaining that his previous
'lenitie hath bred . . . rather encouragement then obedience', and
that the protesters 'have presumed to gather themselves in greater
multitudes, as well in that County, as in some others adjoyning.'
He claimed that from the beginning of his reign he had been
ordinarily careful to prevent enclosures, and was even now engaged
in extraordinary remedial measures, two claims (though the second
contradicted the first) that ought to have prevented 'disordered
persons' from taking the law into their own hands, instead of
trusting to 'the care and providence of their Sovereigne', behavior
which justifies a 'sharper remedie'.[22] Both James's 'care', a term, we
remember, invoked by Menenius Agrippa and mocked by the First
Citizen, and Hirst's 'surprising understanding' become suddenly
inappropriate when, on 8 June, one thousand levellers who had
assembled at Newton, Northamptonshire, to dig out enclosures,
and who refused to disperse when this proclamation was read to
them, were attacked by Sir Anthony Mildmay's soldiery, both
cavalry and foot. Fifty of the protesters were killed outright, 'a

great many wounded, and many captured and later hanged and quartered, as exemplary punishment.'[23] And on 3 July was issued another proclamation, drafted by Cecil, which even as it reiterates the 'Princely care and providence to preserve our people from decay or dimunition' threatens 'execution (even to present death)' of those who continue to show resistance.[24] Most significantly, James himself here introduced the possibility that the protest had spread 'either by secret combination . . . or by ill example of the first beginners', two equally threatening alternatives.

While enclosures were the immediate cause of the Rising, the documents of its aftermath indicate that food shortages were also a major issue. The arable price index, it is true, reflects nothing comparable to the catastrophic crop failures of 1596 (the context of *A Midsummer Night's Dream*), when prices of all kinds of grain were more alarming than at any time since 1317; it does, however, show a sharp rise in wheat prices in 1608, and in 1609, when wheat recovered, a corresponding rise in the price of barley, the poor man's grain.[25] But there is other evidence that in 1607 both the authorities and those whom they would restrain made a theoretical connection between enclosures and dearth, even before the signs of the latter were powerful enough to register in the national statistics. On 24 July 1607, a royal proclamation, whose primary agenda was to *revoke* the threats issued three weeks earlier, and to promise pardon to all who would submit before Michaelmas, complained that 'there was not so much as any necessitie of famine or dearth of corne' to excuse the offenders.[26] But in late August 1607, James issued a proclamation against the use of corn for starch, since this practise '(especially in times wherein the plentie of Corne shall not be very abundant) must needs encrease both the scarcitie, and the prices thereof.'[27] In yet another proclamation of 1 June 1608, James addressed complaints of grain hoarding, engrossing, the export of grain, unfair pricing, quality control and even unemployment. He appealed to justices of the peace to ensure 'that the poore may bee served of Corne at convenient and charitable prices', and 'that the richer sort be earnestly mooved by Christian charitie, to cause their Graine to be sold under the common prices of the Market to the poorer sort.'[28] This was the recall of a 'moral economy' with a vengeance. Not surprisingly, the appeal seems to have failed, if one can judge by popular ballads that appeared in November: 'A new ballad exhortinge all synners to require Gods commiseration and mercy for the great famine and plague which at this instant we justly suffer'; and 'A just complaint made by the poore people of England against the covetousnes of gredy fermours whiche cause a Dearth of plentifull thinges – being an old ballad prynted by Yarath James.' And in January 1609, another proclamation prorogued the parliament (for the fourth time, and for a further eleven months) citing the royal reasons: 'forasmuch as the dearth and scarcitie of all kinde of Victuall is at present great, And if it should draw so great a concourse of people hither as the Parliament will bring, it would not onely more increase the prices of al things hereabouts (which are already very high) but also draw many Gentlemen out of their Countreys, where their hospitality will give much reliefe to their poore neighbours.'[29]

We can, therefore, reasonably infer that when Shakespeare began work on *Coriolanus*, probably in 1609, the issue of the Rising had merged in the public consciousness[30] with the problem of dearth (in both its senses). And while the records indicate that James's policy began and ended in leniency and a corrective, rather than a repressive social policy, they also indicate a stage of panic, with correspondingly draconian language and reactions. There was evidently a public perception, which *Coriolanus* exhibits in its own way, that the country had experienced not a ritual protest but a major test of the government's ability to maintain order, which in turn was structurally connected to its ability to feed its citizens; and this perception produced at least one other account of the Rising that matches *Coriolanus* in its analysis, and possibly even in its intentions.

Between official statements (which tend to survive) and direct expressions of the popular voice (which survive only in shreds) there exists another category of documents, in which the system itself records the protests against it. Sometimes, as in contemporary accounts of Robert Kett's rebellion in 1549, the popular voice and its grievances are ventriloquized with the intention of refuting and ultimately silencing them. But in the case of the Midlands Rising, between the royal proclamations and the popular ballads, there happens to survive a pamphlet that intended for itself a mediatorial status. On 21 June, shortly after the Northamptonshire massacre, a clergyman named Robert Wilkinson preached a sermon 'before the Lord Lieutenant of the County, and the rest of the Commissioners there assembled upon occasion of the late Rebellion and Riots in those parts.'[31] And before the end of the year, he published the sermon and dedicated it to Thomas Cecil, earl of Exeter and baron Burleigh, styling himself Cecil's 'late Chaplaine', and directing his admonitions equally at the 'Oppression of the mighty, and Rebellion of the manie' (A3v). Wilkinson appealed to Cecil, precisely because he had been 'meanes for the due execution of justice upon the rebellious, so likewise . . . to promote the cause & complaints of the expelled, half pined, and distressed poor, that they rebell no more' (A4r). And he read the lesson of the moral economy to 'all states generally, not to grind the faces of the poore (Esa. 3) but the master to wage his servant that he may live; & the work-master so to wage the laborer, that he may live, & the land-lord not to rack, but so to rate his tenant that he may live, *not miserably*' (D2r; italics added).

Like Menenius Agrippa, Wilkinson cited the perennial fable of the body, but with a different allocation of body parts and responsibility:

> I know ye thinke it horrible, that (as in this late Rebellion)
> Mechanicall men are come to beard Magistrates, . . . but as it is an ill
> foot that kicketh at the head, and an ill hand that beateth it, so is it
> an ill head that wisheth the hand cut off, or diviseth a way to have
> fewer fingers on the hand.
>
> (C4v)

Further, Wilkinson implicitly connected his own body fable to the belly theory of popular protest, confirming the Rising's connection to experience or fears of dearth. His text for the sermon, in fact, was Matthew 4:4, 'Man shall not live by bread alone', for which he produced a remarkably materialist exegesis: 'That man liveth by bread, is inferred out of the very text; for even where [the apostle] saith, "not by bread onely," it followeth of necessitie, that amongst other meanes, yet bread for one' (C2v). 'For,' he continued, 'the belly sayth that bread must be had, and the soule subscribeth . . . and though reason may perswade, and authoritie command, and Preachers exhort with obedience and patience to sustaine the want of bread, yet for all that, *Venter non habet aures* [the belly has no ears], in case of extreame hunger men will not be perswaded, but they will have bread' (D2v).

And Wilkinson underlines the occasional nature of his chosen text at every turn: 'Because we are fallen into a time, wherein poverty without patience hath much disordred us,' he wrote, 'I have therefore chosen to speak of the hungry temptation, & yet not of the temptation neither . . . but rather of the answer to it' (B2r). Christ found himself in a place 'where was neither bred nor corn, as may be *now*', precisely that hypothesis that the king's proclamation would two months later deny. But the contemporary version of the temptation is, Wilkinson imagines, socially bivalent. Some the devil 'tempteth to turne bread into stones, that is, to decay the plenty of the earth, as many rich & greedy minded men do *now*; and some he tempteth to turne stones into bread, that is, to use unlawful meanes for their own releife, as the mad & rebelious multitude doth *now*' (B1v). The three-times repeated *now* and the causal construction ('because we are fallen into a time') invite us to situate this sermon centrally in any viable theory of topicality in Jacobean texts; while the astonishing move that makes Christ in the wilderness an appropriate analogy to the Midland Risers as well as to the authorities who put the Rising down is only the first of the essentially *literary* strategies by which Wilkinson

119

invokes sympathy for the insurgents even as he delegitimates their intervention. Later, by an eloquent shifting of personal pronouns, he will move from the denoting the 'mad and rebelious multitude' as 'they' to addressing them as 'yee' and even 'good people', and even to syntactical incorporation with them. Arguing for Job as a model, he advises the Risers that sometimes God, 'for the exercise of *our* patience', will send men to take away our daily bread, 'and no marvell if it be thus now, that the cruell and *tyrannos*, . . . the mighty, and men of authority have the earth in possession' (E3v); and, more startling still, the communal *we* remains when Wilkinson turns to describing how the Risers have abandoned patience for protest: 'yea, bearing is come to bearding, and because of a little want, men have buried their patience as they buried hedges. Yea, we are come to banding . . . & now at last we are come to flat resisting' (F1r).

And in this last construction the radical import of Wilkinson's sermon as a whole and its importance for *Coriolanus* becomes manifest. Even in arguing for what Shakespeare's First Citizen had ambiguously designated 'sufferance'. Wilkinson testifies simultaneously to the scale of the Rising, to its efficacy ('A King of three great kingdomes must capitulate with a Tinker', F1r) and, most significantly, to its motives:

> let men set what pretence & colour they will, yet this hath bin from time to time the common proceeding of popular mutinies; first to murmure upon some just cause . . . Afterward . . . they murmured not for want, but for wantoness . . . But . . . their murmuring came to that, that they would change the state, . . . they would have no head at all; right as in the daies of the Judges, wherein 'there was no King in Israell, but every man did what was right in his own eyes' (Judges 17.6). Thus we find in Scripture, thus in [hi]stories, yea and in our owne English stories, and I do not thinke it would have bin otherwise now, unless it had bin worse. First like Adams sonnes they come forth with shovels and spades, like simple men to reduce the earth to her ancient and native tilladge, but afterward they come forth like Tubal-kaines sonnes, armed with swords and weapons of yron . . . First they professe nothing, but to throw downe enclosures, though that were indeed no part of common powre, but afterward they will reckon for other matters . . . and counsell is given to kill up Gentlemen, and they will levell all states as they levelled bankes and ditches: and some of them boasted, that now they hoped to worke no more.

> (F2r–3v)

Not only does this passage defy the assertion of Hirst and others that protesters 'never challenged the social order' as such; it actually identifies the model of rational argument that the protesters are reported (or imagined) to have used. One thing leads to another. From the experience of local hardship ('some just cause'), they can generalize to the injustice of the socioeconomic structure as a whole, and finally imagine a utopian inversion ('they hoped to worke no more') that is ultimately far more threatening than republicanism, more daring even than imagining the body politic without the head. To argue, as a revisionist social history would need to, that Wilkinson's fears were exaggerated is to ignore the work that his sermon was intended to do, to *negotiate* between the authorities and the protesters; and if this model of reasoning had not been available to the Midland Risers before May Day, 1607, it was certainly available to them, in print, by the end of the year.[32]

Perhaps the most crucial phrase in Wilkinson's sermon, however, occurs in his statement that levelling enclosures, though the most justified first stage in the conceptual structure of protest, was 'no part of common powre'. For the phrase itself, by imagining other parts that common power might appropriately subsume, adopts the same strategy as 'not by bread only', which permits the materialist solution 'amongst other meanes, yet bread for one'. More centrally, it destabilizes the standard assumption that the common people had no power at all, nor desire for power, and hence removes from 'common power', and by extension 'commonwealth', their hegemonic self-contradictions. Sir Thomas Smith's constitution had been seemingly unruffled by the giant oxymoron at the heart of the system he described. But between 1583 and 1607 much had occurred to make political theory a matter of broader public interest; and between 1607 and 1610, while the country was reflecting on the Midlands Rising, 'common power' and 'common wealth' were the lexical signs of an ideology in trouble. In *Coriolanus* Shakespeare sent them wheeling through the play-text with an interrogatory, repetitive and contradictory force that is unequalled in the canon. The *plot* of *Coriolanus* pits political power and the difficulties of its sharing against that militarist sense of the word 'power' which Coriolanus himself represents, and which he ultimately pits against the state as the rough and ready alternative to constitutional checks and balances; but the play as a whole worries more about the constitution, and how it is possible to define and limit such a previously unspeakable concept as common power.

This brings us back to the political vocabulary of Shakespeare's play. Not only is *Coriolanus* the play whose numerical interest in 'power' is by far the greatest in the canon (thirty-eight appearances, as compared to eighteen in *Richard II*, the closest competitor); but also the *primary* usage, again uniquely, is to denote some version of political, that is to say, structural power. In *Richard II* the majority of citations refer to an armed force. But in *Coriolanus* Shakespeare appears to have committed himself to a view of the semantics of power that is not supposed to have been available in political theory, let alone common usage, until half a century later. Again, the plebeians themselves are apparently aware that the term is problematic. 'We have power in ourselves to do it,' worries the Third Citizen in advance of the consular election, 'but it is a power that we have no power to do' (2:3:4–5). The first two 'powers' refer to their *right* to deny Coriolanus the consulship by withholding their votes; the last to their *inability* to deny those votes for fear of seeming ungrateful for his victory, an ingratitude which would lend substance to the invidious view of the 'multitude' that Coriolanus has already circulated. When the tribunes learn of the positive vote, they berate the plebeians for removing Coriolanus from a position where he had 'no power/But was a petty servant to the state', to 'a place of potency and sway o' th'state' (2:3:188). In turn, Coriolanus will berate the patricians for creating the 'power' of the tribunate, which, like Zeefeld, he sees as producing a constitutional imbalance[33] leading to stalemate:

> When two authorities are up
> Neither supreme, how soon confusion
> May enter 'twixt the gap of both and take
> The one by th'other.
>
> (3:1:109–12)

If one follows the semantics of 'power' to their inevitable conclusion, it is surprising how daring Shakespeare has become. He echoes North in having Coriolanus attribute the policy of free distribution of corn to the democratic model of the Greek city states, where 'the people had more absolute power' (3:1:115) than even in Rome at this stage; but there is nothing in North to provoke the multiple distinctions and confusions that follow. Brutus defends the 'authority' of the tribunes as *representing* 'the part o' th' people, in whose power we were elected theirs' (3:1:209–10). Volumnia reproaches Coriolanus for not having put the 'power' of the consulship 'well on' before depriving the people of theirs. It would have been more strategic, she advises too late, 'if/You had not showed them how ye were disposed/Ere they lacked power to cross you' (3:2:22–3). This lends credit to the tribunes' repeated accusation that Coriolanus 'affects/Tyrannical power' (3:3:2, 65), a charge that conceptually separates power from authority and brings it closer to its sole meaning in the last act, that of the military force without which 'authority' as a concept in political theory is finally empty. In one passage the tribunes announce 'in the name o'th'people/And in the power of us the tribunes' that Coriolanus is banished for 'seeking means/To pluck away [the people's] power' (3:3:96, 100), while a few minutes later it is reported that the patricians take the banishment so hard that 'they are in ripe aptness to take all power from the people and to pluck from them their tribunes forever' (94:3:24–5). Following this pattern, as power shifts from mouth to mouth, is to experience conceptual instability – a political vocabulary, in short, in process of evolution. But what remains when these indecidabilities have been fully recognized is that ancient history provided precedents for attributing far more power to the common people than seventeenth-century England; and that Shakespeare exploited these precedents to the utmost by refusing to let the matter drop.

In this late play, then, which may have been his last tragedy, Shakespeare provided a remarkably daring analysis of the sociopolitical system, one that also, like Wilkinson's protesters, imagined the body politic without the head, while retaining some of the head's least attractive attributes (the confidence, in particular, of natural superiority) in Coriolanus himself. He clearly shows us plebeians capable of reasoning from one thing to another, from a local corn shortage to economic injustice in general; and, as a consequence of the changes he made in the Roman historical pretext, he shows us that popular, food-centered protest could *work,* since it resulted in the creation of the tribunate. And however disreputable some aspects of these particular tribunes' behavior, there is nothing in the play to challenge that famous interpretation of the tribunate itself which Livy permitted and Machiavelli made a premise of Renaissance political theory. Did Shakespeare, then, imagine that chance, in the shape of the Midlands Rising, might now be offering England what Machiavelli had denoted 'Fortune's second gift', the opportunity to negotiate needed changes in the sociopolitical structure and so to stabilize it?

In order to complete the answer to that question, we need to go forward in time to the spring of 1610, when James's much prorogued parliament was finally recalled to business. It so happens that in the first weeks of debate the body metaphor appears in parliament in a context that itself emphasizes the problem inherent in the term 'common wealth', that is to say, wealth's distribution, with food standing for the national resources. Since the only reason for recalling parliament was the king's need for funds, Robert Cecil, as Treasurer, had an uncomfortable role to play, given what had occurred during the long prorogation, and perhaps contributed to its length. He chose to ask for a supply by alluding to the venerable image of incorporation:

The king (being the politic head) can receive no other good from the body of this parliament, severed in itself, than the natural head can receive comfort when there is interruption of the passages between the brain and the heart, whereof the best issue can be no other but the effects of a dead palsy which taketh away motion first and life after.[34]

On 3 March, Sir Edwin Sandys, arguing for the crown, developed the metaphor more carefully as one of distribution and digestion:

What his majesty demandeth, supply and support, [are] things so necessary even for a private person that without them no particular man's estate can subsist. All kings in these cases have ever had recourse to parliament. The sun raiseth vapors before it dissolveth them into showers, the liver draweth nourishment before it distributeth blood to the body. The ocean must be filled by the rivers and the head maintained by the members. The sun doth not ingulf the waters nor the liver engross the blood but distributeth where it want, for natura *abhorret a vacuo*. All kings have had ordinary resort to the bounty of their subjects and the people must be as ready to return to the king as the king is ready to distribute to the people.

(2:43)

On 21 March, James himself returned to the metaphor of the body, but in a tone considerably less conciliatory than that of his supporters, and in a medium, since his speech was promptly published, that was generally available to the reading public. 'As for the head of the naturall body,' he said:

the head hath the power of directing all the members of the body to that use which the judgement in the head thinkes most convenient. It may apply sharpe cures, or cut off corrupt members, let blood in what proportion it thinks fit, and as the body may spare.[35]

But the problem was, as every member of both houses must have been aware, that these body fables, whatever their tone, were as 'inept' as the version told by Menenius Agrippa. The national resources have simply not been circulating as the organicist metaphors imply they must, and the people have nothing to return to the king. And, while the Midlands Rising itself is barely alluded to in the debates, it had clearly given rise to a sharpened political consciousness, a more charged political vocabulary, and indeed to a sense of the responsibilities of the House of Commons as representatives not only of the nation at large but especially, perhaps, of those least capable of effective self-representation. Sir Francis Bacon, with his eyes set on the Great Contract which would obviate such debates in the future, saw what was coming and warned against over-explicitness in constitutional relations: 'Questions which concern the power of the king and the liberty of the subject,' Bacon protested, 'should not be textual, positive and scholastical, but slide in practice silently and not be brought into position and order'.[36] But the king warned the Commons not to 'meddle' with his 'power of government', for, he said, 'If a king be resolute to be a tyrant, all you can do will not hinder him' (p. 103). And the opposition leaders whom he had accused of creating a tribunate[37] in England for their turn cited Magna Carta, the 'ancient liberties' and the common law, all of which were, they claimed, 'plainly set forth to be for restraining great and mighty men from wronging or oppressing the common people' (p. 196).

As the debates wore on the concept of the popular, and of popular representation, emerged into lexical audibility and some theoretical clarity. The king desired the Commons to distinguish between genuinely popular grievances and their own, and 'not to buzz those things into the people's heads which they never thought grievous,' (2:61), a warning that might equally have applied to Robert Wilkinson and William Shakespeare. And on 14 November, at a conference between the Lords and the Commons, Northampton finally articulated that version of the body fable that was most appropriate to the dissentious tone of this parliament and the national crisis that led up to it. 'Some say,' he began, 'that the king must begin to relieve himself out of the riches of his own best means and not to depend only upon the supplies of state':

> The like quarrel was made once to the belly, as we read in the Roman histories, by all other parts, for that it engross'd and consumed whatsoever could be gained by the providence and industry of other parts, but finding by experience that upon their envious conspiracy to abstain from offices enjoined by the law of nature for the feeding of that spring which by the timely distribution of nourishment to every part conserves the body, not the belly only but the head, the feet, the arms, the legs, and every part that first began the quarrel fell into decay, they fell again to their old offices and grew very much ashamed of the mutiny.[38]

This speech confirms the intuition that Shakespeare's version of the body fable comes late in the discursive formation begun by the Midlands Rising and ending, in February 1611, with the collapse of the Great Contract and the dissolution of parliament, which was not to meet again until the spring of 1614. Implicitly, in Northampton's version, the king has become the belly of the state, however much he himself insisted on the head's authority; and although there is no textual indication that Shakespeare was aware of Northampton's speech, or the earl of Shakespeare's play, our interpretation of both is richer if we assume a horizontal force field of connections between them, an intertextuality authorized by historical circumstances, and by the intensity of the concerns that revitalized old metaphors and carried them, on the popular circuits, from mouth to mouth and from mind to mind.

Two days later, Samuel Lewknor, speaking for the opposition, declared that it is 'now a fit time to speak plainly and let the King know the voice of his commons'. For, and like Shakespeare and Wilkinson, he puts words into their mouths:

> They complain already that such are their extremities as they are fallen into a gulf of necessity, that they are the anvils whereon all sorts of people do strike. Alas, what gain is this, when the benefit that the King has by a subsidy comes out of the tears of the people?
> (Foster, 2:333–34)

So the term 'commons' shifts downwards in the social register, from the third estate generally to the underclasses, to incorporate that 'fourth sort of men' whom the constitution, as defined by Sir Thomas Smith, had utterly excluded. It was no doubt with some sense of where his eloquence had taken him that Lewknor closed his speech by requesting 'that no evil exposition' be made of anything he said, and that it had not been motivated by any 'affectation of popularity' (2:335).[39] But his words, along with those of Wilkinson and Shakespeare, had entered the discursive formation whose beginning was the Midlands Rising, and whose conclusions, in the slow evolution of political practice, we today take for granted. And if Shakespeare's play appeared in London in late 1609 or early 1610, he too might have hoped, not only that 'no evil exposition' might be made of it (a hope that went unfulfilled), but that the theater, as well as the pulpit and parliamentary bench, might 'speak plainly and let the King know the voice of his commons'; at the very least, if the few require the support of the many, 'the price is, to ask it kindly'.

Notes

1. Compare Richard Wilson, ' "Is this a holiday?" Shakespeare's Roman Carnival,' *English Literary History*, 54 (1987), pp. 31–44 [see chapter 2 in this volume], who, as in his treatment of *Henry VI, Part 2* in relation to the

feltmakers' uprising in 1592, reads 'the first scene acted at the Globe [i.e. the opening scene of *Julius Caesar*] . . . as a manoeuvre in the campaign to legitimize the Shakespearean stage and dissociate it from the subversiveness of artisanal culture' (p. 33).

2. Charles Gildon, *Remarks on the Plays of Shakespeare in Works of Shakespeare*, ed. Rowe, vol. 7 (London, 1710), pp. 362–3.

3. Grass, *The Plebeians Rehearse the Uprising* (trans R. Manheim, Harmondsworth: Penguin, 1972), xii.

4. See Christopher Hill, 'The Many-Headed Monster', in *Change and Continuity in Seventeenth-Century England* (Cambridge, Mass., 1975), pp. 181–204; and Jonathan Dollimore, *Radical Tragedy: Religion, Ideology and Power in the Drama of Shakespeare and his Contemporaries* (Brighton: Harvester Wheatsheaf, 1984), pp. 223–6.

5. See also Coriolanus's complaint that the Senate has 'given Hydra here to choose an officer, . . . the horn and noise o' th' monster's' (3:1:92–4). It must be acknowledged that the playtext includes one stage direction 'Enter a rabble of Plebeians with the Aediles' (3:1:179), although in the scene of confusion that follows it is hard to distinguish one disordinate group from another.

6. Michel Foucault, *Power/Knowledge* (New York, 1980), p. 97.

7. Grass, *The Plebeians Rehearse the Uprising*, p. 31.

8. E.P. Thompson, 'The Moral Economy of the English Crowd in the Eighteenth Century', *Past and Present*, 50 (1971), 76–136.

9. Philip Brockbank, ed. *Coriolanus* (London: Routledge, 1976), p. 38; and see also: Andrew Gurr, ' "Coriolanus" and the Body Politic', *Shakespeare Survey*, 28 (1975), 63–9; Thomas Sorge, ' "Body Politic" and "Human Body" in *Coriolanus*: Ein Beitrag zur Commonwealth-Thematik bei Shakespeare,' *Shakespeare Jahrbuch*, 115 (1979), pp. 89–97; Robert S. Miola, *Shakespeare's Rome* (Cambridge, 1983), pp. 167–8.

10. We might note in this connection that in 1986 President Reagan deferred funds allocated by the Congress for transporting surplus food to homeless people, despite the fact that the transportation costs, $28 million, were a fraction of the $365 million spent annually to store this food in limestone caves in Kansas and elsewhere. See Jonathan Kozol, *Rachel and her Children: Homeless Families in America* (New York, 1988), pp. 59–60.

11. Karl Marx, *Value, Price and Profit*, in Karl Marx and Friedrich Engels, *Collected Works*, Vol. 20 (New York, 1985), pp. 104, 106. See also *The Condition of the Working-class in England*, *C.W.*, Vol. 4 (New York, 1975), p. 510, where Engels complains of Dr Andrew Ure, 'the most furious enemy of the Unions', who had cited the belly fable in his Philosophy of Manufactures (London, 1835), p. 282; and adds, 'A pity that the English working-men will not let themselves be pacified so easily with thy fable as the Roman Plebs, thou modern Menenius Agrippa!' I owe this additional evidence of the fable's 'modern' vitality to Peter Stallybrass.

12. Bloom, *The Closing of the American Mind* (Harmondsworth: Penguin, 1988), pp. 110–11.

13. Grass, *The Plebeians Rehearse the Uprising*, pp. 80–1.

14. Fredric Jameson, *The Political Unconscious* (Ithaca, NY, 1981), p. 34.

15. E.C. Pettet, '*Coriolanus* and the Midlands Insurrection of 1607', *Shakespeare Survey*, 3 (1950), 39.

16. See Buchanan Sharp, *In Contempt of All Authority: Rural Artisans and Riot in the West of England, 1586–1660* (Berkeley, 1980), p. 42.

17. Derek Hirst, *Authority and Conflict: England, 1603–1658* (Cambridge, Mass., 1986), p. 51. I wish to record, however, that Hirst subsequently felt that his position was overstated.

18. See especially Edwin F. Gay, 'The Midland Revolt and the Inquisitions of Depopulation of 1607', *Transactions of the Royal Historical Society*, New Series, 18 (1904), 195–244. The most extensive account of the Revolt is by John E. Martin, *Feudalism to Capitalism: Peasant and Landlord in English Agrarian Development* (London, 1988), pp. 161–215.

19. See James F. Larkin and Paul L. Hughes, eds, *Stuart Royal Proclamations*, 2 vols (Oxford, 1973), 1:153, n.1; and Martin, *Feudalism to Capitalism*, p. 163, who cites the Warwickshire petition from J.O. Halliwell, ed., *The Marriage of Wit and Wisdom* (London, 1846), pp. 140–1.

20. See David Underdown, *Revel, Riot and Rebellion: Popular Politics and Culture in England 1603–1660* (Oxford, 1985), p. 115.

21. See Andrew Charlesworth, ed., *An Atlas of Rural Protest in Britain 1548–1900* (Philadelphia, 1983), pp. 33–4.

22. See 'A Proclamation for suppressing of persons riotously assembled for the laying open of Inclosures, 30 May 1607', in *A Booke of Proclamations* (London, 1609), p. 139.

23. Larkin and Hughes, *Stuart Royal Proclamations*, p. 155, n.2.

24. *A Proclamation signifying his Majesties pleasure aswell for suppressing of riotous Assemblies about Inclosures, as for reformation of Depopulations. 28 June 1607*, in *A Booke of Proclamations* (London, 1609), p. 140.

25. See Joan Thirsk, *The Agrarian History of England and Wales (1500–1640)*, 8 vols (Cambridge, 1967) 4:820. I am grateful to Derek Hirst for reading the message of these figures to me. See also Martin, *Feudalism to Capitalism*, who argues that whereas in national terms harvests were good until 1607, from the 1590s onwards the Midlands 'experienced a chronic scarcity of grain', and that by April 1607 'the peasantry would have been aware that even harder times were on the way, owing to the meagre condition of the coming harvest' (pp. 161–3).

26. Larkin and Hughes, *Stuart Royal Proclamations*, 1:161.

27. Larkin and Hughes, *Stuart Royal Proclamations*, 1:163.

28. *Orders Appointed by his Majestie to be straigtly observed for the preventing and remedying of the dearth of Graine and other Victuall. June 1, 1608* (London, 1608), p. 13.

29. Larkin and Hughes, *Stuart Royal Proclamations*, 1:202.

30. One can be confident of using this phrase when proclamations are involved, since their very function is to bring to public consciousness a particular aspect of governmental policy. Indeed, these proclamations were collected and republished in *A Booke of Proclamations* in 1609, a move interpreted by the Commons as a statement of royal intent to *govern* by proclamation while suspending parliamentary process.

31. Robert Wilkinson, *A Sermon Preached at North-Hampton the 21 of June last past, before the Lord Lieutenant of the County, and the rest of the Commissioners there assembled upon occasion of the late Rebellion and Riots in those parts committed. Pro.22.2 The rich & the poore meete together, the Lord is the maker of them all* (London, 1607). The existence of this document was briefly noted by Brents Stirling, *The Populace in Shakespeare* (New York, 1949), p. 107, who, however, saw it merely as proof of social unrest that would have stirred Shakespeare to law-and-order activity. See also Martin, *Feudalism to Capitalism*, pp. 163, 176, 179, who, however, assumes that Wilkinson's sermon 'reflects the thinking of the government'.

32. If Wilkinson really intended his sermon to be bipartisan, he must have assumed that at least some of the Risers were literate.

33. W. Gordon Zeefeld, '"Coriolanus" and Jacobean Politics', *Modern Language Review*, 17 (1962), pp. 323–4.

34. See Elizabeth Read Foster, ed., *Proceedings in Parliament: 1610*, 2 vols, (New Haven, 1966), 2:10–11.

35. *The Kings Majestie's Speach To the Lords and Commons . . . on Wednesday the xxi of March, Anno Dom. 1609* (London, 1610), B2.

36. Foster, *Proceedings*, 2:98.

37. The term 'tribunes' was still being used pejoratively for the opposition leaders in the Commons on 16 June 1614, when Sir Ralph Winwood wrote to Dudley Carleton: 'Never saw so much faction and passion as in the late unhappy Parliament . . . The impositions were the great grievance, also a speech of the Bishop of London taxing the Commons with sedition, and the Kings messages were thought to abridge the liberty of the House. The break-neck was some seditious speeches which made the King impatient, and it was whispered to him that they would have his life and that of his favourites before they had done, on which he dissolved them. Four of their tribunes, Sir Walter Chute, Christopher Neville, Hoskins and Wentworth, are sent to prison . . .' See *Calendar of State Papers Domestic*, James I, Vol. No. 77.

38. Henry Howard, Earl of Northampton, Lord Privy Seal, in Foster, *Proceedings*, 1:268.

39. See also Kenneth Muir, 'Shakespeare and Lewkenor', *Review of English Studies*, 7 (1956), 182–3.

9 Lenten Butchery: Legitimization Crisis in *Coriolanus**

MICHAEL D. BRISTOL

Michael Bristol's study of *Coriolanus* is a wide-ranging engagement with the play, which takes up a number of different issues, including the question of the way in which power seeks, and, in certain circumstances, fails, to legitimise itself. Bristol also takes up the issue of what he calls 'the politics of carnival', mapping the traditional oppositions between carnival and Lent on to the political oppositions which operate within the text. In this, Bristol's article can usefully be placed beside the selections included here from Richard Wilson and John Drakakis, both of whom explore carnivalesque elements within *Julius Caesar*. Bristol also engages with the way in which the text of *Coriolanus* has been 'mobilised' within criticism, tracing patterns of interpretation within critical analyses of the play.

The general political form of the Coriolanus legend

Since antiquity, the historical fiction of Coriolanus, his rise to power, his expulsion by a tribunal of the people, and his tragic death, has provided material for a political theodicy. Much of the story is, of course, sheer invention (Lehman, 1952). Many of the details of the legend, however, do correspond to historically concrete elements within the Roman state, and, more broadly, to elements of political and social struggle that persist through the emergence of absolutist states and their successors in modern national sovereignties (Anderson, 1974a, 1974b; Guenée, 1985; Nicolet, 1980; Poggi, 1978; Richard, 1978; Strayer, 1970; Yavetz, 1969). The legend articulates a comprehensive vocabulary for the representation of the state. First, Rome is defined as a territory through the story of the war against the Volscians. Second, the internal administrative coherence of the *res publica* is accomplished

*JEAN E. HOWARD AND MARION F. O'CONNOR (EDS), *Shakespeare Reproduced: The Text in History and Ideology* (London: Methuen, 1987), pp. 207–24.

through the interaction of three primary sociohistorical categories – Coriolanus, patricians, and plebeians and tribunate – that constitute a typology of political structure. State formation is conceived in terms of enmity and division. The solidarity of the whole is expressed through the compelling distinction between friend and foe (Poggi, 1978; Schmitt, 1976). But within that negatively determined solidarity, relations among men and women are differentiated according to a division of labor that is itself inimical and invidious (Gramsci, 1957; Marx, 1973; Poggi, 1972). Because of this orientation toward struggle, negativity, and historically determinate action, the Coriolanus legend always exceeds the boundaries of any conservative project of simple apologetics for a given historical condition of the Roman *res publica* or for any of the institutions of political domination that claim succession from this origin.

The antagonism between Coriolanus and the tribunes who represent the common people suggests that something more fundamental is at stake in this narrative material than a difference of opinion over Coriolanus' fitness or unfitness to rule. That difference of opinion could presumably be settled by an appeal to a normative order of some kind. It is, however, the nature and purpose of that normative order, and not merely the appropriate role of one individual within an agreed-upon political structure, that is the central issue inscribed within the material. The historical fiction is, then, always at hand as a parable for what Jürgen Habermas calls legitimation crisis (1975, 1979). Such a crisis typically involves conflict at the deepest levels of social reality.

Legitimation crisis is a phenomenon that divides society over issues much more basic and enduring than factional strife over division of the spoils. First, there is likely to be profound divergence over the question of the derivation of authority and the source of social initiative. Second, there will be a general contestation of the allocation of authority and of the predominant mode of social organization. Third, the ethical horizons of social organization, the purpose or general *telos* of economic and political praxis, informs the other levels of the conflict by generating opposed general metaphors of social existence of 'images of the good life' (Habermas, 1979; Jameson, 1981; McCarthy, 1978; Wallerstein, 1974; Walzer, 1976). What makes the Coriolanus legend so effective as the metaphorical embodiment of the general form of legitimation crisis is the distinctive role taken by the plebs or citizens (Nicolet, 1980; Richard, 1978; Scullard, 1935; Treggiari, 1969; Yavetz, 1969). This anonymous, collective player in the drama of political struggle represents not only a full and coherent alternative political culture, but also the will to power of that political culture.

Coriolanus, as the protagonist in the legend that bears his name, objectifies the principle of charismatic authority (Weber, 1947, 358 ff.).

His claim to political and ethical priority rests on his exceptional powers as a military leader, most specifically his extraordinary personal valor and technical skill in combat. He is the embodiment of an ideal of *virtus,* manly excellence or prowess; the complementary and offsetting ideal of *pietas* comes into play only at the last minute and then in an oddly displaced and distorted form. His charisma rests exclusively on his quasimagical capacity for violence rather than on any prophetic or persuasive gifts, but it is a genuine charisma in that it derives from collectively sustained values. The sudden emergence of a charismatic figure within the *mise-en-scène* of a lawfully constituted political structure is inherently destabilizing; it is certainly ominous in that such a figure can act as the center for politically radical mass movements. In the Coriolanus material, however, it is the party in power, the patricians, who embrace Coriolanus, whom they see as a useful and reliable instrument for the defense of their own class interests.

Opposition to the principle of charismatic authority comes from the institution of the tribunate. That opposition is not merely negative, an intransigent resistance to a resented arrogation of civil authority. It is, on the contrary, an opposition founded on an opposing view of authority as derived from the force of social tradition and customary practice (Weber, 1947, 341 ff.). As E.P. Thompson has pointed out, a plebs is not a working class in the modern sense (1968, 1974). On the other hand, it is not an unorganized population of helots either, and still less a mob or rabble (P. Burke, 1978; Davis, 1975; Harrison, 1984; Richard, 1978). The plebs, or their cognates in the early modern period – Shakespeare's 'citizens' – is a complex ensemble of producing classes. It is also a political entity, nominally excluded from the function of rule but nevertheless a collective agent within the dynamic of political life (Bristol, 1985). The plebs characteristically views authority as derived from local custom and from settled ways of doing things. As 'theoreticians' or 'onlookers' vis-à-vis official politics, the common people tend to view the objectively topmost positions not as a pervasive and ordered hegemony, but as a finite, rigorously bounded and precarious setting forth of an ideology of order and mastery surrounded by a 'sea of productive labor.' This implies a severe curtailment of the centralized function of state power in favor of a general dispersal of authority. Law takes precedence over decree, but custom takes precedence even over law on this view. The plebs thus acts on the conviction of its own prior authority, its expropriation by an elite, and on the need for redressive action to restore an original state of affairs when its constituencies had not yet become 'the unprivileged' (Davis, 1975, 152 ff.).

Opposition over the derivation of authority is elaborated in the further opposition over the allocation of authority and the general form of social organization. In these terms, Coriolanus stands for a principle of hierarchically ordered and centrally administered social structure. It is unfortunate that so much of the critical literature on the best known of all the versions of the Coriolanus legend tends to collapse the terms hierarchy and order into a single category. This obscures the highly specialized character of the type of orderliness favored by Coriolanus. It also denies the possibility of other types of ordering principle and even of the broad range of hierarchizations available within social practice. Coriolanus' allegiance is not to 'hierarchy' in general, but specifically to a vertical command structure of an exclusively military type. The general rationale for his vision of *l'état policier* is, not surprisingly, the idea that the mass of common people is lawless, predatory, and incapable of ordered social relations in the absence of a severe and rigorously enforced external discipline (Poggi, 1978, 5 ff.; Schmitt, 1976). This is the justificatory ideology of the regime of *Herrschaft* or lordship, which depicts itself as the exclusive source of order set over against internal as well as external foes (Le Roy Ladurie, 1979, 299–302).

The tribunate opposes this ideology not with an idea of subversion or derangement, but with an alternative (though not widely acknowledged) conception of social order based on solidarity, a regime of *Genossenschaft* in which the members of a group participate on a more or less equal footing (Durkheim, 1935; La Capra, 1985; Le Roy Ladurie, 1979; Poggi, 1972). Within this regime, of course, temporary pragmatic hierarchies may be recognized, but these differentiations are made for functional reasons, and do not symbolize a permanent and ideal framework of categories. Since there is no speciality of rule it can hardly be neglected. From this perspective it is possible to develop a full and cogent critique of the command structure advocated by Coriolanus, one that goes beyond the observation that he is too proud or that his adventurism might prove too costly. For it is central to the project of any command structure to forbid any countervailing system of imperatives, and specifically to deny the pertinence and the validity claims of any dispersed communal authority. However, if such a logic of domination is actually implemented, then it is clear that the existence of a 'rabble' is one of the more important consequences of its functioning, since the command structure itself would entail the suppression of self-regulating norms and practises that promote and sustain communal solidarity. Rigid insistence on a vertical chain of command creates a situation where the only thing that matters is who's on top. Common people, normally organized in corporate bodies, sink into the condition of rabble as the result of material deprivation and of cultural violence (Durkheim, 1935). Plebeian culture has resources that enable it to resist such a process of internal colonization and the suppression of their own diffuse authority by the figure of the greater personality or *Führer*. The self-exclusion of the great public figure from the body of the people evokes 'choric recrimination' (Styan, 1976, 102). Such anger and violent recrimination speaks to social and cultural norms deeply embedded in the practical consciousness of the plebs. The plebeian forms of *Genossenschaft* thus imply an absolute and radical reversal of the terms order and disorder, in which it is maintained that any hypostasis of the topmost positions in the form of an external disciplinarity is a fundamental derangement in the direction of an endless chain of violent actions.

The most fundamental opposition, then, between Coriolanus and his opponents is at the level of the generative metaphor, *telos*, or goal-value of social life. For Coriolanus, the fundamental *raison d'être* of social life is the state of affairs known as war. The body politic is thus envisioned as perpetually constrained by conditions of austerity and athletic self-discipline oriented toward the geopolitical Other in a posture of aggression (Jorgensen, 1956; Schmitt, 1976). This condition is not thought of as a 'necessary evil,' or even as the means toward some end such as, let's say, peace; it is, on the contrary, an end in itself, and in fact the only possible state of political well-being. This then gives rise to the cognate therapeutic metaphor in which injury and destruction are recuperated by images that refer to the discharge of excessive and superfluous political matter, or to the surgical elimination of pathological growth. The durable ideological appeal of this notion is itself part of the Coriolanus material, in that the legend suggests that the plebs is willing to follow Coriolanus into battle against the Volscians. However, a fundamental misunderstanding takes place as soon as this campaign has ended.

The plebs views war as at most an instrumental and purely temporary value. It constitutes a transient condition of political arousal, not a state of social health. For the plebs the governing metaphor of social life cannot be war; it can only be subsistence, the constellation of homeostatic processes of production, reproduction, and renewal most often represented by images of a living organism. This orientation gives rise to the speech type of popular culture, an idiom that grants special importance to what Bakhtin has called the 'lower bodily stratum,' and to those processes that mark the individual body as open, unfinished, and traversed by the activities of social production (Bakhtin, 1968, 368 ff.). One reason for the success of Menenius' speech to the angry plebeians is his ability to make use of their own characteristic idiom of the 'grotesque body' and to appeal directly to the distinctive goal-values of plebeian culture by positing social health as homologous with the visceral satisfaction of bodily needs. His speech is, of course, tendentious, shaped by an ideology fundamentally alien to the aspirations of the social horizons of the plebs, but the legend suggests that an intervention of this type can be effective, at least in the short run, as a strategy of containment. The very effectiveness of the intervention tacitly acknowledges, however, that the plebeians have a distinctive outlook or world-view and that their consciousness is not merely an absence of political ideas, but a full and coherent mode of being-in-the-world, as well as a mode of being-with-others.

The opposition between Coriolanus and the tribunate is, of course, mediated by the framing social reality of the *res publica* as a lawfully constituted form of social life that finds its origins in the historical expulsion of the Tarquins, and the rejection in principle of absolute, individual rule. It is this 'state' that suffers through legitimation crisis. In the distinct works that concretize the materials of the legend it is the *res publica*, an entity with a historically specific constitution that emerges from the turbulent cross-currents that threaten both its territorial integrity and its internal cohesion. The achievement of a constitutional settlement brings with it a more or less stable legitimation of an ensemble of power relations. In itself, however, a constitution does not resolve the conflicts built into the division of social labor. Active and open conflict is suspended and deferred; sociocultural and discursive antagonism persists, however, and one or another party to the ongoing process of legitimation may at any time withhold consent. Ideas of chronic social antagonism and incipient crisis are intrinsic to the Coriolanus material, and for that reason the story retains its potentially explosive character.

Shakespeare's *Coriolanus* and the politics of carnival

Shakespeare's full-scale dramatization of the Coriolanus legend begins with a scene depicting the community of citizens decisively entering into the sphere of political action that Fernand Braudel refers to as *l'histoire événementielle* (1977). The common people are always present as part of the nearly immobile level of history, the slow unfolding of material culture and everyday life (Braudel, 1981, 23–5). The emergence of the body of citizens into the more eventful dimension of history takes the dramatic form of a crowd or chorus surging onto the stage to enact their anger, their desire for social and economic restitution, and the will to power of a heretofore mute constituency. It has frequently been asserted that the common people are presented unsympathetically in this and subsequent scenes (Ide, 1980; MacCallum, 1967; Pettet, 1950; Rabkin, 1967; Rossiter, 1961; Simmons, 1973; Zeeveld, 1962).

Stated in this form, the proposition is logically incoherent, since the quality of sympathy refers to intersubjective relations, but not to discrete objects or representations. If the claim is made in the more precise form – the plebeians are represented in a manner intended to evoke antipathy – then the ideologically contingent nature of the assertion becomes immediately apparent (Charney, 1963; Dollimore, 1984). The quality of sympathy or of antipathy would depend far less on the dramatic rhetoric as such, and far more on the prevailing social outlook of those present at the moment of reception.

Sympathy is, of course, a relative form. The response of shared feeling is likely to be governed by collective predispositions, often unconscious, much more than by a purely neutral and disinterested reaction to artistic language and mimetic action. The intersubjective condition of sympathy corresponds to a particular social experience, namely that of class-conscious solidarity. In reading *Coriolanus* it is, of course, extremely pertinent to ask who feels sympathy or its lack and for what reason. But this question requires that general criteria of 'social goodness' or 'social badness' be made explicit. The tendency to view the crowd of citizens unsympathetically reflects a specific ideological orientation. If this is not simply an unreflective elitism, it is most likely to be an orientation in which the dominant criterion of 'social goodness' is a comprehensive order in which integration of disparate interests and rationalization of authority, power, and wealth are achieved by means of an uncontested hegemony. In this orientation, toleration for conflict and thus sympathy for those who appear to initiate it is extremely low. The ambient level of social violence ideally approaches zero by virtue of a rationally integrated apparatus that maintains a monopoly of coercive force. The idea of society or collective life is thus collapsed into the idea of the state as the indispensable objectification and agency of social order, the only possible barrier to the condition of interminable civil war. Within this tradition, spontaneous popular initiative can only be interpreted in one way, that is as an instance confirming a particular social dread, the war of all against all.

It may well be that Shakespeare's own ideological alignments fall within this tradition and that *Coriolanus* is precisely what traditional historicism has always claimed, that is, a theodicy of the absolutist state (Phillips, 1940; Honig, 1951; Rossiter, 1961; Simmons, 1973). If this is the case, then it seems that criticism might assume responsibility for making explicit both the grounds of this orientation and its consequences for social practice. This might entail the abandonment of a hermeneutics that simply keeps faith with tradition in favor of a critique of that tradition in which the authoritarian character of valued literacy material is contested rather than simply confirmed as 'beyond ideology' (Adorno, 1967; Gadamer, 1976; Giddens, 1977; Habermas, 1971; Hjort, 1985; McCarthy, 1978). There is, however, another way to challenge the confirmatory ideology of normal literary criticism, and that is to show how *Coriolanus* might be read as situated within an alternative political culture such as the one objectified in the crowd scenes and in the speeches of the unnamed citizens. Such a reconsideration would entail a more sympathetic view of the plebeians, not so much with the intention of assessing the justice of their claims, but rather with the aim of elucidating a distinctive political discourse. This seems particularly appropriate in light of the outbreaks of popular unrest during the early years of James I's reign, and more generally of the conditions of incipient revolution throughout the period (Charney, 1963; Dollimore, 1984; Goldberg, 1983; Sharp, 1980; Stone, 1972; Walzer, 1976).

In *Coriolanus* the ambient condition of political uncertainty and of gathering resistance to lawfully constituted authority is expressed in a complex and ambivalent rhetoric based on the traditional *topos* of the body politic (Cavell, 1984; Danson, 1973; Gurr, 1975; Hale, 1971). The image of the body is, of course, a familiar topic in the critical discussion of *Coriolanus*. The play is saturated with concrete situations in which the fate and condition of bodies is of paramount importance. Both literal and symbolic implications of the analogy between the private individual body and the body politic are elaborated in nearly every scene.

Menenius' great rhetorical set piece on the belly and the other members restates a commonplace of Renaissance political rhetoric that correlates the natural body and its functions with the body of the community and its social processes. The analogy suggests an organic view of society in which every member has an ascriptive status and function; social well-being depends on each member fulfilling his own duties and obligations. The fable of the belly itself derives ultimately from Aesop (Muir, 1952). Equally pertinent, however, is the image of the community of believers as articulated in *First Corinthians*:

> For as the body is one, and hath many members, and all the members of that body, being many, are one body, so also is Christ. For by one Spirit are we all baptized into one body. . . . . If the foot shall say, because I am not the hand, I am not of the body; is it therefore not of the body? And if the ear shall say, Because I am not the eye, I am not of the body; is it therefore not of the body?
>
> (12:15–19)

Obviously physical health depends on the unity and coordination of the whole body; similarly the health of a community depends on

137

a stable and harmonious division of labor and on the appropriate distribution of subsistence. In the normative use of this metaphor, harmony and orderly differentiation require the clear subordination of the 'lower organs' to the higher faculties of reason and spiritual understanding. The belly cannot be in charge, and when the fable is used by such writers as Sidney, William Camden, or Edward Forset the political discordancy among the lower faculties of the body is reconciled by the superior agency of the head (Hale, 1968). *Coriolanus* can be read exclusively in light of such a normative tradition, but the text reveals that the lower bodily stratum continues to assert itself against the imperatives of vertical order and control.

The language of Coriolanus accords particular prominence to images of the viscera, digestion, mouth, tongue, food and eating, as well as to instances of thrashing, wounds, injury, and violent death. This constellation of images constitutes the system of the 'grotesque body' (Bakhtin, 1968; Cavell, 1984; Bristol, 1985; Stallybrass and White, 1986). The visceral or lower-bodily orientation provides for the elaboration of an ethos in which abundance of material life and the continuity of processes of production and reproduction are both the primary agencies *and* the fundamental criteria of social well-being. The abundance of the material principle is the characteristic goal-value of plebeian culture, a horizon present throughout *Coriolanus* as a general speech type containing and surrounding other class discourses. Menenius appropriates this speech type in his 'fable of the belly' performance, and again in his conference with the tribunes when he characterizes himself as a 'humorous patrician . . . that converses more with the buttock of the night than with the forehead of the morning' (II. i. 47–53). No genuine political accommodation can be reached, however, by the superficial exchange of ideological currency. The imagery or language of the grotesque body is more than simply a novel and picturesque vocabulary; it corresponds to the way the body is actually lived.

The grotesque body is lived 'together with others;' it is most fully expressed in the energetic confusion of the popular festive crowd, in feasts, and in the life of the public square (Bakhtin, 1968, 1981). This is, of course, exactly what Coriolanus himself finds most intolerable. Since Coriolanus lives his own body in accordance with the canons of a radical, voluntaristic, and proprietary individualism, the intimacy and physical actuality of the collective, grotesque body can arouse only disgust. His sense of the integrity of the private body, and the plebeians' demand for familiarity and crude contact, are mutually incompatible modes of social existence. That incompatibility is objectified in Coriolanus' response to the customary demand that

he show his wounds in public. 'I cannot / Put on the gown, stand
naked, and entreat them, / For my wounds sake, to give their suffrage'
(II. ii. 138–9). His personal modesty and physical reticence that confine
acknowledgement and disclosure of the body to private, domestic space
are a deliberate expression of contempt and mockery for the values of
plebeian culture. These attitudes represent his refusal to understand the
compelling ethical force of tradition and the equally compelling value of
solidarity expressed by the public exposure of his body. His calculated
self-exclusion from the experience of the grotesque body corresponds
to a commitment to the ruthless suppression of the political culture of
the plebs. Unlike Menenius, who seeks an ideological appropriation
of plebeian culture and its integration with the *res publica* on terms
favorable to his own party, Coriolanus seeks the comprehensive
disciplinary control of popular energy. The implicit aim of his political
sensibility would be a form of authoritarian populism based on terror
and coercion. He is, however, unable to achieve such a dispensation;
his intentions are thwarted by the actions of the aroused citizens, who
make of him the exemplary victim of a popular festive scenario of
crowning and uncrowning (Bakhtin, 1968, 275).

In the context of early modern Europe, the central event of popular
festive life is the battle of Carnival and Lent. The battle, as it was
enacted in the traditional scenarios in streets and public squares,
articulates various symmetrical oppositions, beginning with the contrast
between fat and lean, that is, between two different, seasonal cuisines.
Carnival celebrates meat; Lent celebrates fish. The pattern of abstinence
from meat and the shift to a diet of fish during Lent is a religious and
spiritual discipline, a 'burying of pagan ways' as part of the purification
of the spirit in preparation for Easter (Le Roy Ladurie, 1979, 285). But
the relationship of Carnival to Lent, or *Carême–carnaval*, has secular
importance as well.

The battle of Carnival and Lent dramatizes permanent conflicts
within the practical experience of the early modern European
economy. During Carnival, surplus livestock that cannot be wintered
is slaughtered and preserved; meat is consumed in abundance
and butchers enjoy prosperity. As Carnival ends and Lent begins,
butchers are required to close their shops. This coincides with travel
into the countryside to begin purchase of cattle for the spring.
While the butchers are inactive fishmongers claim their market. In
due course, however, the butchers return and all the dogs 'howl
for joy' at the renewed abundance of meat. The annual ceremonial
combat opposes two complementary social elements – Carnival/Lent;
butchers/fishmongers; war/peace – that coexist in dynamic equilibrium.
These contrasts between different times of year, different sources of
wealth and abundance, different métiers, represent the complexity of
social life as a dialectical tension between the persistent drive toward

material abundance and the requirements of social discipline. Closely connected with this is a corresponding dialectic between violence in the form of Carnival butchery and social peace in the form of the Lenten Truce of God.

In the recurrent rhythms of Carnival's battle with Lent, the figure of Carnival is closely identified with butchers and thus with the complex and ambivalent interconnection of slaughter with the abundance of the material principle (Bristol, 1985). The interval of abstinence and intensified social discipline known as Lent is the period during which the butchers' shops are closed. This interval is framed by two periods of climactic ascendancy for butchers, first in the Carnival feasting itself, and then, after the Easter Sunday observances, in the triumphal return of the butchers and the annual compensatory expulsion of Lent.

> Then pell-mell murder in a purple hue,
> In reeking blood his slaughtering paws imbrue:
> The butcher's axe (like great Alcides' bat)
> Dings deadly down, ten thousand thousand flat:
> Each butcher (by himself) makes marshall laws,
> Cuts throats, and kills, and quarters, hangs, and draws.
>
> (Taylor, 1630, 19)

This is, in fact, celebratory imagery of renewed material abundance, but it suggests the very deep ambivalence and complexity that must be acknowledged in and through the productive processes that sustain collective life. The forms of *Carême–carnaval* can be regarded, not as the discharge of accumulated energy, but as the collective balancing and coordination of antagonistic elements within productive life and the channeling along familiar lines of chronic and irreducible social violence. The apparent lawlessness of these proceedings can also be read as an alternative law of coexistence. In this model of being-with-others, *Carême–carnaval* requires that every moment of ascendancy be checked, that every claim of domination be thrashed and regularly expelled. The aim of this social process is not the definitive resolution of conflict through rationalized administration, but the dynamic reenactment of traditional allocations of wealth and authority that nevertheless permits customary practice to be altered. The process is 'conservative' in the sense that there is a diffuse collective will to conserve social wealth, established communal autonomy, and other elements that make up the horizons of the 'good life.'

Coriolanus follows the normal pattern of crowning and uncrowning/expulsion until halfway through the action, at which point the patterns of *Carême–carnaval* are disrupted. Unlike the expulsion of the butchers, who are scattered and dispersed into the countryside, only to return later to reassert the 'bodily-material principle,' Coriolanus' expulsion is made permanent, his attempted return at the head of a hostile army is prevented by the intervention of his mother. In order to understand this general pattern of political action, it is useful to compare Coriolanus with the ominous figure of the Lenten Butcher.

The categorical framework of *Carême–carnaval* maps the sociopolitical order into opposing domains depicted agonistically. The abundance of the material principle as manifested in the forces of production is projected as the Carnivalesque figure of the Butcher. Over against this is the principle of social discipline and restraint objectified in the Lenten Fishmonger. Obviously the kingdoms of Carnival and Lent must remain separate and the inhabitants of each domain kept apart. Nevertheless within the social landscape of Elizabethan and Jacobean England there is actually such a person as a Lenten Butcher. Such a figure transgresses the boundaries between Carnival and Lent. Equally important, he appears both within the criminal underworld as the supplier of contraband flesh, and also within the sphere of legally privileged economic monopoly. The Lenten Butcher who is granted a royal 'license to kill' is permitted to practise his trade in accordance with secular imperatives that override the religious prohibition against the consumption of meat. The figure of the Lenten Butcher cuts across the boundary between Carnival and Lent, between law and its transgression. A Lenten Butcher does his work

in Sir Francis Drake's ship at Deptford, my Lord Mayor's barge, and divers secret and unsuspected places, and there they make private shambles with kill-calf cruelty and sheep slaughtering murder, to the abuse of Lent, the deceiving of the informers, and the great griefe of every zealous fishmonger.

(Taylor, 1630, 13)

Under this institutional sanction, violence not only persists without periodic remission, it is in fact invested with immense preemptive authority 'for reasons of state.' The secular demands that require, for example, that naval vessels be provisioned during the Lenten period lead to a general curtailment of the traditional *Carême–carnaval* alternative. The grotesque ambivalence of the Carnival Butcher gives way to the principle of selectivity and rationally administered violence that finds its source not in the 'abundance of the material principle' but in the *projets de grandeur* of the state apparatus.

In *Coriolanus* the conquest of *res publica* by charismatic authority and rationally administered violence embodied in the ascendancy

of a Lenten Butcher is averted by Coriolanus' extraordinary act
of self-cancelation. Legitimation then takes the form of a class
compromise, in which the party in power is able to reestablish
dominance over the popular element. The *res publica* – or is it only
the party in power? – is saved from utter and calamitous defeat at the
hands of military absolutism. And the threat of calamity provides
the means for incorporating and channeling the energy of popular
initiative. The outcome is clear, though not, I think, exactly what we
are to make of it. Is this an authentic and exemplary resolution of
crisis? Is it a case of making the best of a bad situation? Or is it an
instance of the thwarting of a genuine collective will by a dominant
minority, using a general strategy of dramatized crisis, sacrifice, and
the claims of a 'national emergency' to control and redirect the energy
of a popular majority?

Coriolanus and the patterns of ideological mobilization

To interpret *Coriolanus* is to engage is critical reflection on the
legitimation problem of the modern state, especially if the state is seen
as a constellation of balanced interests challenged on the one hand
by the '*Führer* principle,' or cult of personality, and, on the other,
by a radical collective will that threatens a general appropriation of
the means of production. That discussion does not, it would appear,
permit ideological neutrality. Furthermore, the general institutional
setting in which that discussion takes place is one in which there has
already been a general appropriation of Shakespeare for the 'national
interest.' For this reason, orientations that entail a strong critique of
the existing sociocultural order, or that are subversive in some other
way, are the only ones likely to appear overtly ideological. Normal
readings are not particularly likely to reveal themselves as tendentious.
In general, however, normal readings assume that the state must exist
as the uncontested principle of sovereignty; 'social goodness' is possible
only within such a political formation and criticism is limited to the
adjustment of contending interests and the therapeutic elimination of
'social badness'.

It would not be difficult to demonstrate the general recruitment
of Shakespeare for the purpose of fostering the diffuse mass loyalty
necessary for the continuing legitimation of state power and the class
interests represented by that power (Dollimore, 1984). There are of
course overt and external forms of appropriation, for example in the
use of Shakespeare's plays in the English system of state examinations
(Dollimore and Sinfield, 1985, 134–57). Just as direct is the expression

of diffuse sentiments about the need to promote the heritage of
'western values' as the *raison d'être* of literary scholarship generally and
Shakespeare studies in particular.

[. . .]

The recruitment of Shakespeare is mediated by a disciplinary
ideology that sets forth a constellation of interests and goal-values
which either directly underwrite the aims of a general mobilization
or channel oppositional energies so as to curtail any possibility of
effective dissemination. Space does not permit a full elaboration of
that disciplinary ideology here, but any account of its salient features
would certainly include the following points. To begin with, there
is a high value accorded to the integrity of the dramatic work of art
and to the achievement of a higher order of resolution within those
works of historically specific conflicts. This view leads to the endlessly
recurring universalistic claim that Shakespeare is 'beyond ideology.'
Although this has the occasionally useful effect of offering resistance
to entrenched doxological formulations, it also carries with it the desire
to escape from the nuisance of real history. By transcending history
both Shakespeare and the scholarship that would contemplate his
work are excused from participation in historically contingent political
life. Closely connected with the consensus as to the integrity of the
dramatic work of art is the view of Shakespeare's authority in terms
of an ahistorical conception of the 'exceptional subject.' This entails a
view of the cultural producer as a singularity; the producing subject
is characterized as a proprietary, autonomous, and voluntaristic
self, distinguished from ordinary men and women. In the case of
Shakespeare, the thematics of a contemporary achievement ideology
finds an abundant reservoir of examples in the complex structure of his
works. Value-laden propositions can then be authorized by attribution
to this exceptional individual who is carefully set apart from anything
that resembles a collective will. One important consequence of this is
the shift from politics to sensibility. Criticism discovers in Shakespeare
a higher loyalty to the human imagination and to universalistic
higher-order integration. This corresponds to criticism's renunciation of
partisan political engagement (Gilbert, 1968).

Within the range of interest generally authorized by a disciplinary
ideology, contending voices can certainly be heard. It is even possible
to challenge the disciplinary ideology itself. However, what I hope
to indicate in the following remarks is that most of the spectrum
of legitimate contention rehearses the stance of civil and vocational
privatism that either endorses the goal-values of the existing political
structure and of the sociocultural order that supports it *or* confines the
function of critical intervention to relatively narrow channels. I shall

try to develop this by considering two kinds of normal readings of *Coriolanus*: first, readings mainly concerned with analysis of Coriolanus' character, and second, 'balanced views' of the forces at play within the text.

There is no doubt that the Coriolanus that is represented in the Shakespearean text is a fascinating character. Like other Shakespearean tragedies, *Coriolanus* can certainly be read exclusively in light of the pathos of the exceptional subject. The case of Coriolanus is, like a number of others, sufficiently complex to have generated abundant controversy. One type of reading in this tradition concentrates on developing some basis for sympathetic identification with Coriolanus, or at least respect for the worthiness of his character (Bradley, 1912; Ide, 1980; MacLure, 1955; Rossiter, 1961). Alternatively, a reading might seek to give an account of his character in which his strengths are somehow compromised by one or more personal shortcomings, so that he fails to convey to his antagonists any sense of his true value (Adelman, 1978; Berry, 1973; Cavell, 1984; Sicherman, 1972). Or his character may be depicted as containing a deeper inner contradiction of some kind, so that the virtues he possesses are themselves the cause of his undoing (Cantor, 1976; Honig, 1951; McCanles, 1967). The tension between tragic and ironic reading represents a concern with the question of Coriolanus' personal fitness to rule, the nature of his ideals, and the pattern of his motivations. Whatever specific judgements may be rendered on this question, however, all these accounts of the 'exceptional subject' rehearse the stance of civil/vocational privatism (Habermas, 1975; McCarthy, 1978). Critical intervention confines itself to an evaluation of leadership qualifications and to assessments of leadership performance. Neither the goal-values of institutions nor their organizational structure is called into question. The channeling of interpretation and criticism into controversy over highly visible individual personalities is a powerful way to sustain consensus in relation to broader issues of institutional structure and public policy.

Balanced views of *Coriolanus* are typically more concerned with Shakespeare as the source of a complex and aesthetically satisfying elaboration of conflict than they are with description of a singular character. One pattern of balance depicts the common people in light of their genuine need for subsistence over against the potential for 'greatness' embodied in Coriolanus (Cantor, 1976; Charney, 1963; Paster, 1981; Rabkin, 1967; Simmons, 1973). The tragedy lies in the failure of these two elements to achieve reconciliation. 'If he cannot help being greater than they are – and in his greatness alone – they cannot help being less. Thus, although we would not have the community die for Coriolanus, it survives diminished, starved by feeding' (Paster, 1981, 143). On this view, Coriolanus serves as the

sacrificial victim for the sake of a circumscribed communal harmony
which no doubt would have been much richer had Coriolanus himself
been able to call forth a more stable and generous collective will. But
Paster gives no account of a community's need for heroes, nor does
she explain how singular instances of greatness enhance communal
well-being or promote 'social goodness.' In fact, the 'great individual'
may be fundamentally incompatible with genuine solidarity; the
connection of towering personalities with pathological forms of social
life is certainly familiar in contemporary political experience (Suvin,
1980). In the darker version of balanced reading neither Coriolanus
nor the common people deserve any sympathy, since they represent
equally ignoble forms of narrow self-interest (Goldberg, 1983; Goldman,
1972; Kott, 1966). In every case, however, the equation of complexity
and artistic sophistication with balance entails a prior, usually implicit
distribution of values that constitutes the spectrum necessary for
discovering the balanced position (Ryan, 1982). In the variations on
the balanced position, the extremes of the spectrum turn out to be the
opposing claims of individual achievement or 'greatness' on the one
hand, and a diffuse, leveling collective will on the other. The balance
point will always take the form of a class compromise usually endorsed
only conditionally as a necessary evil. As with the civil privatism of
interpretation of Coriolanus' character, balanced readings constitute
a gesture of political renunciation. Since neither side is ever seen to
embody a plenitude of social goodness, disengagement and critical
appreciation of complexity 'beyond ideology' are to be preferred to
active participation in discursive will formation (Habermas, 1971, 1975).

In my opinion it is extremely difficult to foster and sustain an
alternative political culture within the dispensation of diffuse mass
loyalty and civil/vocational privatism (Habermas, 1975). And in the
absence of an effectively organized alternative political culture it is
difficult to see how to articulate an oppositional or subversive discourse
in the elaboration of our cultural history. Simply to say 'forbidden
things' about Shakespeare or to connect his work to an ideologically
subversive discourse remains bound up in the politically weak and
practically insignificant corporate goal-values of pluralism unless the
critique of tradition breaks out towards an active constituency (Erlich,
1986; Jameson, 1981; Mitchell, 1986; Ohmann, 1976; Rooney, 1986).
Nevertheless, I think there is some real point in rearticulating the
institution of Shakespeare as a strategic encounter with the hegemonic
cultural order. But such a rearticulation must transgress the frame
of the play itself, moving from specifically literary interpretation to
a consideration of the effective history of the Shakespearean canon.
And it must, in addition, come to terms with the political and social

foundations of critical scholarship by examining the terms of a 'post-war settlement' of institutional claims.

Although a full account of such a post-war settlement is beyond the scope of an essay of this length, a brief sketch may suggest why critical scholarship is likely to result in legitimation rather than in practically effective critique. To begin with, the agencies of national publicity – newspapers, magazines, radio and television – are powerfully oriented toward legitimation rather than critique. Thus even a debacle like Watergate may be editorially processed so that it 'proves that the system works.' In the university, on the other hand, critique is permitted, but only insofar as it is mandated by the imperatives of pluralism. Marxist or socialist opposition to the existing sociocultural order is thus limited to the status of an 'approach' or a 'point of view'; such opposition must submit to the discipline of 'objective revisionism' – in other words theory is not to be translated into a practical program (Erlich, 1986; Jameson, 1981). Universities thus remain depoliticized. The critical authority of scholarship has no direct bearing on the public sphere. Finally, the working-class movement, partly through self-policing, partly through statutory repression, renounces its own distinctive political goal-values in the form of a socialist alternative and confines its activities to struggling for a greater share in the North American standard of living. The weakening or depoliticizing of these large institutional structures has made the task of general ideological mobilization very much easier for the hegemonic sociocultural order. In the light of these massive constraints the prospect of rallying effective cultural opposition appears disheartening, to say the least. But it is only in an accurate appraisal of the tactical situation that a practically significant deployment of the possibilities of tradition can begin.

Works cited

ADELMAN, JANET (1978) ' "Anger's My Meat": Feeding, Dependency, and Aggression in Coriolanus," *Shakespeare, Pattern of Excelling Nature,* ed. Bevington, David and Halio, Jay, Newark, University of Delaware Press.

ADORNO, THEODOR (1967) 'Culture Criticism and Society,' *Prisms: Cultural Criticism and Society,* trans. Samuel and Shierry Weber, London, Verso.

ANDERSON, PERRY (1974a) *Lineages of the Absolutist State,* London, New Left Books.

—— (1974b) *Passages from Antiquity to Feudalism,* London, Verso.

BAKHTIN, MIKHAIL (1968) *Rabelais and his World,* trans. Hélène Iswolsky, Cambridge, Mass., MIT Press.

—— (1981) *The Dialogic Imagination,* trans. Michael Holquist and Caryl Emerson, Austin, University of Texas Press.

BERRY, RALPH (1973) 'Sexual Imagery in *Coriolanus,' Studies in English Literature 1500–1900,* 13, 301–16.

BRADLEY, A.C. (1912) '*Coriolanus*: British Academy Lecture 1912,' in *A Miscellany* (1929), London, Macmillan.

BRAUDEL, FERNAND (1977) *Afterthoughts on Material Civilization and Capitalism*, trans. Patricia Ranum, Baltimore, Johns Hopkins University Press.

—— (1981) *The Structure of Everyday Life: The Limits of the Possible*, trans. Sian Reynolds, New York, Harper & Row.

BRISTOL, MICHAEL D. (1985) *Carnival and Theatre: Plebeian Culture and the Structure of Authority in Renaissance England*, London and New York, Methuen.

BROWER, REUBEN (ed.) (1966) *Coriolanus* by William Shakespeare, Signet edn, New York and Scarborough, Ontario, New American Library.

BURKE, KENNETH (1966) '*Coriolanus* and the Delights of Faction,' in Burke, Kenneth, *Language as Symbolic Action*, Berkeley, University of California Press.

BURKE, PETER (1978) *Popular Culture in Early Modern Europe*, New York, New York University Press.

CANTOR, PAUL A. (1976) *Shakespeare's Rome: Republic and Empire*, Ithaca, NY, Cornell University Press.

CAVELL, STANLEY (1984) ' "Who Does the Wolf Love?" *Coriolanus* and the Interpretations of Politics,' *Shakespeare and the Question of Theory*, ed. Patricia Parker and Geoffrey Hartman, London, Methuen.

CHARNEY, MAURICE (1963) *Shakespeare's Roman Plays*, Cambridge, Mass., Harvard University Press.

DANSON, LAWRENCE, K. (1973) 'Metonymy and *Coriolanus*,' *Philological Quarterly*, 52, 30–42.

DAVIS, NATALIE Z. (1975) *Society and Culture in Early Modern France*, Stanford, Ca., Stanford University Press.

DOLLIMORE, JONATHAN (1984) *Radical Tragedy: Religion, Ideology, and Power in the Drama of Shakespeare and his Contemporaries*, Chicago, University of Chicago Press.

DOLLIMORE, JONATHAN and SINFIELD, ALAN (eds) (1985) *Political Shakespeare: New Essays in Cultural Materialism*, Manchester, Manchester University Press; Ithaca, NY, Cornell University Press.

DURKHEIM, EMILE (1935) *The Division of Labor in Society*, New York, Free Press.

ERLICH, BRUCE (1978) 'Structure, Inversion, and Game in Shakespeare's Classical World,' *Shakespeare Survey*, 31, 53–63.

—— (1986) 'Amphibolies: On the Critical Self-Contradictions of "Pluralism",' *Critical Inquiry*, 12, 521–50.

GADAMER, HANS-GEORG (1976) *Philosophical Hermeneutics*, Berkeley, University of California Press.

GIDDENS, ANTHONY (1977) *Studies in Social and Political Theory*, London, Hutchinson.

GILBERT, JAMES BURKHART (1968) *Writers and Partisans: A History of Literary Radicalism in America*, New York, John Wiley.

GOLDBERG, JONATHAN (1983) *James I and the Politics of Literature*, Baltimore, Johns Hopkins University Press.

GOLDMAN, MICHAEL (1972) *Shakespeare and the Energies of Drama*, Princeton, Princeton University Press.

GRAMSCI, ANTONIO (1957) 'The Modern Prince: Essays on the Science of Politics in the Modern Age,' in Gramsci, Antonio, *The Modern Prince and Other Writings*, trans. Louis Marks, New York, International Publishers.

GUENÉE, BERNARD (1985) *States and Rulers in Later Medieval Europe*, trans. Juliet Vale, Oxford, Basil Blackwell.

GURR, ANDREW (1975) '*Coriolanus* and the Body Politic,' *Shakespeare Survey*, 28, 63–9.

HABERMAS, JÜRGEN (1971) *Knowledge and Human Interests*, trans. Jeremy Shapiro, Boston, Beacon Press.

—— (1975) *Legitimation Crisis*, trans. Thomas McCarthy, Boston, Beacon Press.

147

—— (1979) 'Legitimation Problems in the Modern State,' in Habermas, Jürgen, *Communication and the Evolution of Society*, trans. Thomas McCarthy, Boston, Beacon Press.

—— (1985) 'Neo-Conservative Culture Criticism in the United States and West Germany: An Intellectual Movement in Two Political Cultures,' in Bernstein, Richard J. (ed.) *Habermas and Modernity*, Cambridge, Mass., MIT Press.

HALE, DAVID J. (1968) 'Intestine Sedition: The Fable of the Belly,' *Comparative Literature Studies*, 5, 377–87.

—— (1971) '*Coriolanus*: The Death of a Political Metaphor,' *Shakespeare Quarterly*, 23, 197–202.

HARRISON, J.F.C. (1984) *The Common People: A History from the Norman Conquest to the Present*, London, Flamingo.

HAWKES, TERENCE (1986) *That Shakespearian Rag: Essays on a Critical Process*, London, Methuen.

HJORT, ANNE METTE (1985) 'The Conditions of Dialogue: Approaches to the Habermas–Gadamer Debate,' *Eidos*, 4, 11–37.

HONIG, EDWIN (1951) '*Sejanus* and *Coriolanus*: A Study in Alienation,' *Modern Language Quarterly*, 12, 407–21.

IDE, RICHARD (1980) *Possessed with Greatness: The Heroic Tragedies of Chapman and Shakespeare*, London, Scolar Press.

JAMESON, FREDRIC (1981) *The Political Unconscious: Narrative as a Socially Symbolic Act*, Ithaca, NY, Cornell University Press.

JORGENSEN, PAUL A. (1956) *Shakespeare's Military World*, Berkeley, University of California Press.

KOTT, JAN (1966) *Shakespeare Our Contemporary*, trans. Boleslaw Taborski, New York, Anchor Books.

LA CAPRA, DOMINICK (1985) *Emile Durkheim: Sociologist and Philosopher*, Chicago, University of Chicago Press.

LEHMAN, ALAN D. (1952) 'The Coriolanus Story in Antiquity,' *The Classical Journal*, 47 (8), 329–36.

LE ROY LADURIE, EMMANUEL (1979) *Carnival in Romans*, trans. Mary Feeney, New York, G. Braziller.

MACCALLUM, M.W. (1967) *Shakespeare's Roman Plays, and their Background*, London, Macmillan.

MCCANLES, MICHAEL (1967) 'The Dialectic of Transcendence in *Coriolanus*,' *Publications of the Modern Language Association*, 82, 44–53.

MCCARTHY, THOMAS (1978) *The Critical Theory of Jürgen Habermas*, Cambridge, Mass., MIT Press.

MACLURE, MILLAR (1955) 'Shakespeare and the Lonely Dragon,' *University of Toronto Quarterly*, 24, 109–19.

MARX, KARL (1973) *Grundrisse: Introduction to the Critique of Political Economy*, trans. Martin Nicolaus, New York, Vintage Books; Harmondsworth, Penguin.

MITCHELL, W.J.T. (1986) 'Pluralism as Dogmatism,' *Critical Inquiry*, 12, 494–503.

MUIR, KENNETH (1952) 'Menenius' Fable,' *Notes & Queries*, 198, 240–2.

NICOLET, C. (1980) *The World of the Citizen in Republican Rome*, trans. P.S. Falla, Berkeley, University of California Press.

OHMANN, RICHARD (1976) *English in America: A Radical View of the Profession*, New York, Oxford University Press.

PASTER, GAIL KERN (1981) 'To Starve with Feeding: The City in *Coriolanus*,' *Shakespeare Studies*, 11, 135–43.

PETTET, E.C. (1950) '*Coriolanus* and the Midlands Insurrection of 1607,' *Shakespeare Survey*, 3, 34–42.

PHILLIPS, JAMES EMERSON (1940) *The State in Shakespeare's Greek and Roman Plays*, New York, Columbia University Press.

POGGI, GIANFRANCO (1972) *Images of Society: Essays on the Sociological Theories of Tocqueville, Marx, and Durkheim*, Stanford, Stanford University Press.

—— (1978) *The Development of the Modern State: A Sociological Introduction*, Stanford, Stanford University Press.

RABKIN, NORMAN (1967) *Shakespeare and the Common Understanding*, New York, Free Press.

RICHARD, JEAN CLAUDE (1978) *Les Origines de la plèbe romaine: Essai sur la formation du dualisme patricio-plébéien*, Rome, École Française de Rome.

ROONEY, ELLEN (1986) 'Who's left out? A rose by any other name is still red; or, The Politics of Pluralism,' *Critical Inquiry*, 12, 550–64.

ROSSITER, A.P. (1961) *Angel With Horns*, ed. Graham Storey, London, Longmans, Green.

RYAN, MICHAEL (1982) *Marxism and Deconstruction: A Critical Articulation*, Baltimore, Johns Hopkins University Press.

SCHMITT, CARL (1976) *The Concept of the Political*, trans. George Schwab, New Brunswick, Rutgers University Press.

SCULLARD, H.H. (1935) *A History of the Roman World From 753 to 146 B.C.*, London, Methuen.

SHARP, BUCHANAN (1980) *In Contempt of All Authority: Rural Artisans and Riots in the West of England, 1586–1660*, Berkeley, University of California Press.

SICHERMAN, CAROL (1972) '*Coriolanus*: The Failure of Words,' *English Literary History*, 39, 189–207.

SIMMONS, J.L. (1973) *Shakespeare's Pagan World: The Roman Tragedies*, Charlottesville, University Press of Virginia.

STALLYBRASS, PETER and WHITE, ALLON (1986) *The Politics and Poetics of Transgression*, London, Methuen.

STONE, LAWRENCE (1972) *The Causes of the English Revolution: 1529–1642*, New York, Harper & Row.

STRAYER, JOSEPH, R. (1970) *On the Medieval Origins of the Modern State*, Princeton, Princeton University Press.

STYAN, J.L. (1967) *Shakespeare's Stagecraft*, London, Cambridge University Press.

SUVIN, DARKO (1980) 'Brecht's *Coriolan*, or Stalinism Retracted: The City, the Hero, the City that does not need a Hero,' *Fiction and Drama in Eastern and Southeastern Europe*, Columbus, Slavica.

TAYLOR, JOHN (1630) *Iacke a Lente*, London, facsimile edn, in *The Works of John Taylor, The Water Poet*, ed. Charles Hindley (1872), London, Reeves & Turner.

THOMPSON, E.P. (1968) *The Making of the English Working Class*, Harmondsworth, Penguin.

—— (1974) 'Patrician Society, Plebeian Culture,' *Journal of Social History*, 7, 382–405.

TREGGIARI, SUSAN (1969) *Roman Freedmen During the Late Republic*, Oxford, Clarendon Press.

WALLERSTEIN, IMMANUEL (1974) *The Modern World System: Capitalist Agriculture and the Origins of the European World Economy in the Sixteenth Century*, New York, Academic Press.

WALZER, MICHAEL (1976) *The Revolution of the Saints: A Study in the Origins of Radical Politics*, New York, Atheneum.

WEBER, MAX (1947) *The Theory of Social and Economic Organization*, trans. E.M. Henderson and Talcott Parsons, ed. Talcott Parsons (1964), New York, Free Press.

WOLF, ERIC R. (1982) *Europe and the People without History*, Berkeley, University of California Press.

YAVETZ, Z. (1969) *Plebs and Princeps*, Oxford, Clarendon Press.

ZEEVELD, GORDON W. (1962) '*Coriolanus* and Jacobean Politics,' *Modern Language Review*, 57, 321–34.

10 Shakespeare and the General Strike*

TERENCE HAWKES

Where Michael Bristol closes his essay on *Coriolanus* by examining the way in which the play has been mobilised within the world of scholarship, Terry Hawkes in his essay looks at the history of other kinds of political mobilisations of the play. In particular, he examines the function of the play within the context of the General Strike in England in the mid-1920s. In taking this approach, Hawkes has much in common with Alan Sinfield in his piece on *Julius Caesar*, in that both critics stress the way in which Shakespeare is continually re-appropriated and re-deployed over the course of the twentieth century. This emphasis on the modern as well as the early modern is central to the project of cultural materialism.

Our England is a garden that is full of stately views,
Of borders, beds and shrubberies and lawns and avenues,
With statues on the terraces and peacocks strutting by;
But the Glory of the Garden lies in more than meets the eye.

(Kipling, *The Glory of the Garden*)

Criticism on strike

There is a particular statue in the centre of the city of Cardiff whose inscription has always seemed to me to offer a text suitable for the most stringent critical analysis. Its six words are pithy and pointed. 'John Cory', it says, 'Coal-Owner and Philanthropist'.

Any person memorialized in such a fashion must surely have been a connoisseur of the oxymoron. I hope that the similarly opposed polarities of the present essay's title would have appealed to him. For both texts, as befits their South Wales provenance, are rooted in coal, and the concerns of mine are apparently no less contradictory than those of his. After all, 'Shakespeare and the General Strike' links on the one hand Art (for which Shakespeare

---

*TERENCE HAWKES, *Meaning by Shakespeare* (London: Routledge, 1992), pp. 42–60.

can stand as an appropriate symbol), something that in social terms may be said to be binding, bonding, and reinforcing; and on the other hand Politics, of which industrial action, or the strike, is an apt representative. The contradiction comes about because a strike, with the abruptness that the word suggests, represents an immediate refusal, an incisive severing of the social, political and economic bonds that supposedly bind human communities together.

Any strike is always an astonishing moment in human history. Suddenly, often violently, the event reaches beyond the polite, tacitly agreed, philanthropic surface of society to lay bare what some would call its real foundations. And in its brusque refusal of some of the basic assumptions of those foundations, the strike seems almost to threaten their dissolution. The term itself proposes fundamental disruption. It offers, in miniature, what Fredric Jameson calls 'the figure for social revolution'.[1]

So the title 'Shakespeare and the General Strike' presents a contradiction of a radical kind. Art and Politics, in our culture, are not just opposites, they rank as the organizing epicentres of two quite contrary discourses. Hence the sense of an unbreachable wall separating one from the other. Hence the outcry normally raised against the very idea of any conjunction, or any common ground. To propose that such a possibility exists is almost to sanction some illicit act of transgression in which a grubby 'Politics' may be 'dragged' across a threshold to sully the otherwise sacrosanct shrine of Art. Worse, reversing the process, Shakespeare himself might even be 'dragged into politics'.

Of course, the trap of essentialism lies in wait for the unwary critic here. 'Art', it can be said, has no necessary commitment to binding, bonding, affirmation. Any work can be *read* in an oppositional mode, or to a subversive purpose. Equally, a 'strike' often generates bonding amongst its participants: it can and does develop its own kind of affiliative unity. These are important considerations. However, my focus here is on ways in which the world is experienced and understood as meaningful in terms of the 'common sense' which all cultures habitually and uncritically endorse as the basis of existence. And Art – particularly the art of Shakespeare – is certainly understood by our society on that 'common-sense' level as wholly capable of unsullied transcendence over the everyday sphere of profit margins, market forces, redundancies and wage settlements. Strikes, on the same level, are deemed to be quintessentially of that world and in it. The separation seems absolute. But the central concern of this essay is not just to confirm that this is the way things appear to be. It also – in so doing – implies a challenge to and a questioning of that arrangement. Perhaps what it calls for is a strike against common sense.

Over the top

In fact, Shakespeare presents an immediate opportunity for that and in precisely those terms. Of all his plays, *Coriolanus* seems so regularly and so provocatively to connect with political events outside the text that it immediately offers to undermine the common-sense separation with which we began. The process has a long history, dating from the play's composition. Some scholars argue that it possibly bears some imprint of the riots of 1607–8 in the Midlands.[2] The fundamental opposition it constructs between patricians and plebeians, and the involvement in that of an arrogant and charismatic military hero whose final march to sack Rome is stayed only by the pleas of his mother, suggests links with various aspects of post-Renaissance class conflict.

Certainly, by the nineteenth and early twentieth centuries the play regularly seems to chafe against the boundaries of that 'Art' category to which common sense so earnestly wants to consign it. It has been noticed above that, long before the advent of New Historicism or Cultural Materialism, the radical eighteenth-century activist John Thelwall argued that the Elizabethan theatre was 'in reality a question of politics', both in its own day and subsequently. Right-wing critics took the point. William Hazlitt's disturbing essay on *Coriolanus*, already mentioned, was roundly condemned with the rest of his Shakespearean criticism as 'seditious' in 1817 by William Gifford, the most powerful London editor of the day, because it offered an example of what Jonathan Bate calls a 'new kind of political criticism'. Bate rightly places Hazlitt and Thelwall on one side and Coleridge on the other in what amounts to an ideological tussle for ownership of the National Poet.[3]

The process continued. In Charlotte Brontë's novel *Shirley* (1849), chapter VI is entitled 'Coriolanus'. Caroline Helstone and Robert Moore read the play together in the presence of his sister Hortense, as a way of passing an evening, and as a significant stage in their courtship. They proceed to discuss it against a clear background of political and industrial unrest: that of the novel's own plot (1811–12), and that of its actual composition (1848).

Robert, a mill-owner whose new frames have been destroyed by Luddite workers, admires and sympathizes with Coriolanus, but Caroline calls that a 'vicious point': 'you sympathise with that proud patrician who does not sympathise with his famished fellow-men and insults them'. Despite this 'brotherhood in error', she persuades him that, since Coriolanus's major sin was pride 'you must not be proud to your workpeople; you must not neglect chances of soothing them, and you must not be of an inflexible nature, uttering a request as austerely as if it were a command.' 'I never wish you to lower yourself', she continues, 'but somehow, I cannot help thinking it unjust to include all poor working people under the general and insulting name of "the mob" and continually to think of them and treat them haughtily.'[4]

March on Rome

In the twentieth century, Coriolanus's disdain of the mob connects intimately with anti-democratic developments in Europe after the First World War and further deepens the play's material involvement in the politics of everyday. Between December 1933 and February 1934, a production of René Louis Piachaud's version of *Coriolanus* at the Comédie-Française, sponsored by the right-wing party Action Française, sought to present it as a Fascist denunciation of democracy and provoked riots in the streets of Paris. School editions and performances of the play along similar lines were popular in Nazi Germany throughout the 1930s and *Coriolanus* was banned by occupying American forces when they reached Berlin in 1945.[5] A famous production planned by the Berliner Ensemble in 1962/3 proposed using Brecht's unfinished adaptation of the play to present it as a denunciation of Fascism in which the working classes, educated by their tribunes, rise to overthrow their patrician oppressors.[6] The ironies of that (in the light of previous developments in East Germany, in which an actual rising against the rigidities of Communist rule had occurred) were later explored and slightly fictionalized in Günter Grass's play *The Plebeians Rehearse the Uprising* (1966) which dwells specifically – if not incisively – on the complexity of the barrier between Art and Politics and the difficulties encountered by any attempt at transgression.[7]

In short, with the opposition between Art and Politics still our central concern, the twentieth century offers a number of opportunities for a yet narrower focus on the issue, and in pursuit of it, it might be helpful now to close in on a particular day in a particular year. Since our interest is with Shakespeare on the one hand and political/industrial action on the other, the coordinates to some extent choose themselves. Let the day be 23 April, Shakespeare's Birthday. Let the year be 1926, the occasion of the General Strike, one of the major political upheavals of modern times in Britain.

And, for good measure, we can add an appropriately symbolic place: Stratford-upon-Avon, Shakespeare's Birthplace, right at the centre of England.

Of course, the period 1925 to 1926 was one of unprecedented political and social tension in Britain and it is worth trying to recall some of the details. So-called 'Red Friday', 31 July 1925, offers an appropriate point of departure. On that day, the Prime Minister, Stanley Baldwin, agreed to continue subsidizing the faltering coal-mining industry and thus to protect miners' wages. One of the reasons for what his enemies saw as a major retreat was the fear of civil strife: different political groups within the country were said to be spoiling for a fight, and in a report to the King, the Permanent Secretary to the Cabinet, Maurice Hankey, had claimed that 'Fascists numbering anything from fifty to a hundred thousand are organized for different reasons.'[8]

Fascists in Britain! The movement known as the British Fascists had been founded just two years previously, in 1923, by a young woman called Rotha Lintorn-Orman.[9] Initially known as the 'British Fascisti', they were incorporated in 1924 as a limited company, with the not overly bellicose title of 'British Fascists, Ltd.', their main object being to counter reiterated trade-union threats of industrial action by proposing schemes to 'maintain public order and guarantee essential services'.[10] The example of Mussolini was a potent one. His much-trumpeted, Coriolanus-like 'March on Rome' in 1922 had presented Fascism as the means of saving Italy from Bolshevism, and by 1926 those two terms were being used to nominate the polarities for political squaring-off in Britain at a popular level. The enrolment form for the British Fascists required an entrant to undertake to 'render every service in my power to the British Fascisti in their struggle against all treacherous and revolutionary movements now working for the destruction of the Throne and Empire', and conditions were certainly ripe for conflict at this slightly hysterical level.[11] On 2 August 1925, the Home Secretary, Sir William Joynson-Hicks, opined that 'Sooner or later this question has got to be fought out by the people of the land. Is England to be governed by Parliament and the Cabinet or by a handful of Trade Union leaders?'[12]

On 8 October 1925, at the annual conference of the Tory party at Brighton, Baldwin had promised to consider prosecuting the Communist Party. On 14 October 1925, Joynson-Hicks announced (at an evening performance of an amateur dramatic society) 'I believe that the greater part of the audience will be pleased to hear that warrants have been issued and in the majority of cases have been executed for the arrest of a certain number of notorious Communists.' There followed what one historian has called 'the first overtly political trial in England since the days of the Chartists'. Sentences of between six and twelve months imprisonment were imposed on a dozen people. By 24 October, George Lansbury, the Socialist leader, was asserting that the Communists were part of 'the indivisible movement of the working class'. Within days, more than two hundred South Wales miners were sentenced to terms of between fourteen days and twelve months for acts of violence during a strike in July.[13] No doubt, by now, even John Cory's philanthropy might have been feeling some slight strain.

Let us move into 1926. On 7 February of that year, the so-called 'Release the Prisoners Day', massive demonstrations took place throughout the country. In London a crowd of 15,000 marched to Wandsworth Prison. At the end of February, Shapurji Saklatvala, a Communist MP, presented Parliament with a petition for the prisoners' release signed by 300,000 people. And less than a month later, a meeting at the Albert Hall ('one of the biggest meetings ever held in London') rose to its feet and repeated after Lansbury the seditious slogans for which the Communists had been jailed;

> We call upon all soldiers, sailors and airmen to refuse under any circumstances to shoot down the workers of Britain, and we call upon working class men to refuse to join the capitalist army. We further call upon the police to refuse to use their batons on strikers or locked out workers during industrial disputes.[14]

On 12 February 1926, both the Miners' Federation and the Industrial Committee of the Trade Union Congress considered Walter Citrine's 'Memorandum on the Impending Crisis', which spoke of 'unmistakeable evidence of preparation for possible public disorder. The Fascisti movement is drilling and organising its forces'.[15]

It is in this atmosphere of potential civil strife, in which Bolsheviks are supposed to be squaring up to Fascists, and in which class warfare seems at long last about to burst openly upon the streets of Britain, that it becomes both proper and interesting to inspect the Shakespearean coordinates mentioned above. Within the Shakespeare Festival at Stratford, there is a central highlight: the celebration on 23 April of the Bard's Birthday, marked by a civic luncheon, various public ceremonies, and the performance in the evening of a special Birthday Play at the Shakespeare Memorial Theatre. Less than two weeks after Citrine's alarming forecast of violent public disorder, there appeared in *The Times* of 25 February 1926 a simple but slightly disturbing announcement: 'For the Birthday Play . . . the Governors of the Theatre have chosen *Coriolanus*.'

Just over a week later, on 6 March 1926, and in mysterious circumstances, the Shakespeare Memorial Theatre at Stratford was burned to the ground.

Birthday Bard

By the end of the first quarter of the twentieth century, largely as
a result of the sort of educational processes I have outlined above,
Shakespeare had undoubtedly become established as a pillar of
the existing social and political order in Britain; the linchpin of an
education and examination system which, with the academic subject
called 'English' at its centre, 'Englished' the world in a particular
political mould. There is even a well-known comic verse which records
a potent link between the study of Shakespeare, as determined by one
of his most influential academic intermediaries, and the machinery of
government accessible through the civil service examinations:

> I dreamt last night that Shakespeare's Ghost
> Sat for a civil service post.
> The English paper for that year
> Had several questions on King Lear,
> Which Shakespeare answered very badly
> Because he hadn't read his Bradley.

This appeared in *Punch* on 17 February 1926. Its author was Guy Boas
(1896–1966), Vice President of the English Association and originator
and Associate Editor (1935–65) of its journal *English*. Clearly, the flames
which, less than three weeks later, consumed the Memorial Theatre in
Stratford, also licked tentatively at a power–knowledge nexus lying at
the heart of a national, not to say imperial culture.

Charged with the awesome duty of preserving and presenting work
of such monumental design, the Shakespeare Company at Stratford
showed commendable spirit. Undaunted by the fire, it took over a
cinema, the Stratford Picture House, and continued its preparations for
the season. Then, on 12 April, on the day the Festival opened, another
bombshell exploded. The headlines of a local paper, the *Wolverhampton
Express*, give the essence of it. 'Shakespeare Dragged into Politics' they
cried. 'Inner Story of Strange Conflict'.

What the inner story revealed was that the Soviet Union had recently
requested that it should be permitted to join that large group of
nations whose flags are flown in the centre of Stratford in honour of
Shakespeare, at the Birthday celebrations. Incensed at what she was to
term a proposal for a 'profanation' of the town of the National Poet's
birth, the wife of the Vicar of Stratford, a Mrs Melville, had organized a
petition, collecting over 2,000 signatures, which demanded in vigorous
terms that the Hammer and Sickle should not in any circumstances
appear at the ceremony. The barrier between the Bard and Politics was
suddenly breached, and the noise was deafening.

The redoubtable Mrs Melville pulled no punches. And in the course
of her denunciation of the Soviet Union in the press, interesting aspects
of her began to emerge. Not only was she vocal. Not only was she
tough-minded. Not only was she (as the *Wolverhampton Express* felt
compelled to inform its readers) 'Eton Cropped', and not only did
she have strong objections to the socialist Bernard Shaw's frivolous
suggestion that the burning down of the theatre was 'very cheerful
news' (he offered to provide a list of other theatres which might,
with profit, be similarly destroyed), she was also, she announced with
pride, 'A Fascist and a Conservative'. And this said nothing of her role
as chairperson of the local branch of the right-wing and notoriously
anti-Semitic association known as the National Citizens' Union.[16]

'Will Soviet Red Flag be Unfurled?' 'Strong Attitude of Fascist
Woman' screamed the *Wolverhampton Express*. Other papers, including
The Times, were more temperate, but *The London Mercury*, edited by
Sir John Squire, whose strong admiration for Fascism and whose 'overt
championing of Mussolini' was well known, was highly approving.[17]
But few of them stressed what is perhaps most interesting from our
present point of view: Mrs Melville was also one of the governors
of the Shakespeare Theatre, and thus presumably amongst those
responsible for the choice of *Coriolanus* as the Birthday Play.

It is time to move to that occasion itself: 23 April 1926, and the
performance of the Birthday Play, on the occasion of Shakespeare's
Birthday, in Shakespeare's Birthplace. As we do so, perhaps it is worth
pausing to ponder two of the fundamental implications of that time
and that place.

First, Shakespeare's Birthday undoubtedly has a symbolic aura
by reason of its date: 23 April. This is St George's Day, the patron
saint of England. That national dimension of the Bard's beginning is
reinforced by the standard biographical assertion that he obligingly
died – no less symbolically – on the same day in 1616: 23 April.
He is thus, by calendar, neatly consecrated top and tail, entrance
and exit, to his native land in something of the same way that
other great artists find themselves fused to their countries of
origin. Louis Armstrong, for instance, always used to give as
his birthday the entirely fictitious but no less significant date of
4 July 1900.

Second, the notion of birthplace, or seat of origin, as somehow a
location of special sanctity and source, ultimately, of authority and
authenticity, is a crucial matter. The example of Bethlehem is the most
obvious of many. For if birthplaces can be said to fix, formulate and
guarantee forever, they can stand as major fortifications against flux.
They can be said to make us what we 'really' are, and to promise that
nothing ever 'really' changes. Locating Shakespeare firmly and finally

in Stratford is, like placing God in his heaven and the Queen on her throne, curiously comforting.

Against the willed permanence of these arrangements, the concrete change-making events of 23 April 1926 begin nevertheless remorselessly to lap. And the sound that insistently recurs is that of the crumbling of the barrier between Art and Politics. We can hear it most clearly if we interlace the events of the Birthday celebrations – as it were stereophonically – with those other incidents taking place in the world beyond Stratford, to which Stratford nevertheless felt itself to be speaking and of which it certainly thought itself to be representative. The major occurrences in that world were, of course, the political manoeuvrings that constituted the build-up to the by now inevitable General Strike. Sparked by the clash between coal-owners (their philanthropy for the moment distinctly in abeyance) and miners (fighting for a living wage), this finally began only ten days later, on 3 May. It lasted until 12 May. The General Strike was, it is worth recalling, the major public political demonstration of the century in Britain. Whatever the final outcome, at the time it provoked genuine fears of a Bolshevik revolution.

At 11 a.m. on 23 April, in London, Stanley Baldwin was presiding over a tense joint meeting of coal-owners and miners. In Stratford, at approximately the same time, the Birthday celebration ceremonies began. The flags of sixty-three nations (including that of the Soviet Union) were unfurled without incident. Indeed, a placatory wreath of violets, lilacs, roses and wistaria had already been received at Stratford from Soviet headquarters, and was placed on Shakespeare's tomb.[18]

There followed a public luncheon during the course of which the traditional toast to 'The Immortal Memory' of the Bard was proposed by Mr James Montgomery Beck, a former Attorney-General of the United States. Beck's right-wing politics were well known. An apostle of extreme individualism, he would later resign from one of Roosevelt's New Deal committees, aghast at what he saw as its radical tendencies. No doubt, when he told his fellow diners that 'a large body of Shakespeare's matchless verse reflected his own views on the moral problems of life', their digestive systems gurgled accord.[19]

That afternoon, in London, at 5.45 p.m., Baldwin and his Cabinet colleagues met a committee representing the coal-owners. Thomas Jones, Baldwin's Secretary, noted in his diary the 'contrast between the reception which Ministers give to a body of owners and a body of miners. Ministers are at ease at once with the former, they are friends jointly exploring a situation.' Somewhat taken aback, he asks whether it would be 'better to precipitate a strike or the unemployment which would result from continuing the present terms.'[20] At 7.15 p.m., Baldwin went to dinner – perhaps, on this evidence, having almost colluded in a decision to precipitate the strike. At roughly the same moment in Stratford, 'a company of mutinous Citizens, with staves, clubs, and other weapons' ran on to the stage of the Picture House. *Coriolanus* had begun.

Enter 'Shakespeare'

The *Morning Post* review of the next day (24 April) was characteristic of many responses in being oddly lame. Perhaps dissolution of the barrier between Art and Politics scarcely warrants the salute of a bang. What it certainly received was a cautious whimper: 'a play of arguments . . .' the reviewer pronounced, 'that in many ways seem strangely up to date'.

Coriolanus of course has its own 'political unconscious', and perhaps bears the marks of the social tensions surrounding its origins in 1607/8. In 1926, other pressures were certainly at work and the very choice of the play – perhaps the first move in an attempt, putting it baldly, to leap the Art–Politics divide and to hijack Shakespeare for a right-wing cause – could not help but make it seem 'strangely up to date'. But for it to function as the ideological weapon its promoters presumably wanted, then in the name of integrity and coherence specific aspects of its text would, in the event, have to be foregrounded at the expense of others.

For the text plunges us immediately into an arena where choices are urgently required: with concrete political confrontation occurring at street level, it has an urgency to match anything on offer outside the theatre. Uniquely amongst plays of the period, *Coriolanus* opens with a scene of public violence: the entry of that 'company of mutinous Citizens, with staves, clubs and other weapons'. This ever-present physical challenge to and questioning of the ties which bind a society together ironically undercuts all of its subsequent expositions of 'organic' theories of society, such as the fable of the belly presented by Menenius (I, i, 95ff.).

In short, there is no doubt that the play's central concern is the political one raised on the streets both in 1607 and in 1926: can mutually exclusive class interests ever be appeased? These political dimensions are reinforced by the central spectacle the play consistently presents of a figure who, contemptuous of society's demands, tries to 'opt out', to rise above it: one who himself undermines the co-operative imperatives of the fable of the belly by his habit of insulting his fellow organs and threatening to 'Hang 'em' (I, i, 180–204).

159

Caius Martius's concerted efforts to distinguish and separate himself from his society are marked not just by his use of such terms of strong rejection. The very feat on which his fame rests sees him entering the city of Corioles on his own, as a single morsel thrown in 'to the pot' (I, iv, 47) and being locked in there 'himself alone / To answer all the city' (ll. 50–1). And this singularity receives a confirming rhythmic stress throughout. His followers are urged 'alone' to follow him, to cry 'O me alone! Make you a sword of me!' (I, vi, 73–6). His reminder, 'Alone I fought in your Corioles walls' (I, viii, 8) is regularly taken up by others, 'alone he enter'd / The mortal gate of the city', 'aidless came off' (II, ii, 110–14) and on his return to Rome, that city is urged to 'Know Rome, that all alone Martius did fight' (II, i, 161). Faced with his greatest challenge, when his mother comes to plead with him finally to spare Rome, he reminds us in resonant terms of his continuing project: to stand at last absolutely alone, 'As if a man were author of himself / And knew no other kin' (V, iii, 36–7). The power of this validation of unique, personal identity, this sense of ultimately being true to an inner, self-authenticating subjectivity, finally enables Coriolanus to override the banishment to which Rome harshly subjects him. In the end, it fuels an astonishing conceptual reversal which completes the self-authoring, and decisively cuts him off from any contact with society:

> You common cry of curs! whose breath I hate
> As reek o' th' rotten fens, whose loves I prize
> As the dead carcasses of unburied men
> That do corrupt my air: I banish you!
>
> (III, iii, 120–3)

Absolute, even heroic, self-commitment in the face of a contemptible world in this manner, assertion of the individual solitary will as the ultimate and only valid instrument of power and morality, has of course been a feature of a range of political stances in Europe since the early modern period and is probably specifically linked with the thinking of Nietzsche. It readily produces the sort of creature described by J.P. Stern:

> The Will – not the common will of a body politic but *his* individual solitary will, mythologized to a heroic dimension – is his instrument. He is a maker of his kingdom: the powerful embattled personality . . . imposes its demands upon the world and attempts to fashion the world in its own image . . . His acts are judged according to a criterion of immanent, inward coherence: that is, according to the degree to which a man's utterances and actions express his total personality and indicate his capacity for experience.[21]

Stern is describing here not the character of Coriolanus, but the ideological seedbed from which sprang the phenomenon of Hitler. He proposes the German word *Erlebnis*, which refers to living experience, inner authentic conviction (*inneres Erlebnis*) to suggest the sense of that 'immanent inward coherence' on which such terrifying power rests. Coriolanus evidently possesses and glories in *Erlebnis* of this sort in ample measure. His celebration of it reaches its climax with his magnificent reminder to Aufidius of the distinctive basis of his fame. It lies precisely in what Hitler used to call *Front Erlebnis*, the personal, authentic, living experience of battle, crystallized in the moment when

> like an eagle in a dovecote, I
> Flutter'd your Volscians in Corioles.
> Alone I did it.
>
> (V, vi, 114–16)

'Alone I did it.' Words, no doubt, to gladden Mrs Melville's heart. Of course, the temptation to hear in this ultimate distillation of Coriolanus's megalomania the faintest striking of a political and psychological note whose furthest pitch sounds in the very title of Hitler's *Mein Kampf* should obviously be resisted. Nevertheless, as we have seen, the rise of Fascism in Germany during the period immediately preceding the General Strike in Britain certainly informed the political atmosphere in which that event took place. It even happens that the second and final volume of *Mein Kampf* was published in 1926.

Yet to present *Coriolanus*, chosen as the 1926 Birthday Play, as a validation, even a justification of this sort of lone, self-endorsing independence, to draw out the assertion of single subjectivity and unique heroic individualism in the face of the contemptible masses as its essence and its 'message' – as one kind of right-wing reading surely must – it is necessary at the same time to suppress other dimensions of the text. And, in fact, a contradictory case can easily be discerned, deployed no less forcefully in the play, which questions whether true independence is ever possible and suggests to the contrary that human beings are inescapably involved in mutuality and defined by reciprocity.

Coriolanus may, as his nomenclature allows, virtually become a city, but so after all do the plebeians. 'What is the city but the people?' says the Tribune Sicinius. 'The people are the city', they answer (III, i, 197–9). In effect, the apparent polarity 'Individual – Society' is constantly undercut (even deconstructed) in the play in a kind of counter-rhythm which syncopates with the assertions of 'alone'-ness and singularity. Gradually, the process expands to undermine a wide range of the oppositions on which Coriolanus's view of the world depends. Once Antium's enemy, he finds himself entering that city offering friendship, and saying 'O world, thy slippery turns . . . / My birthplace hate I, and my love's upon / This enemy town' (IV, iv, 13–24). In this text, 'slippery turns' predominate and finally characterize: everything seems capable of turning into its opposite. This is true both sexually (IV, v, 115–19) when Aufidius seems to love Coriolanus like a woman and when 'Our general himself makes a mistress of him' (IV, v, 199ff.: see also I, vi, 29–32) and socially when Coriolanus, perceived by servants as a beggar, turns into a hero in front of their eyes to the cry of 'Here's a strange alteration!' (IV, v, 149). By the end of the play, when we see the spectacle of 'patient fools, / Whose children he hath slain . . . giving him glory' (V, vi, 52–4) we realize that 'strange alteration' pinpoints the existential mode of someone who has finally been both a hero and a traitor on each side in the same war.

In short, Coriolanus can never finally be 'alone', or be the 'author of himself', because the very concepts at stake can only be generated in and be relevant to a society which must be presupposed. To mount the classic deconstructive argument, the opposition 'Individual–Society' has no validity. Only within the social structure, and conceived in its terms as its opposite, can 'alone' be meaningful. The very idea of individual subjectivity requires a society to validate it. And that requirement brings with it a commitment to language and thus to interlocution. To speak at all involves dialogue, the very condition of society. Nobody can speak meaningfully in a vacuum, because meanings are dialogically and socially – that is, politically – constructed. As a result, and as the play's 'slippery turns' and 'strange alterations' indicate, they are by no means fixed or permanent. What *Coriolanus* shows above all is that, lying at the heart of social structures and thus of politics, meaning is constantly in dispute, under discussion, and the battle for it is never-ending. Indeed, politics is to a large degree the name we give to that battle.

Of course, any 'reading' of a text can only be achieved by a suppression of the pluralities of which all texts are composed. That is how texts, and indeed languages, work. But there is a sense in which this latent plurality is exactly what *Coriolanus* finally makes overt. As a result, every attempt simply to shackle the play to a specific party-political position must run into crucial difficulties; something which Brecht discovered and which Günter Grass makes the subject of his own critique. Party-politics will always seek coherence. Yet few texts manage so blatantly as *Coriolanus* to promote those aspects of themselves that any coherent reading will try to suppress in order to establish its validity. The play doesn't simply focus on political struggle, it embodies political struggle. It isn't that it can be 'read' in a number of ways. It is that it can't be coherently read in any single way. And with this in mind, it's worth looking again at Caius Martius's magnificent assertion of his singularity, of his personal *Erlebnis*: his reminder that

> like an eagle in a dovecote, I
> Flutter'd your Volscians in Corioles.
> Alone I did it.

(V, vi, 114–16)

Now, 'flutter'd' certainly seems to characterize the action of the heroic embattled individualist. An individual eagle pitted against a society of complacent doves, Coriolanus relentlessly harries them in the name of their enemy, just as he had proposed to do in the case of Rome. Yet the fact is that 'flutter'd' – to some degree the semantic fulcrum of this reading of the play – is a late emendation to the text which first appears in the Third Folio. The First Folio text of the play has 'flatter'd'.

However much ingenuity may be expended on justifying this emendation (almost universally adopted in modern editions), certain aspects of the situation are immediately clear. 'Flatter'd' makes perfect sense and needs no emendation if we accept the arguments made just now about Coriolanus's actual relation to his enemies and to society at large. The word suggests a much more complex interactive engagement with the Volscians than the imperiously dismissive 'flutter'd'. It implies comparison, evaluation and negotiation (the eagle's pre-emptive ferocity hinting at an unrealized potential in the doves) and thus a considerable degree of societal awareness and involvement. In short, it bespeaks a kind of baffled reciprocity and it acknowledges a degree of impotent mutuality, even whilst it manifests the wholesale hostility to which Coriolanus is undoubtedly committed. In this sense, 'flatter'd' is not simply different from 'flutter'd', it offers a completely opposed dimension of meaning. To refuse that dimension is deliberately to choose to impose a single and specific reading on the indeterminacy and multiplicity fostered by the First Folio text. The most obvious effect of replacing 'flatter'd' by 'flutter'd' is strongly to promote an uncomplicated sense of Coriolanus as unique individual pitted alone against society. Coriolanus the individualist, the single subject, the author of himself, would certainly 'flutter' the Volscians. But to 'flatter' them subtly undercuts and questions that role. In a play in which that kind of 'flattering' relationship is made an issue throughout, there is a sense in which the heart of the text lies here.

Some statistics may therefore be relevant. A glance at a *Concordance* reveals that the word 'flatter'd' (or 'flattered') appears fifteen times in Shakespeare's plays. Various forms of the verb 'to flatter' appear forty-seven times (seven of them in *Coriolanus*), together with a number of derivations such as 'flatterer', 'flatteries', 'flattery', etc. In *Coriolanus* the count for all the words in this category is as follows: 'flatter', 7; 'flatter'd' 1; 'flatterers', 2; 'flattery', 2. On the other hand, the word 'flutter'd' appears only once in the entire Shakespearean canon: here. There are no other occurrences of the word or its derivatives in any form, whether as noun, verb, adjective or anything else: no 'flutter', no 'flutter'd', no 'fluttering', no 'flutterers'.

What, then, are we to make of the decision of editors to replace 'flatter'd' by 'flutter'd'? The editor of the Arden edition of the play, for example, announces directly that the 'ambiguity' of 'flatter'd' strikes him as 'startling' and that he has changed it to 'flutter'd' in order 'to avoid eccentricity'.[22] This, of a play in which flattery, its complexities and its political and moral dimensions, is obviously a major consideration! Of course, any attempt to appropriate the text must appropriate this moment above all, and must do so by containing its ambiguity. Given this, the emendation of 'flatter'd' to 'flutter'd' perhaps begins to seem slightly less than innocent and even to hint at a tiny, occluded political dimension.

Conservative or right-wing readings of the play seem rooted in the nineteenth century where interpretations of it formed part of the 'struggle for possession of the national poet' mentioned by Jonathan Bate. In the middle of that century, it was the actor Samuel Phelps who drained the lines of all duplicity and famously nailed the text down to a single meaning at this point by means of a reinforcing and deliberately delimiting gesture which Godfrey Turner describes as follows:

> A fine action of Phelps's accompanied his utterance of the word 'fluttered', which came after a seemingly enforced pause, and with that lifted emphasis and natural break in his voice, remembered, I dare say, by all who admired him in his prime. Lifting his arm to its full outstretched height above his head, he shook his hand to and fro, as in the act of startling a flock of doves.[23]

Let me be briefly outrageous. Let me suggest that Phelps's kinesic reinforcement of – indeed insistence upon – what for Shakespeare would at best be a nonce-word, 'flutter'd', represents a crucial moment of containment and enlistment. In it, the play is finally and irrevocably recruited to a conservative project in which the claims of single subjectivity are asserted against the collective demands of the state. It is not insignificant that Phelps's performance was first given in 1848, the year in which Charlotte Brontë wrote *Shirley* and, of course, the year of European revolutions. You might even say – as the faint echo of *Mein Kampf* drifts scandalously in and out of earshot – that the arm lifted in that vengeful salute has more than once found chilling echoes in the choreography of right-wing politics in our own century.

Yet, to retreat from the outrageous to its opposite in the English Midlands, how can we account for the apparent lameness of the response to the play's production in the charged atmosphere of Stratford in 1926? What is it that subverts – let us be bold – Mrs Melville's attempt to hijack it for the Fascist cause? Can it really be the case that, despite what we now know about events surrounding the Birthday celebrations, the machinations of Baldwin, the miners' leaders, the coal-owners, the theatre itself in flames, that the play's ultimate plurality finally drains away all its political force and leaves us just with – well, just with 'Shakespeare'?

For drain away it apparently did. On 7 May, two weeks after the Birthday Play had opened, and had entered the season's repertory, with the General Strike by now in full swing, angry crowds in the streets of large cities, volunteers driving buses and trains, food shortages, and provocative troop movements, the *Stratford-upon-Avon Herald* delivered itself of an editorial comment on the subject of the Shakespeare Festival and the Strike, in which its view of the barrier between Politics and Art, so precariously at stake in all the events of that Stratford spring, is nothing if not clear: 'It would be no bad thing', it fulminates, 'if the strikers themselves were brought in relays to see some of the Shakespearean productions.' The experience, it urges, 'might induce them to look beyond the paltry advantage of the moment and hitch their wagons to something more substantial than the will-o-the-wisp which is at the moment leading the country to irreparable ruin.'

You ain't heard nothing yet

No doubt the *Stratford-upon-Avon Herald* spoke for England. But perhaps it is mistaken to assume that its dismissal of the 'will-o-the-wisp' of the General Strike and its recommended embrace of the 'more substantial' figure of Shakespeare constitutes, in the rather overheated atmosphere of the times, a bluff, good-hearted British rejection of Politics in favour of Art. Indeed, in its determined re-erection of the barrier dividing them, its own politics are perfectly clear. There are, after all, no such things as straightforward 'Shakespearean productions' in our society. Quite the reverse: a distinct political option exists which the invocation of 'Shakespeare' both commends and promotes. By and large it involves tradition, individualism, patriotism and permanence, all the ingredients of Mr Beck's Birthday luncheon speech dedicated to the 'Immortal Memory'. And it is far more powerful, seductive and acceptable than the politics any mere right-wing reading of *Coriolanus* could command. The medium, in this case, is certainly the message, and the essence of what might be called the 'Shakespeare Effect' lies in the more subtle, but also chilling principle that, whatever his plays say, 'Shakespearean productions' are always good for us. Their simple presence – like that of the Bard in Stratford – is enough.

Thus, the notion of *Coriolanus* as in itself a 'political' play is something of a nonsense. Of course, its overt 'subject' is politics. But a more genuinely disturbing prospect is the possibility that *all* Shakespeare's plays in our society have a political function, regardless of what their 'subjects' may be. In any case, we can never know what the exact response of the Stratford audiences to the production of *Coriolanus* in 1926 actually was. For instance, it could be said that, since *Coriolanus* is a play, it must in the end affirm the priority of society, in the very presupposition its nature makes manifest of a theatre in which and an audience before which it is performed. To the extent that it shows the assertion of individualism on the stage in front of an audience, it may enact the paradox which it explores, but it finally functions as an instrument of social cohesion.

But, and here a more complex dimension of the events of 1926 perhaps unexpectedly emerges, we should also remember that this particular Shakespearean production did not take place in a theatre at all. In fact, a deep-seated irony invests its actual venue and maybe the truly political dimension of the affair lies there. Hindsight – history's poor relation – tells us that the cinema is in many ways the theatre's opposite, and that it was also then to some extent its future. We might go even further and see in the advent of the cinema the perceptual and psychological outcrop of a material social revolution, unnoticed by Fascist and Bolshevik alike: the darkened auditorium and its lighted silver screen appropriate symbols for our modern society's growing paradoxical commitment to the sanctity of the inner – indeed the unconscious – life of the individual. It is not insignificant that by 1926 the expanding popularity of the medium meant that the Stratford Picture House offered the only hall large and central enough in the town for the production of *Coriolanus*.

A modern audience, committed to the cinematic mode, might well seek and find the fulcrum of that play in a moment which flatters (rather than flutters) its own preconceptions: the moment when, at the end of his mother's impassioned speech imploring him to desist from his intentions of sacking Rome, Coriolanus silently reaches for her hand, begins to weep, and then finally and famously capitulates to her wishes. In 1926, the Stratford Picture House was surely capable of lending those gestures a heightening cinematic quality. This is individualism in full cry, as it were, and the words 'O mother, mother! / What have you done?' (V, iii, 183–4) are surely the most suitable of all of Shakespeare's lines to appear as a caption on the silent screen, apparently offering insight into and validation of the purely individual dimensions of their utterer's agonized soul.

But if that remains a moment worthy only of D.W. Griffith, hindsight offers the further suggestion that the manipulative use of Art for political purposes was then only, in the massive terms in which we have since experienced it, in its infancy. The production of *Coriolanus* in Stratford, in 1926, in that cinema, designed though it undoubtedly was to link with the glorious past, was surely in effect also being propelled willy-nilly towards the inglorious future by a technological wind of change of which it knew little. But *we* know that within twelve months of that 1926 production, a series of frantic experiments that were taking place in Hollywood, California, finally bore fruit. And we can be fairly sure that the spectacle of another errant protagonist, kneeling at his mother's feet – indeed with an American version of 'O mother, mother!' on his lips – would shortly be able to yoke its audience, far more firmly than any Shakespearean productions could, to a set of comfortable stereotypes by which their political aspirations might be even more safely contained.

Notes

1. Frederic Jameson, *The Political Unconscious: Narrative as a Socially Symbolic Act*, London, Routledge, 1981, p. 193.

2. See *Coriolanus*, ed. Philip Brockbank (Arden edn), London, Routledge, 1976, p. 26.

3. See Jonathan Bate, *Shakespearean Constitutions: Politics, Theatre, Criticism 1730–1830*, Oxford, Clarendon Press, 1989, pp. 160–78.

4. Charlotte Brontë, *Shirley*, London, Dent, Everyman's Library, 1955 (first pub. 1849), pp. 70–2.

5. See Oscar James Campbell and Edward G, Quinn (eds), *The Reader's Encyclopedia of Shakespeare*, New York, Crowell, 1966, pp. 146–7. Also *Coriolanus*, op. cit., pp. 84–6.

6. See Bertolt Brecht, 'A study of the first scene of Shakespeare's *Coriolanus*', in *Brecht on Theatre*, trans. and ed. John Willett, London, Methuen, 1964, pp. 252–65.

7. See Günter Grass, *The Plebeians Rehearse the Uprising: A German Tragedy*, trans. Ralph Mannheim (with an introductory address by the author), London, Secker & Warburg, 1967.

8. Christopher Farman, *The General Strike*, 2nd edn, London, Panther Books, 1974 (first pub. 1972), p. 42.

9. See Richard Griffiths, *Fellow Travellers of the Right*, London, Constable, 1980, pp. 85–6.

10. ibid., p. 86.

11. ibid.

12. Farman, op. cit., p. 46.

13. ibid., pp. 54–6.

14. ibid., p. 81.

15. ibid., p. 72.

16. See Griffiths, op. cit., pp. 354–5.

17. ibid., p. 24. See also *The London Mercury*, May 1926, pp. 1–2.

18. *The Times*, 23 April 1926, p. 12.

19. *The Times*, 24 April 1926, p. 10.

20. See Thomas Jones, *Whitehall Diary*, vol. II, ed. Keith Middlemass, Oxford, Oxford University Press, 1969, pp. 18–19.

21. See J.P. Stern, *Hitler: the Führer and the People*, London, Fontana, 1975, pp. 43–4.

22. See *Coriolanus*, op. cit., pp. 8, 308.

23. ibid., p. 82.

11 *Cymbeline*: Beyond Rome*

PAUL A. CANTOR

As indicated in our introduction, this piece by Paul Cantor, like the
work of Derek Traversi, serves to provide a contrast with the more
radical work included in this anthology. Cantor's book, though
published in 1976, exemplifies significant continuities with Traversi's
approach, and demonstrates a particularly respectful allegiance to
earlier authorities – such as G. Wilson Knight – who are usually
treated oppositionally by contemporary critics. At the same time,
Cantor's less historicist and more formalistic perspective enables
him to recognise *Cymbeline* as a 'Roman' play, and to explore, in
a play usually extrapolated out of history into 'late romance', the
ways in which genre interacts with historical form.

Generally regarded as a tragicomedy or romance (each genre
defined differently by different critics) and studied in the context
of Shakespeare's last plays, *Cymbeline* has attracted little attention
as Shakespeare's final Roman work.[1] Tacitly most assume that the
incarnation of Rome in *Cymbeline* is insignificant next to that in *Lucrece,
Titus Andronicus*, and the Plutarchan tragedies. After all, the titular
figure is a British king ruling in Britain, and Rome is merely the
other place in opposition, domain of an Emperor we never see and
of characters who seem more like Renaissance Italians than classical
Romans. The play affords only the briefest glimpse of the ancient city,
that strangely unmoored scene (III.vii) in which the senators serve
the tribunes a commission to levy soldiers for the upcoming war.
The Capitol is mentioned only once in a blatant lie (I.vi.106), and no
other familiar landmarks create atmosphere or establish place. Physical
detail is kept to a minimum, and only one character, Caius Lucius,
embodies anything like the stalwart *Romanitas* we observe in *Lucrece,
Titus*, Brutus, Antony, Caesar, and Coriolanus. The seriousness of
Shakespeare's previous Roman efforts, resulting from an abiding

---

*PAUL A. CANTOR, *Shakespeare's Rome: Republic and Empire* (Ithaca, NY: Cornell
Univ. Press, 1976), pp. 206–35.

interest in character and politics, here yields to a cavalier nonchalance that tolerates inconsistencies, eschews political analysis, and trumpets its own artifices.[2] *Cymbeline*'s liberal mixing of incompatible characters, plots, themes, conventions, and styles has largely disqualified it as successor to the masterful *Antony and Cleopatra* and the carefully wrought *Coriolanus*.

Yet, Rome is undeniably present in *Cymbeline*. The city is a major locality in the play, and its historical skirmishes with Britain make up a good part of the action. What is more, *Cymbeline* incorporates and transforms (sometimes almost beyond recognition) many of the scenes, characters, images, and allusions from previous Roman works. By so doing, the play dramatizes the liberation of Britain from Roman domination, from the hazy past of Sicilius's Roman service, Cymbeline's knighting by Caesar, Caesar's invasion, and Cassibelan's promise of tribute. It celebrates an assertion of British independence as well as the creation of a new alliance with Rome, one in which Britain will be ascendant.[3]

The Roman elements in *Cymbeline* color the entire play and appear unexpectedly at various places. Analysis of these elements illuminates the drama and, in addition, reveals the conclusion of Shakespeare's Roman vision. *Cymbeline* demonstrates that Britons can meet Romans on Roman terms – on the battlefield. The play acknowledges the grandeur that was Rome, but suggests that such grandeur is past, superseded by that of a young nation, awakening to its strength and potential. In some ways Britons live like Romans, but in some ways they are quite different. In the best of them Roman pride is balanced by humility, Roman courage by the qualities of mercy and forgiveness, Roman constancy by a capacity for flexibility, growth, and change.

The play opens with a curious mixture of elements – comic and tragic, Roman and non-Roman. As often in Shakespearean comedy, an angry father blights his daughter's budding romance by separating her from her beloved and by championing the suit of another. Cymbeline, however, is no mere *senex iratus*, but the king of Britain. His actions create in himself and the court a potentially tragic rift between form and feeling, between external appearance and internal reality. Though outwardly he shows only grief and rage, he still loves and pities Imogen: He is 'touch'd at very heart' (I.i.10), as the First Gentleman puts it. Though outwardly the courtiers follow the king and frown, all are really 'glad at the thing they scowl at' (15). This early emphasis on heart mysteries, implicit as well in the story of Imogen's secret marriage to Posthumus, is proleptic. *Cymbeline* will attempt to explore these mysteries as it reconciles internal feeling with external form by transforming both.

Various Roman analogs underlie the situation in the British court and greatly sharpen its tragic potential. Recently, David M. Bergeron has discussed the ways in which Roman history influences Shakespeare's conception of British characters in this play.[4] He notes the parallels between Augustus and Cymbeline, both lacking male heirs and angry with their daughters; between Posthumus and Agrippa, both possessed of two older brothers, both banished, and both ultimately reconciled with the king; between Posthumus and Germanicus, two valorous men who are respected by the people. Cloten, he observes, has much in common with Tiberius, the lusty, vengeful, and cruel stepson to the ruler. And the Queen resembles remarkably the infamous Livia – ambitious, cruel, and dissimulating dealer in poisons.

[. . .]

The First Gentleman's account of the Leonatus genealogy strikes other familiar Roman notes. We hear the Latinate names, Sicilius, Tenantius, and Leonatus, the last an agnomen like 'Coriolanus.' The name 'Posthumus' obviously derives from unhappy circumstances of birth, but it may owe something as well to Raphael Holinshed's mention of Posthumus, son of the first Roman, Aeneas, and Lavinia.[5] There is also here the characteristically Roman emphasis on fame achieved by military exploits, on 'honor' (29), 'titles' (31), 'glory and admir'd success' (32).

Like many of Shakespeare's Romans, Posthumus is heir to a tradition of honor and military excellence. Demonstrating his mettle early, he confronts Cloten and advances 'forward still' (I.ii.15) toward the enemy's face. Imogen refers to Posthumus as an 'eagle' (I.i.139), a metaphor here as in *Coriolanus* associated with the Roman eagle, symbol of the city's strength, courage, and superiority. Confident in Posthumus's marital skill and courage, Imogen wishes that he and Cloten could fight it out in 'Afric' (I.i.166–9). Volumnia, of course, expresses similar confidence in Coriolanus against the tribunes: 'I would my son / Were in Arabia, and thy tribe before him, / His good sword in his hand' (IV.ii.23–5).

As parts of a larger, more complex whole, Roman elements in *Cymbeline* appear with a difference: they are continually balanced and modified by non-Roman elements. Although Sicilius certainly lives like a Roman patriarch, he dies in a distinctly non-Roman manner. After his sons died 'with their swords in hand . . . their father, / Then old and fond of issue, took such sorrow / That he quit being' (I.i.36–8). Sicilius's response to the death of his sons pointedly contrasts with the response of a Roman parent such as Titus, who proudly contemplates his sons' honorable burial. Valuing his sons' lives as much as their honor, Sicilius

Anglicizes Roman *pietas*. This transformed virtue manifests itself throughout the play, often in the form of intuitive and powerful familial sympathy.

Son of such a father and a 'gentle' mother (38) (unlike Volumnia), Posthumus has a non-Roman capacity for romantic affection. We first encounter him many fathoms deep in love with Imogen. Their tender parting differs sharply from the leave-takings of Brutus and Portia, Caesar and Calphurnia, Coriolanus and Virgilia, wherein the men sternly subordinate private emotion to public duty. Nor does Posthumus recall here Bassianus or Antony, who valiantly assert their right to love with their swords. Instead, he appears a Lysander or Romeo – naive, innocent, fervent, amorous, fallible, and young. What Shakespearean Roman could emphatically declare that the exchange of his 'poor self' for his beloved works to her 'so infinite loss' (I.i.119–20)?

When in Rome Posthumus appears as a Roman and does as Romans do. At Philario's house, the Frenchman describes him as an eagle, as one who can behold the sun with firm eyes (I.iv.12). Before refusing to 'story him' further (33), Philario remembers serving with Posthumus's father, Sicilius, when Britons and Romans fought side by side. After Posthumus enters, he defends the honor of his lady against Iachimo's verbal attacks.

[. . .]

Superbly paced and dramatically exciting, the wager scene is very complex. The force of literary tradition works to exonerate Posthumus for his part, suggesting that he is a perfect lover and gentleman.[6] According to the conventions of chivalry and medieval romance, Posthumus is a knight who champions his lady's virtue. And yet, Shakespeare does not rest content with received traditions. As Homer Swander argues, Shakespeare's treatment of the traditional wager story puts Posthumus in a bad light.[7] The unique recollection of a past quarrel makes his praise of Imogen seem arrogantly proud, his defense of her chastity contentiously aggressive, especially as he promises to make Iachimo answer with 'sword' (163). Shakespeare also adds to the typical wager scene the common sense of Philario, who opposes the bet and tries to stop it. Like Enobarbus, Philario functions to point up the folly of Roman boasting and self-assertion. We note that the words 'honor' and 'constancy,' evoking two central Roman virtues in Shakespeare's conception, and sound throughout the scene. As Imogen's ring becomes part of the wager, Posthumus vows:

If you
make your voyage upon her and give me directly to
understand you have prevail'd, I am no further your
enemy; she is not worth our debate.

(157–60)

How unlike the perfervid lover a few scenes earlier! Posthumus's
inconsistency of character is precisely the problem he must work out in
the play. From the disparate parts of his personality he must learn to
forge a new, well-integrated identity. In other words, he must learn to
reconcile his British heart with his Roman arms.

[. . .]

Both Iachimo's and Cloten's amatory sieges of Imogen, who is
described by G. Wilson Knight as 'Britain's soul-integrity,'[8] are parallel
to the military siege and invasion of Britain. In the background of this
threat looms the past invasion of Britain by Julius Caesar, a Roman
victory that Shakespeare in this play takes pains to diminish and
finally expunge. The conversation between Philario and Posthumus in
Act II, Scene iv prepares the audience for the confrontation between
Cymbeline and Caius Lucius in Act III, Scene i. Philario predicts that
Cymbeline will concede the tribute because remembrance of Roman
conquest is 'yet fresh' in British grief (14). Posthumus disagrees,
asserting that 'not-fearing Britain' (19) will make known 'to their
approvers they are people such / That mend upon the world' (25–6).

The conflict between the past tyranny of Rome and the present
struggle of the British for a new future receives fuller articulation in
Act III, Scene i. Caius Lucius begins by invoking the talismanic name
of Julius Caesar, 'whose remembrance yet / Lives in men's eyes, and
will to ears and tongues / Be theme and hearing ever' (2–4). Here
Lucius pithily enunciates the familiar Roman view of history, of the
past that Caesar rules and that originates all present and future action.
The Britons directly confront and contradict this view of history by
supplying their own version of the 'kind of conquest / Caesar made'
(22–3). According to the Queen, Caesar suffered two shameful defeats
at British hands and had his ships cracked 'like egg-shells' (28) on
British rocks. Were it not for 'giglet Fortune' (31), Cassibelan, who
made London bright with rejoicing and filled Britons with pride, would
have mastered Caesar's sword. The great conqueror was merely a lucky
mortal, one, as Cloten reminds us, with a crooked nose.

That the Britons write their own past up as they write the Roman
past down is hardly surprising.[9] Revisionist history always
accompanies revolution. And like most revolutions, Britain's assertion
of independence from Roman domination excites and perplexes

onlookers. At a loss to reconcile the Queen's and Cloten's nationalism
in Act III, Scene i with the later reunion with Rome, many have judged
their outbursts to be self-serving, part of a dishonorable scheme to gain
power. According to this view, Jacobean audiences would not have
cheered the patriotic sentiments expressed on stage, but instead would
have perceived iniquity in the speakers and loathsome uxoriousness
in the king.[10] But surely this reading expands some difficulties and
introduces many new ones. Cymbeline's refusal to pay tribute (46–61)
shows firmness and courtesy, qualities not likely to alienate an
audience or indicate moral turpitude. Moreover, the claims for Cloten's
patriotism are exaggerated. Boorishly, Cloten insults the dignified
Lucius by repeating the puerile joke about Italian noses (14, 37). He
interrupts his mother (34–8), and in pointed contrast to Cymbeline,
dismisses Lucius with a jeering threat: 'If you fall in the adventure, our
crows shall fare the / better for you; and there's an end' (81–2). Finally,
this reading of the scene ignores the connection between the imminent
Roman siege and the amatory ones. Because the emphasis of the play
is on the wager plot, the Roman invasion appears as a reflection of
Iachimo's, as another example of Roman pride and arrogance. In both
invasions we witness Roman self-assertion, manifested variously in the
attempt at military domination and in the degenerate modern Italian try
at amorous conquest.

The scene of British defiance is crucial to the play as it outlines the
ambivalences in Britain's relationship with Rome. Clearly, Britain is
proper heir to Roman civilization and values. Cymbeline says:

> Thou art welcome, Caius.
> Thy Caesar knighted me; my youth I spent
> Much under him; of him I gather'd honor.
>
> (68–70)

And yet, it is equally clear, the time has come for Britain to declare its
independence of Rome and Roman values. The play depicts Britain's
struggle to come into its own as a strong but gentle nation, seasoned
with courtesy, humanity, and a respect for the human heart.

Imogen's journey to 'Blessed Milford' removes her from the potentially
tragic British court to what Alvin Kernan calls the 'second place' of
Shakespearean drama, a natural spot of imagination and
transformation.[11]

[. . .]

Faced with Pisanio's letter from Posthumus and with death, Imogen
initially acts the part of Lucrece. Like the chaste Roman matron, she
invokes the tale of Troy as an analog to her own desperate situation:

True honest men being heard, like false Aeneas,
Were in his time thought false; and Sinon's weeping
Did scandal many a holy tear.

(III.iv.58–60)

[. . .]

The scene recalls as well characters and incidents from the Roman
plays. After the revelation of Posthumus's murderous intention, for
example, Pisanio evokes Cleopatra in her most Roman moment: he
talks of slander, 'whose tongue / Outvenoms all the worms of Nile'
(III.iv.34–5). And when Imogen, sword at her breast, beseeches
Pisanio to strike home, we remember the similar scenes enacted by
Cassius and Pindarus, Brutus and Strato, Antony and Eros. Imogen
here is no weak, pleading, and pitiful girl, but a brave Roman ready
to end her life honorably. She orders the servant, 'Prithee dispatch'
(95), and reminds him several times of his duty to his master. When
he whimpers that he hasn't slept a wink since receiving Posthumus's
command to kill her, she curtly answers, 'Do't, and to bed then' (100).

The expected end to the Roman scene never takes place. Instead
of participating in a bloody ritual for honor and fame, Pisanio and
Imogen resort to disguise and deception. Instead of boldly asserting her
identity by death and consecrating her name for all posterity, Imogen
decides to lose both identity and name. She bids easy farewell to the
old self, restricted by responsibility, burdened by sorrow, and takes on
a new one, Fidele. The conventions of comedy completely reverse the
tragic Roman momentum. In so doing, they reveal the brittleness of
Roman egotism and the importance of British flexibility. Sometimes one
must lose oneself in order to be found.

Significantly, Imogen decides not to return to Britain, but to reside in
'other place':

Hath Britain all the sun that shines? day? night?
Are they not but in Britain? I' th' world's volume
Our Britain seems as of it, but not in 't;
In a great pool a swan's nest. Prithee think
There's livers out of Britain.

(136–40)

Such an alternative, of course, is unthinkable for Shakespeare's
Romans, for whom all roads lead directly home. For them, Rome is the
world; they must either live in the city or die. Antony cannot find in all
the earth's spaces room enough for him and Cleopatra; he leaves the
world and seeks a place with her in another life. Coriolanus vows to
find 'a world elsewhere' but discovers that there can be no honorable

life for him outside Rome. Imogen, however, dons a doublet, hat, and
hose, and cheerfully decides to live in Wales. Comedic vivacity and
flexibility work to ensure survival and to achieve a resolution. These
qualities are fostered by Pisanio, the faithful servant who refuses to
play the part of his staunch Roman counterparts. Instead, he exhibits
kindness, mercy, and a strong faith that Fortune, as he later puts it,
often 'brings in some boats that are not steer'd' (IV.iii.46).

When the disguised Imogen comes upon the cave of her long-lost
brothers, she has a Roman thought:

> Yet famine,
> Ere clean it o'erthrow nature, makes it valiant.
> Plenty and peace breeds cowards; hardness ever
> Of hardiness is mother.

> (III.vi.19–22)

The curious soldierly sentiment, perhaps an echo of *Coriolanus*
(IV.v.217ff.), serves to reveal the differences between the British
maiden and the Roman warrior, between the cave of Belarius and
the battlefield.[12] the ensuing scene illustrates not her capacity for
'hardiness,' but her (and her brothers') capacity for love – intuitive,
overpowering, and familial. Witness the following exchange:

Guiderius
Were you a woman, youth,
I should woo hard but be your groom in honesty:
I bid for you as I do buy.

Arviragus
I'll make't my comfort
He is a man, I'll love him as my brother:
And such a welcome as I'ld give to him
After long absence, such is yours. Most welcome!
Be sprightly, for you fall 'mongst friends.

Imogen: Aside.
'Mongst friends?
If brothers: would it had been so, that they
Had been my father's sons.

> (III.vi.68–76)

The Britons immediately respond to each other and instinctively
grasp the hidden truth about their relationship. Later, both princes
assert that they love the gentle youth as much as they do their father

(IV.ii.16ff.). The repeated expression of such miraculous perception and affection suggests the innate capacities of the British heart; it asserts the sacredness and naturalness of familial love and sympathy.[13]

Shakespeare carefully balances British and Roman elements in the princes as well as in the play. The scenes of family harmony alternate with scenes of military confrontation and battle. Cloten arrives in Wales and insults Guiderius. Guiderius staunchly rebuffs him, finally cutting off his head. Thus he demonstrates his natural nobility in high Roman style, through use of a strong right arm. Arviragus envies his brother the valorous deed while Belarius again ruminates on the innate honor of the princes:

> 'Tis wonder
> That an invisible instinct should frame them
> To royalty unlearn'd, honor untaught,
> Civility not seen from other, valor
> That wildly grows in them but yields a crop
> As if it had been sow'd.
>
> (IV.ii.176–81)

In this play, however, such Roman regard for honor and military prowess is Anglicized in important ways. Guiderius, it is plain, fights Cloten in self-defense, using the aggressor's sword against him (IV.ii.149–51). Not only does Cloten start the trouble, but, we are told, he also threatens to kill Belarius and Arviragus as well (120–3). The implausibility of this threat (how could Cloten know that the others existed?) raises no doubts about Guiderius's veracity, but justifies his actions as self-defense. He is not a Roman, seeking glory and conquest, but a Roman Briton, courageously defending himself, his home, and his family.

The differences between British and Roman warriors are also apparent in the funeral service for Fidele, not really dead but drugged. Belarius and the princes decide to inter Cloten with their friend, magnanimously granting the enemy the courtesy of princely burial. Guiderius and Arviragus recite poignant obsequies over Fidele's body. Their exquisite dirge, 'Fear no more the heat o' th' sun' (VI.ii.258–81), reflects upon the dangers and difficulties of life and extolls the peace and quiet of death, the inevitable end: 'Golden lads and girls all must, / As chimney-sweepers, come to dust' (262–3). The evocative 'golden', richly suggestive of health, youth, wealth, and perhaps the lost golden age, combines with the homely detail of 'chimney-sweepers' coming to dust to soften grief into bittersweet resignation. Unlike the various Roman funerals previously encountered – those of Lucrece, the Andronici, and Caesar, for example – this service is personal, intimate, and familial. Three times it is iterated that the princes performed the same ritual for Euriphile, their 'mother,' many years ago (190–1, 223–4, 236–8). There is no recognition here of civic meaning in death, nor is the corpse a spur to political or military action. Instead, the princes quietly consign their beloved to the earth with flowers and song.

[. . .]

The comedic process outlined above, here as always in Shakespeare, requires the assistance of the human heart. Imogen's forgiveness of Posthumus's treachery prepares for an important turning point in the play – Posthumus's own repentance and sorrow.

[. . .]

The resolution to amend life and perform penance perfects Posthumus's contrition.[14] The penance he has in mind, however, is unusual. Posthumus plans to change into the costume of a British peasant and to fight for Imogen:

> Let me make men know
> More valor in me than my habits show.
> Gods, put the strength o' th' Leonati in me!
> To shame the guise o' th' world, I will begin
> The fashion: less without and more within.

> (V.i.29–33)

At first glance, Posthumus's resolution to fight, to live up to his noble ancestry, seems a most Roman way of making reparation, reminiscent, perhaps, of Antony after Actium. Yet, Posthumus is un-Roman in a number of important particulars. Disguised as a British peasant, he does not seek in battle self-aggrandizement, but self-abnegation. Posthumus hopes to die not for country, but for his wife.

Posthumus's intention to 'shame the guise o' th' world' by starting a new 'fashion' aims directly at overturning the Roman military ethos that encourages destruction of life for fame and glory. The difference between Posthumus and his Roman predecessors, Roman enemies, and former Roman self (who wanted Iachimo, himself, or both killed in combat [II.iv.58–61]) becomes evident in the ensuing battle. After vanquishing and disarming Iachimo, he leaves him unharmed, pointedly refusing to exalt himself over the body of an enemy. Posthumus rejects the Roman vanity of personal honor for the exercise of British mercy and compassion.

Posthumus's expression of Anglicized *Romanitas* is balanced by additional proof of Roman excellence in Britain, that provided by

Belarius and the princes. Unable to hide in the mountains and watch their country invaded, this trio helps rescue Cymbeline and rout the Romans. Like Coriolanus, they encourage fleeing companions and inspire them to fight on to honor and victory. Stout-hearted Britons thus overcome mighty Romans, a triumph that surely excited original audiences. The young challenger finally breaks the hold of Roman history. The defeat of the Romans on the battlefield, their own proving ground, marks the end of their domination and the beginning of a new regime. Though heir to Roman traditions, this regime, as Posthumus's story intimates, will be different, more merciful and humane, 'less without and more within.'

The joy of British conquest is not for Posthumus, however, whose search for death leads to further self-denial, penance, and purification. 'No more a Britain' (V.iii.75), he withdraws from the victory celebration and puts on Roman clothing. This change from British to Roman appearance covers the opposite internal change from Roman to British. In non-Roman fashion, Posthumus refuses to claim due honor and receive public recognition. Instead of enjoying victory and hard-earned fame, he chooses anonymity, suffers capture, and endures unceremonious imprisonment. In soliloquy Posthumus expresses sincere sorrow and again offers his life in exchange for Imogen's, this time in accents reminiscent of the earlier exchange of his 'poor self' to her 'so infinite loss' (I.i.119–20): 'For Imogen's dear life take mine, and though / 'Tis not so dear, yet 'tis a life' (V.iv.22–3). The Briton who exercised Roman virtue in British costume now, in Roman costume, shows a British capacity for humility and spiritual growth.[15]

[. . .]

The dizzying revelations of the last scene of the play accomplish first the reunion of the lovers, Posthumus and Imogen. With Cymbeline's help the disguised Imogen prompts Iachimo to reveal his treachery. He tells the whole tale of how his 'Italian brain' (V.v.196) operated in 'duller Britain' (197) and cost Posthumus his wager and his wife. Enraged, Posthumus breaks off the account and reveals his identity. After Imogen unmasks, the lovers embrace, and the daughter receives her father's blessing. Thus, form and feeling are finally reconciled in Britain. What is more, Posthumus demonstrates that he has finally learned to harmonize Roman aggression and British compassion. After explaining that he was the 'forlorn soldier,' he accepts his due honors and the King's gratitude. Instead of claiming the life of his enemy as he first threatened, Posthumus spares Iachimo a second time:

> Kneel not to me.
> The pow'r that I have on you is to spare you;
> The malice towards you, to forgive you. Live,
> And deal with others better.
>
> (417–20)

Cymbeline's recovery of his daughter and his acceptance of Posthumus as son-in-law begin the reconstitution of the royal family. The evil Queen dies despairing off-stage, killed by her own shameless desperation. Guiderius's account of the fight with Cloten permanently settles the question concerning the ignoble Prince's whereabouts. The dying of the old family, of course, is a necessary prelude to the rebirth of the new. Intuitive familial sympathy manifests itself again in Cymbeline's knighting of the princes, now 'companions to our person' (21), and in his instinctive attraction to the disguised Imogen: 'What wouldst thou, boy? / I love thee more and more' (108–9). Miraculously, Cymbeline regains his lost children and his identity as parent. Amazed, he exclaims: 'O, what, am I / A mother to the birth of three? Ne'er mother / Rejoic'd deliverance more' (368–70). The references to himself as mother and to the process of birth suggest the intensity of the moment and the power of the love that binds.[16] Like Posthumus earlier, Imogen resides in the middle of a warm family circle, this one consisting of Cymbeline (who is father and mother), and two long-lost brothers. Fittingly, the circle widens to include Belarius, whom Cymbeline embraces as a 'brother' and Imogen accepts as another 'father' (399–401).

The reconciliation and reunion of the royal family in *Cymbeline* leads directly to the reconciliation and reunion of nations. Initially, it appears as though the Britons will be barbarous victors. The kinsmen of the slain demand the lives of the Roman captives so as to appease the souls of the dead 'with slaughter' (72). Lucius's calm and courageous response, 'Sufficeth / A Roman with a Roman's heart can suffer' (80–1), points up the primitive cruelty of the request. The scene closely parallels the opening of *Titus Andronicus*, wherein victorious Romans butcher Alarbus '*ad manes fratrum*' (I.i.98).[17] Significantly, however, the sacrifice of the Romans in *Cymbeline* never takes place. Inspired by Posthumus's forgiveness of Iachimo, Cymbeline pardons all the prisoners. The contrast between the early and late sacrifice scenes graphically illustrates the differences between Roman and British civilization, the one founded on self-assertion, revenge, and bloodshed; the other, on forgiveness and mercy.

'Although the victor' (460), Cymbeline promises of his own free will to submit to Caesar and send the tribute. Shakespeare may have found precedent for Cymbeline's actions in Heliodorus's *Aethiopica*, wherein

King Hidaspes freely restores his defeated enemy's lands in order to
keep and foster 'amity.'[18] Like Hidaspes's, Cymbeline's donation does
not cancel out the triumph, but demonstrates the victor's generosity
and nobility. As Frank Kermode comments: 'We are meant to conclude
that the valour of the British royal family is "gentle", and not simply
a brute toughness which must set the nation against the forces of
civility and religion.'[19] The gift of tribute completes the comic ending,
dissolving rather than resolving the differences between opposing
nations.

For his earlier kindness to Imogen and his present show of courage,
Lucius is included in the final comic circle. His presence there
symbolizes the greater harmony now existing between nations. This
harmony is familial in nature, not only because it derives from the
reunion of Cymbeline's family, but because it unites both the Roman
and British descendants of Priam and Aeneas.[20] The grand conclusion of
Cymbeline, then, reconciles the warring factions of the larger, extended
Trojan family and thus creates the blessed peace that descends upon
all, Briton and Roman alike.

Shakespeare's increasingly critical scrutiny of Rome concludes in
Cymbeline. British valor triumphs over Roman might, but more
importantly, British flexibility and humility overcome Roman constancy
and honor. The siege and invasion motif, appearing here on both the
sexual and national levels, articulates no vision of impious violation.
Instead, it leads to a scene of toleration and forgiveness, wherein
each side accepts the other in human kindness. Romans may hold to
'*suum cuique*' as their justice, but Britons, Shakespeare demonstrates,
share their victories. The halcyon peace that closes the play results
from the integration of opposites and the gathering of enemies into
familial harmony. In Shakespeare's Rome *pietas* demands the honoring
of family, country, and gods, that series of concentric and increasingly
important values. In Shakespeare's Britain, however, the smallest circle,
the family, expands outward to include the rest and to eliminate the
possibility of conflict with them. Private and public obligations become
one and the same.

The differences between Roman Britain in *Cymbeline* and the Romes
of Shakespeare's other works come into focus upon recollection of
Titus Andronicus, a play much in the dramatist's mind during the
construction of his last Roman effort. In that early tragedy private
emotion sharply conflicts with public obligation, and the resulting battle
rages through scenes of ghoulish bloodletting and barbaric ritual. On
stage and in language the pastoral world, symbolic of the nonurban,
un-Roman, and therefore, private sphere, is repeatedly violated,
its innocent life hunted and maimed, its branches lopped, its green

shade turned red with blood.[21] In *Cymbeline*, however, the pastoral world withstands the Roman invasion unscathed. Indeed, the air itself subdues the enemy:

> *Iachimo*
> The heaviness and guilt within my bosom
> Takes off my manhood. I have belied a lady,
> The Princess of this country; and the air on't
> Revengingly enfeebles me.

(V.ii.1–4)

Noble pastoral residents conquer the would-be destroyers and proceed to take their place in a new civilization, wherein natural and Roman, private and public join in accord. The conflict between the two worlds results not in mutilation, but in magical restoration and growth.[22] The lopped branches of the stately cedar revive, become jointed to the old stock, and freshly grow. In Shakespeare's Roman vision, the eagle flies westward and vanishes in British sunlight.

Notes

1. The exceptions are Hugh M. Richmond, 'Shakespeare's Roman Trilogy: The Climax in *Cymbeline*,' *Studies in Literature*, 5 (1972), 129–39; and David M. Bergeron, '*Cymbeline*: Shakespeare's Last Roman Play,' *SQ*, 31 (1980), 31–41. Some have made in passing interesting comments on *Cymbeline* as a Roman play: Roy Walker, 'The Northern Star: An Essay on the Roman Plays,' *Shakespeare Quarterly*, 2 (1951), 287–93; A.P. Rossiter, *Angel with Horns* (London: Longman, 1961), p. 252; J.L. Simmons, *Shakespeare's Pagan World: The Roman Tragedies* (Brighton: Harvester Press, 1974), p. 10, 165–6. Walker speaks of Shakespeare's Rome as devolving to degenerate Italian brilliance; Rossiter, of *Cymbeline* as an escape from the darkness of history evident in *Coriolanus*; and Simmons, of the providential Roman peace with which the play ends.

2. On the self-conscious theatricality of the play, see R.A. Foakes, *Shakespeare: The Dark Comedies to the Last Plays: From Satire to Celebration* (Charlottesville: University Press of Virginia, 1971), pp. 98–118; Barbara A. Mowat, *The Dramaturgy of Shakespeare's Romances* (Athens: University of Georgia Press, 1976), pp. 51ff.

3. In taking this approach I follow the leads of G. Wilson Knight, *The Crown of Life* (1947; rpt. London: Methuen, 1961), pp. 129–67; and J.P. Brockbank, 'History and Histrionics in *Cymbeline*,' *ShS*, 11 (1958), 42–9.

4. '*Cymbeline*: Shakespeare's Last Roman Play.'

5. 'The First Booke of the Historie of England,' in *The First and Second Volumes of Chronicles* (1587), p. 7. There is also a Posthumus in Ben Jonson's *Sejanus* (1603).

6. See William Witherle Lawrence, *Shakespeare's Problem Comedies* (New York: Macmillan, 1931), pp. 174–205.

7. '*Cymbeline* and the "Blameless Hero,"' *English Literary History*, 31 (1964), 259–70. Below, I follow the First Folio and read 'Iachimo' for Evans's 'Jachimo.'

8. *Crown of Life*, p. 148.

9. Rewriting the story of Julius Caesar's invasion was a common activity in Europe from ancient times onward. See Homer Nearing, Jr., 'The Legend of Julius Caesar's British Conquest,' *PMLA*, 64 (1949), 889–929.

10. See variations of this interpretation by Warren D. Smith, 'Cloten with Caius Lucius,' *Studies in Philology*, 49 (1952), 185–94; Robin Moffet, '*Cymbeline* and the Nativity,' *SQ*, 13 (1962), 207–18 (209–10); D.R.C. Marsh, *The Recurring Miracle: A Study of Cymbeline* (Pietermaritzburg: University of Natal Press, 1962), pp. 51–2; Joan Hartwig, *Shakespeare's Tragicomic Vision* (Baton Rouge: Louisiana State University Press, 1972), pp. 187–8. Cymbeline's later remark that he was 'dissuaded' from paying tribute by the 'wicked Queen' (V.v.463) simply clears the way for reconciliation; it can hardly be used post facto to discredit the patriotism of Act III, Scene i and the battle scenes.

11. 'Place and Plot in Shakespeare,' *Yale Review*, NS 67 (1977), 48–56. Alexander Leggatt, 'The Island of Miracles: An Approach to Cymbeline,' *Shakespeare Survey*, 10 (1977), 191–209, sees all of Britain as the 'second place,' not distinguishing between the court and Wales; more perceptive in J.S. Lawry, '"Perishing Root and Increasing Vine" in *Cymbeline*,' *ShakS*, 12 (1979), 179–93, who regards Britain and Rome as fixed 'in static malevolence' and Milford Haven as 'a third direction, place, "way", and metaphor' where lies the possibility of 'gainful loss' (p. 183). Recent commentators have made much of the fact that Milford Haven was the landing place of Henry Tudor en route to the throne and was celebrated as such in Jacobean masques. See Emrys Jones, 'Stuart Cymbeline,' *Essays in Criticism*, 11 (1961), 84–99; Glynne Wickham, 'From Tragedy to Tragi-Comedy: "King Lear" as Prologue,' *ShS*, 26 (1973), 33–48 (44–5); Frances A. Yates, *Shakespeare's Last Plays: A New Approach* (London: Routledge & Kegan Paul, 1975), pp. 41–61.

12. These differences have often been emphasized in performance by Imogen's comical timidity and fear. See Arthur Colby Sprague, *Shakespeare and the Actors: The Stage Business in His Plays (1600–1905)* (Cambridge, Mass.: Harvard University Press, 1944), p. 62.

13. The reunion of Imogen and her brothers in the cave may owe something to Torquato Tasso's story of Erminia and the shepherds, *Jerusalem Delivered*, Book VII. Edwin Greenlaw, 'Shakespeare's Pastorals,' *SP*, 13 (1916), 122–54 (136–47) notes the connections, and Bullough reprints portions from Edward Fairfax's translation (1600) as an 'analogue' to *Cymbeline* (Vol. VIII, pp. 103–11). Renato Poggioli's comment on the Erminia episode, 'the

natural outcome of the pastoral of innocence is the family situation, or the domestic idyll,' is also very apt for the episode in the play. *The Oaten Flute: Essays on Pastoral Poetry and the Pastoral Ideal* (Cambridge, Mass.: Harvard University Press, 1975), p. 12.

14. Robert Grams Hunter demonstrates in *Shakespeare and the Comedy of Forgiveness* (New York: Columbia University Press, 1965) that Posthumus's repentance and renewal are presented as the pagan equivalent to Christian regeneration (pp. 159ff.).

15. On the importance of costuming to the play, see John Scott Colley, 'Disguise and the New Guise in *Cymbeline*,' ShakS, 7 (1974), 233–52.

16. The difference between Cymbeline's perception here and Caesar's vision of himself as *mater patriae*, from whom 'great Rome shall suck / Reviving blood' (*J.C.* II.ii.87–8), is instructive.

17. See Kittredge, *Complete Works*, p. 1332.

18. *An Aethiopian Historie*, trans. Thomas Underdowne (1587), fol. 131. Carol Gesner notes this and other parallels in *Shakespeare & the Greek Romance: A Study of Origins* (Lexington: University Press of Kentucky, 1970), pp. 90–115.

19. *Shakespeare: The Final Plays* (London: Longman, 1963), p. 21.

20. See the British response to Caesar's demand for tribute in 'Caius Iulius Caesar,' in *Parts Added to 'The Mirror for Magistrates' by John Higgins & Thomas Blenerhasset*, ed. Lily B. Campbell (Cambridge: Cambridge University Press, 1946), p. 293. In an appendix to Nosworthy's Arden edition, Harold F. Brooks discusses Shakespeare's indebtedness to the work of Higgins and Blenerhasset in *Cymbeline* (pp. 212–16). Holinshed emphasizes Britain's Trojan connection through Brute.

21. See Albert H. Tricomi, 'The Mutilated Garden in *Titus Andronicus*,' ShakS, 9 (1976), 89–105.

22. The magical process remains inscrutable despite the attempts at Christian and topical explication. The Christian category includes variously Moffet, '*Cymbeline* and the Nativity'; Hunter, *Comedy of Forgiveness*; Felperin, *Shakespearean Romance*; Richmond, 'Shakespeare's Roman Trilogy'; Leggatt, 'Island of Miracles'; Lawry, '"Perishing Root."' The topical category includes Jones, 'Stuart Cymbeline'; Wickham, 'From Tragedy'; Yates, *Shakespeare's Last Plays*; and Bernard Harris, '"What's past is prologue": *Cymbeline* and *Henry VIII*' in *Later Shakespeare*, Stratford-upon-Avon Studies, No. 8 (London: Arnold, 1966), pp. 203–34. The two categories often overlap. For caveats against such interpretation, see Philip Edwards, 'Shakespeare's Romances: 1900–57,' *ShS*, 11 (1958), 1–18; Hallett Smith, *Shakespeare's Romances: A Study of Some Ways of the Imagination* (San Marino, Calif.: Huntington Library, 1972), pp. 211–15.

Notes on Authors

JANET ADELMAN is Professor of English at the University of California, Berkeley. She is author of *The Common Liar* (1989).

MICHAEL BRISTOL is Professor of English at McGill University in Montreal. He is the author of *Carnival and Theatre: Plebeian Culture and the Structure of Authority in Renaissance England* (1985) and *Shakespeare's America, America's Shakespeare* (1990).

PAUL CANTOR is Professor of English at the University of Virginia. He has published extensively on Renaissance and other topics. His books include *Shakespeare's Rome: Republic and Empire* (1976) and *Creature and Creator: Myth-making and English Romanticism* (1984).

JONATHAN DOLLIMORE is Professor of English at the University of Sussex. He is the author of *Sexual dissidence: Augustine to Wilde, Freud to Foucault* (1991), an extended historical exploration of constructions of the figure of the homosexual.

JOHN DRAKAKIS lectures in English at the University of Stirling. He has published numerous articles on early modern literature and is editor of the ground-breaking volume *Alternative Shakespeares* (1985).

TERRY HAWKES is Professor of English at the University of Wales College of Cardiff. He is the author of several books on Shakespearean topics, including *That Shakespeherian Rag* (1986).

ANNABEL PATTERSON is Professor of English at Yale University. She is the author of numerous books, including *Censorship and Interpretation* (1990) and *Pastoral and Ideology* (1987).

ALAN SINFIELD is Professor of English at the University of Sussex. He is the author of a number of different books on early modern and modern topics, including *Literature, Politics and Culture in Postwar Britain* (1989). He is co-editor (with Jonathan Dollimore) of *Political Shakespeare* (1985; 1994).

LEONARD TENNENHOUSE is Professor of Comparative Literature at Brown University in Providence, Rhode Island. He is co-editor (with Nancy Armstrong) of *The Violence of Representation: Studies in Literature and the History of Sexuality* (1989).

RICHARD WILSON lectures in English at the University of Lancaster. His essays on Shakespeare have been collected in the volume *Will Power: Essays on Shakespearean Authority* (1992), which seeks to locate the social logic of Shakespearean texts in relation to Tudor and Stuart political practices.

Further Reading

Recent work on Shakespeare

These texts provide a good indication of contemporary critical and theoretical analysis of Shakespeare's work generally.

DOLLIMORE, JONATHAN and SINFIELD, ALAN (eds) *Political Shakespeare* (2nd edn) (Manchester: Manchester Univ. Press, 1994).

DRAKAKIS, JOHN (ed.) *Alternative Shakespeares* (London: Methuen, 1985).

HOWARD, JEAN E. and O'CONNOR, MARION F. (eds) *Shakespeare Reproduced* (London: Methuen, 1987).

MARSDEN, JEAN I. (ed.) *The Appropriation of Shakespeare: Post-Renaissance Reconstructions of the Works and the Myth* (Hemel Hempstead: Harvester Wheatsheaf, 1991).

PARKER, PATRICIA and HARTMAN, GEOFFREY (eds) *Shakespeare and the Question of Theory* (London: Methuen, 1985).

Older work on the Roman plays

The following selection provides a good sense of more traditional approaches to the Roman plays.

CHARNEY, MAURICE *Shakespeare's Roman Plays: The Function of Imagery in the Drama* (Cambridge, Mass.: Harvard Univ. Press, 1961).

SPENCER, T.J.B. *Shakespeare: The Roman Plays* (London: Longmans, Green, 1963).

WILSON KNIGHT, G. *The Imperial Theme* (London, Methuen, 1965).

Shakespeare Survey 10 (1957) – special issue dedicated to the Roman plays.

Recent work on the Roman plays

The following works provide analyses of the Roman plays which are inflected by contemporary theoretical concerns

ADELMAN, JANET *The Common Liar: An Essay on Antony and Cleopatra* (New Haven: Yale Univ. Press, 1973).

FAWKNER, HARALD *Shakespeare's Hyperontology: Antony and Cleopatra* (London: Associated Universities Press, 1990).

KING, BRUCE *Coriolanus* (London: Macmillan, 1989).

PARIS, BERNARD J. *Character as a Subversive Force in Shakespeare: The History and Roman Plays* (London: Associated Universities Press, 1991).

VIVIAN, THOMAS *Shakespeare's Roman Worlds* (London: Routledge, 1989).

Index